FACE THE MUSIC

A Sailor's Story

Sir John Hayes

Face the Music

A Sailor's Story

by

John Hayes

The Pentland Press Limited
Edinburgh Cambridge Durham

First published in 1991.
Reprinted in 1992 by
The Pentland Press Ltd.,
Brockerscliffe
Witton le Wear
Durham

ISBN 1872795 05 6

Set in 10pt Times by
Print Origination (NW) Ltd., Formby, Liverpool L37 8EG.
Printed and bound by Antony Rowe Ltd., Chippenham.;

For Rosalind
who, over many years, has known and
shared every note of the score.

From "Persuasion" by Jane Austen

1. Miss Musgrove has just decided to be noticed by Captain Benwick R.N. whom she was, eventually, to marry.

"Louisa Musgrove burst forth into raptures of admiration and delight on the character of the navy–their friendliness, their brotherliness, their openness, their uprightness; protesting that she was convinced of sailors having more worth and warmth than any other set of men in England; that they only knew how to live, and they only deserved to be respected and loved."

and

2. Miss Austen's closing words of the novel on the subject of her Anne Elliott's eventual marriage to Captain Wentworth R.N.

"She gloried in being a sailor's wife, but she must pay the tax of quick alarm for belonging to that profession which is, if possible, more distinguished in its domestic virtues than in its national importance."

Acknowledgements

My thanks are due firstly to Lord Carrington for his over-generous foreword. Secondly to the Pentland Press for accepting my efforts and in particular Pamela Grant, their appointed personal editor for my venture. Next, to Roderick Suddaby, Keeper of Documents in the Imperial War Museum, who accepted the original MS and subsequently all my scribblings including my Midshipman's Journals of sixty years ago! Lastly to my family, for their interest and encouragement and in particular to our elder son Colin for his professional help and support in all approaches to publication.

CONTENTS

Part One 1913-1939   The Pre-War Royal Navy

Part Two 1939-1945   War at Sea

Part Three 1946-1988
... and Peace, a Miscellany

List of Illustrations

Author's Preface

I was born in Bermuda, the son of a Lieutenant in the R.A.M.C. who returned there in 1919, a wounded, gassed victim of Ypres. At the age of six I was sent to the converted sail-loft which called itself the Dockyard School. The cruisers of the West Indies Squadron excited me more than arithmetic, so even at that tender age I nurtured an instinct to make the Royal Navy my life if I could.

At twelve I entered the competition to become a naval cadet at Dartmouth. Though diminutive for my age, and to my Headmaster's considerable surprise, I was accepted. That ordeal forms the prologue to the story of my career, which spanned another forty years.

As with everyone of my generation, war became an inescapable experience, in my case an experience which Fate decreed should include several disasters in quick succession: the sinking of *Prince of Wales* and *Repulse*; the last man out of Malaya with the Argyll and Sutherland Highlanders; the fall of Singapore; the catastrophe which overtook the ill-fated Russian Convoy PQ17, and the subsequent and notable libel action of Broome v Irving and Cassels thirty years later in which I was a principal witness. These were the more sombre moments in a life spent mainly at sea.

But war is not what this book is principally about. Nor does it dwell unduly on the years of more senior rank which followed. My generation joined the Royal Navy in the wake of the *Pax Britannica*, believing it to be the peaceful guardian of the high seas and a service which, deeply embedded in our island history, seemed to occupy a particular affection in the eyes of the British people. From start to finish my experience was shaped by the humour and uninhibited commonsense of the sailor. It is the sailor who taught me about himself, and who has mattered to me more than most in this complicated world because of his uncomplicated attitude towards it.

Much of my story is therefore lightly told. It covers a period from the 1920s to the 1960s when the Navy underwent huge changes, technically, politically and socially, yet whose people remained fundamentally the same. It is written as much for the layman, who I hope will find interest here in a great Service, as for those colleagues of my generation or for the present Wardrooms of the Fleet.

Face the music? First and foremost I was a sailor. But music has ever been my other love. I turn to it in times of need, and at several moments in our history face it I hope I did.

Foreword

by

The Rt. Hon. Lord Carrington

Vice-Admiral Sir John Hayes, better known to his friends as Joc, has had a varied and interesting career and in this book he has written about it with style.

There used to be a presumption that Naval Officers were not very well educated. If ever that were true, John Hayes is an outstanding exception. He is a man of many interests and widely read and he writes an evocative account of his life and his days in the Royal Navy. His dedication to the Services is obvious. It is clear, too, that the happiest days of his career were spent at sea.

It so happens that he and I had eighteen months working together. They were the happiest of days. He was a delightful companion, wise in judgement and experienced in the ways of the Services. We travelled the world together and I do not remember a single occasion on which we disagreed or had a difference of opinion. I can, at first hand, recommend both the book and the man who wrote it.

Those of you who read it will find some amusing stories and some sad ones. He writes most movingly and vividly of the sinking of the Repulse, of the misjudgements and the appalling consequences, of the disgraceful story of the surrender of Singapore, of the Arctic convoys and the sinking of The Bismarck. It is a splendid story and splendidly told.

After he left the Navy, John Hayes retired to the Highlands of Scotland where he became Lord-Lieutenant of Ross and Cromarty, Sky and Lochalsh—a singular compliment for someone without any Scottish blood in his veins and, as he himself says, "a comparative newcomer of twenty years!". But then he is a remarkable man who, in his retirement and after a lifetime of public service, has afforded us the pleasure of reading about his happy life.

FACE THE MUSIC

A SAILOR'S STORY

PART 1

1913 - 1939

CHILDHOOD, SUBORDINATE AND
JUNIOR RANK

in

THE PRE-WAR ROYAL NAVY

Chapter 1

Alpha and Omega

The frightening array of stern-faced, plain-clothed gentlemen confronted the thirteen-year-old schoolboy across the long bare table. There had been a staccato exchange of questions before the dormouse at the far end opened his eyes apparently for the first time.

"Can you play Chopin?"

"No, sir."

"Why not? It says here you can play the piano and won a music prize."

"Yes, sir."

"Then why not Chopin?"

"Because there are too many sharps and flats, sir."

"Oh!"

Silence. I had in fact been awarded *Legends of Greece and Rome* and *David Copperfield* for playing something with only one sharp at the age of ten, in embossed bindings unlikely to be afforded by preparatory schools today.

Then, from the large figure confronting me, the inevitable:

"Why do you want to join the Navy? I see your father's in the Army."

"Yes, sir."

"But you don't want to join the Army?"

"No, sir. My father is also a doctor."

"Ah!" came a friendly voice from the end opposite to the dormouse. Here, I felt, was an ally. "I see your middle name is

Osler. Are you any relation of Sir William Osler?"

"Not that I know of, sir."

"A pity. He was a great physician."

"Yes, sir."

Then from the left front: "I am still not clear why you want to join the Navy. You were born in Bermuda and after the War went to the Dockyard School."

"Yes, sir."

"Why was that?"

"Because my father was rather badly wounded and gassed at Ypres, sir, and after the war asked if he could go back to the Bermuda which he loved."

"I see. And is that the only reason you want to become a Naval Officer?"

"I suppose it is, sir. I loved the children's parties in H.M.S. *Calcutta*."

"So you are telling me . . . " when he was interrupted by my ally, *sotto voce:*

"And a very good reason too."

Not to be deterred, my inquisitor opposite continued: "Supposing you do become a Cadet, what would you like to do in the Navy?"

"Be a Navigator, sir."

"Why particularly?"

"Because my father's special friend in H.M.S. *Calcutta* was the Navigator and he took me to sea for a day. He explained how a compass works and how the stars help to find where you are. He was very nice and very quiet, sir. I would like to be like him."

Silence until the dormouse woke up again. "Can you play Chopin?".

"You asked him that before," said his neighbour.

"Of course. How silly of me. What can you play?"

"Not very much, sir."

"Oh!"

A new voice chimed in. "Am I to understand that your reason for wanting to join the Navy is that you lived among the cruisers in Bermuda where your father was a doctor in the Army, you went to the Dockyard School, enjoyed children's parties and clearly became attracted to what a compass could do?"

"Yes, sir. And I liked the Naval Officers who used to come and play charades with my parents in our house when I ought to have been in bed."

"I see," said the person opposite me. "Has anybody got any more questions to ask the lad?"

"Just one," said somebody who had not hitherto spoken. "You realise that the Navy is not just one long children's party, and not all compasses. If we accept you and your father agrees, d'you think you can make the Navy your life? Because that's what it demands."

"I hope so, sir. It's all I've thought of and my father has no other ideas for me."

"Thank you," said the person opposite and after a few more observations among themselves and whispers and nods I was dismissed from my ordeal. There followed an exhaustive and intimate scrutiny of my diminutive naked body which was pummelled and prodded in unlikely places for reasons I did not understand at the time; I jumped up and down on my toes while they felt bits of me and was made to bend over–not for the last time, in the years which were to follow, for different reasons–and was then given a cursory reading of the optician's eye chart. They looked into my ears which look like a taxi coming towards you with both doors open; invited me to write an essay either on charabancs or my favourite hobby, which at the time was toy soldiers, not sailors, and I was ushered out into Tothill Street by one of those leathered, bemedalled dignitaries who was putting my mother at ease while waiting to receive her small son. I was thankful to see her because at that age I leaned on her maternal love while living in some awe of my father.

Our family was happiest in Bermuda, where I was born in Paget under the pencilled tower of Gibb's Hill lighthouse, whose sweeping, penetrating beam from beneath the horizon I was so often to welcome from the bridge during my years at sea. The Army Lieutenant of those days, as I told my interviewing Admirals, was to return as a Captain after the hell of that first war to have his own laboratory for pathology on Boaz Island, half way between the cruisers in the dockyard on Ireland Island and the naval families on Somerset.

The Bermuda of that time was as near paradise as can be imagined. The inhabited islands in an archipelago of some three hundred were then joined only by wooden bridges in a semi horseshoe which enclosed a coral lagoon of some five miles wide, the whole surrounded by a reef through which there is just one channel giving access to large ships, which must thereafter navigate the intricacies into Hamilton, the capital, or elsewhere. No cars were allowed, only bicycles which I was too young to ride. My father's official transport consisted of a pony trap and groom which he was certainly not going to allow his six-year-old son to use to the dockyard school. I therefore walked the three miles there and back, seemingly against the wind always, to join on Boaz Bridge my arch-enemy Albert, my elder and the son of a Bermudian Dockyard official, who would flick the elastic of my hat under my chin by way of greeting.

The school was the old sail loft in which I suppose I must have learnt something; yet I must also have been the despair of my teachers, for my eyes were for ever straying out of the window to the graceful hulls, the light grey funnels and masts of those four cruisers and some sloops which then comprised the North American squadron, my ears forever listening to the pipes and bugles which in some way were subconsciously beckoning me towards a predestined life from the age of six.

The craze obsessed me so that I would linger between the bollards after school, partly to avoid Albert, partly to savour the to-ing and fro-ing of the sailors, but mainly to delay the attention of an odious nurse who had come with us to look after my younger brother, aged nothing. I resented her deeply as a substitute for my own Florence who had left because my parents, to whom it would have been anathema, refused to allow her to bring me up as a Catholic. My father was an agnostic and my mother a Unitarian.

Dawdling homewards along the dusty track, past the tennis courts where my mother was lady champion, past the official residencies of senior naval officers with their brass-funnelled picket boats moored in the creeks, stepping aside for the buggies of the gentry and the antics of the sailor lurching shipwards after all-night leave (and whom I had been taught to avoid!), I would cast my bent hook and dough over any bridge in the hope of luring the small octopus, the shoals of angel fish, aquamarine with golden flutings and so elusive, the shell-pink squirrel fish or the ugly, greedy little black molly-minnows which were the only regulars to my crude bait. I would pause again on the jetty where my father kept his boat in the cove outside our bungalow, to wind the crane up and down, before sauntering among the oleanders and hibiscus, school satchel askew, to be given a friendly grin by Goodall the groom and a scolding from Nanny Turner that I was late. Never mind: I had a tarantula in a box which would make her scream as it clambered on her mosquito net that night.

Next day there was something else to make her scream. So intent was I in leaning as far as I dared over Boaz bridge, having rid myself of Albert, watching the swift flow of the ebb or flood over the coral where lurked my bait, that I had not seen Goodall the groom approaching on his bicycle. He seemed relieved to see me.

"Ah, Master John. Your parents were wondering . . . you'll not be catching an octopus now."

"Why not, Goodall?" (We were great friends.) "What have I done wrong?"

"Nothing as I know of, Master John. But look at that . . . ."

I had, of course, in my absorption, quite failed to notice the threatening banks of indigo and purple cloud gathering beyond the reef on the horizon. I was too young to sense that warning of nature in the wind when it dies from the breeze of orthodox conditions into that ominous and quiet restlessness which presages something violent—like the anticipatory lull which Beethoven captures in those few seconds between the end of the third movement of his great C Minor Symphony and the bursting climax which heralds the last.

"There's a hurricane warning," said Goodall. "You'd best come home." He put me on the back of his bicycle and pedalled me home to anxious parents. Nanny was already hysterical and had managed to plant one of the poles which held out the huge jalousie shutters of the night nursery into her stomach. This amused my two-year-old brother but my mother less so, since she also had to contend with Prunella, the Bermudian maid (whom we adored) and Lucy, the coal-black cook (whom we did not), who were already preparing for emergency under the kitchen table.

"Nanny is hurt," said my mother quietly. "I think she'd be better in bed"—where I helped put her, sobbing, forgetting my tarantula.

The house was eventually battened down, the shutters secured, Prunella and Lucy also, Nanny and my brother under their mosquito nets, Goodall with Sylvia the pony in her stable, as the wind began to rise.

Circular storms are the same the world over, under any name; typhoons in the Far East, cyclones in more middle eastern longitudes, and hurricanes in the western world. They observe the same pattern, reek the same havoc on what presents itself to their path, come as quickly as they go, now rejoice in girls' names as if to give some semblance of feigned romance to their ravages, and have been described in literature by the masters, Joseph Conrad pre-eminent. To a child of seven this one was sheer excitement, and although later I was to experience another ashore, fate spared me the challenge of such at sea. I remember now rejoicing at the calm of my parents and the seeming terror of the others, as the daylight darkened, the wind rose to a scream, the bungalow shook, and the hissing of the rain beat upon us. I remember too wondering where to go; for certainly I would not stay in that room with the whimpering corpse under the mosquito net. After dinner my father used to sing Kipling's words to the music of Edward German in his "Just So" songs:

"When the cabin portholes are dark and green
Because of the sea outside . . .
When the ship goes 'Wop' with a wiggle between
And the steward falls into the soup tureen
And the trunks begin to slide;
When Nannie lies on the floor in a heap
And mother tells you to let her sleep . . . "

Yes, let her sleep! It's so much less trouble in the mind of the small boy trying to assert a feigned early masculinity of independence; and her despised capitulation will stand him in good stead next time she tries to exert any kind of authority. So unkindly I let her be and went out into the hall. It suddenly seemed full of strange people beleaguered between their husbands and their homes, between Ireland Island and Somerset, occupying my parent's attention. No Goodall, no Prunella, no nobody; just the turmoil of the storm.

I don't know how I got out. Probably it was through Prunella's back door while she and Lucy writhed together under the kitchen table. Disobedience was given fuel by that instinct of the young to draw attention to themselves when everybody else is otherwise preoccupied. I remember only an impression of helpless terror as the door whipped away from me and I was sucked out into the vortex. Swept off my feet at once, I was carried as a tiny human cargo in the grip of the wind and horizontal rain in what now seemed to be near darkness. I was conscious of the chicken coop with its squawking occupants bowling along beside me; of flying branches and the dreadful roar; and then a prickly haven, cushioning my spindrift, airborne flight before I was flung against something hard. I lay there bleeding and semi-conscious, imprisoned by the wind.

It was Goodall who found me, enmeshed in the tamarisk against the wall. A few more yards one way and I would have been blown out of the gate to the sea parapet. His strong arms enfolded me as he battled back to shelter and then there was my mother, controlling admonishment, bending over my battered and sodden little body on my bed. My last memory, to my lasting astonishment, was of Nanny Turner, forgetting her own fright for a moment, administering to me as I lost consciousness.

Out at sea, H.M.S. *Valerian*, one of the flower class sloops on the Station, was driven on to the reef and went down with all hands.

*   *   *

Nearly fifty years later I was to stand by that same tamarisk in the corner of the garden, the little bungalow unchanged but now in naval hands, as the Admiral Second-in-Command of the Western Fleet. By some strange quirk of fate, my last voyage at sea was to the West Indies, flying my Flag in the cruiser *Tiger*, to visit the Americans in Bermuda and Puerto Rico and Key West in Florida to further NATO relations. I had been back to my birthplace on and off during my career in varying ranks; but never in such comfort or in such changed circumstances from my beginning.

It was 1966 on a Spring morning that *Tiger* had edged through the hole in the reef off St. David's and wended her way past the sloping lawns of Government House, into Murray's Anchorage off the old dockyard, and then up through the Salt Kettle Cut, past the millionaire's hotels with early risers in their negligés scanning us from their balconies, to berth alongside the Capital's wharf at Hamilton.

It had been a solitary and sometimes stormy voyage across the

Atlantic and when a ship which has been pitched and rolling in the embraces of the oceans suddenly finds peace in the calm of sheltered water, in this case behind that same reef which had destroyed *Valerian*, a sudden ease overcomes the mental and physical faculties of those on board. Mental apathy from scanning an empty horizon is suddenly roused by the sight of land, the fruits of your labours as the naval prayer has it; the release from the automatic flexing of muscles to stay upright while, as in Nannie's cabin, the scuttles are dark and green and the fo'c's'le is an angry scene of foam through the hawse pipes with the spray spewing against the bridge windows above the bow turrets, enhances the deliverance from strain; and so emotion may excusably take hold of the sentimentalist. Looking through my binoculars to find my old home on Boaz on this morning, with the ship slipping gently across a lake of such vivid aquamarine that only sun and coral can invent—a blue that painters are generally accused of exaggerating—I suddenly asked the Flag Captain if he would bring all hands, who were not on duty, on deck, and in any dress.

"Why, sir?" asked my close friend, who commanded a superb Flagship for me and who was frequently tried by my extravagant whims. "We're just getting ready to enter harbour." He gave me that quizzical look which clearly implied I was being unreasonable. The average age of the *Tiger's* ship's company of some 700, including the likes of me, was just over 21.

"How many do you think have seen that coloured sea before?"

"Aye, aye, sir," he said—the classic reply peculiar to the Navy which avoids all argument and does not disclose whether you agree or not—and did so. I took it upon myself to explain my caprice to the sailors, many of whose experience had not been more than the winter seas around their own coast in endless NATO exercises.

"And what do you think of that?" I asked a young mechanical engineer from the boiler room after we had berthed.

"F.....g marvellous," was the reply I had hoped for.

When all the officialdom was over, when all the civic receptions had been accomplished and the inevitable quarterdeck cocktail party with Beat Retreat had passed without a thunderstorm, when the Lesson had been read in the Cathedral and Lord and Lady Mortonmere had been successfully entertained to dinner to the satisfaction of Chief Steward Ferraro (and, I hope, their Excellencies too), when I had watched the football match and visited the

American Air Base – in short, when that blessed moment for an Admiral arrives when he is not making small talk, when he is not eating more than he wants or drinking more than he should, when he has fought off all those who so kindly insist on entertaining him with a repetition of all such excesses – I asked for my car driven by Leading Stoker Mechanic Cavanagh with no flag on the bonnet and with nobody else to accompany me. "Plain clothes and picnic for the two of us, please."

The kindly officer of the Watch was waiting on the gangway to see me off. Poor fellow: how many thousands of hours had I spent around the world, pacing that quarterdeck and longing for something to happen, crises of weather, the odd drunk, even the Admiral going over the side. Anything to relieve the tedium of watchkeeping.

"When shall we expect you back, sir?"

"When do you want me? I won't be on the telephone."

"The Flag Lieutenant asked me to remind you, sir, that you are expected for dinner at Government House at 7.45 in Mess Undress. The Bishop is also dining, sir."

"Reassure the Flag Lieutenant I'll be there," and I joined the waiting Cavanagh respectfully holding open the rear door.

Cavanagh, was an old and trusted friend. A previous generation of Admirals would have had as driver one of the old school, a three-badge Able Seaman, "stripey" as he was affectionately known to the Navy and who lived for his daily tot, his run ashore and his reunion one day with the missus. He neither wished nor courted responsibility of the Leading Seaman's role or that of Petty Officer.

Content with his own caboosh in some obscure gun support where he nurtured his prick of leaf tobacco in spunyarn, pasting his nudes in juxtaposition to his wife and keeping his special pieces of seamanlike equipment in caressing affection against the day when they might be needed, stripey was the sage and character of the lower deck. It was he who brought me up, taught me the codes and language of the lower deck during my years as a Midshipman, explained those values sacrosanct to his calling, rummaged among the anecdotal extravagances of his escapades with women, and taught me the fallacies of socialism in that he wanted no more to be me than I could ever aspire to be him.

But stripey is no more. Modern thinking dictates that you cannot stand still: you must have ambition to promote yourself in any walk of life; and so, if the stripeys of this world will not now try to better themselves in rank, their pay stands still and their bemused rum-sodden wisdom only earns them an early place on the few shelves which still appreciate their classic virtues. Instead we have the young Leading Seaman of a different mould, equally admirable but strenuous and questing, filled with the potential of technological knowledge, properly thinking for himself and his family (which had to take second place for stripey), smart, alert and awake to the social differentials of the modern world. Of such was Cavanagh, a Leading Stoker mechanic qualified in driving, recently married and a father, and who in the hundreds of hours we spent together on the road was not inhibited, at my discretion, in discussing any subject he or I cared to raise, avoiding of course any personality common to our present circumstances. That would have been disloyal and embarrassing which was not in his creed or, indeed, mine.

It was a gentle day as we drove under the lighthouse, the modern hotels leading down to their beach umbrellas sheltering the browning bikini bodies intent upon their drinks.

In some ways there had been no change from the Bermuda I had known through the years–the bent cedars arching their trunks before the prevailing wind, the white spume from the breakers on the reef, the occasional cardinal or blue bird flitting from the oleander hedges, the natives themselves in their smock-like cotton dresses before their ramshackle houses–but the underlying impact of sophistication, born of the days of American prohibition when the shipping lines advertised "Come to Bermuda for an alcoholiday", the prostitution of a natural beauty which I had known unsullied by man's devices, preoccupied me.

So we drove slowly along the road now made fit for cars, over a modernised Albert's bridge, past every childish landmark which had marked my dawdling, "creeping like snail unwillingly to school", and came to the deserted dockyard at the southern extremity of Bermuda's horseshoe. It was an eerie feeling. A scene which I had associated throughout my life with bustle and bugles and bosun's pipes, and all the activity which warships seem to generate by day and night, was deserted and silent. In common with so many of the other foreign stations, the colour of which was the incentive to join the Navy, the West Indies squadron had long gone and the odd visit from a ship like *Tiger* from the U.K. was all that the colony could now expect. Tragically no use seemed to have been found for this relic of an old dockyard. Grass grew between the concrete of the quays. The bollards were still there but nothing else. Like a television documentary with that trick of quick fading, I saw on my imaginary screen the shapes of *Calcutta, Constance, Cambrian, Calliope* of the early twenties give way to *Danae, Dragon, York* and *Exeter* of the thirties; and then to *Vindictive* and *Devonshire,* the cadets' training cruisers out in Murray's Anchorage beyond the basin–*Devonshire* when, as First Lieutenant with my Captain and Commander ashore at some Government House reception, the wind had suddenly escalated from calm to gale in half an hour with a hundred cadets away under sail, all capsizing in minutes but only one drowning whose parents understandably demanded my Court Martial... "Last night I dreamt I went to Manderley," wrote Daphne du Maurier, at the outset of that evocative first chapter of her classic novel.

The old sail loft was boarded up; and yet so well built was it all that there was no sign of decay; just silent emptiness; no living soul; just Cavanagh and me and the breeze.

We drove back rather faster than Goodall and Sylvia used to take us, conversing on safer topics: Mrs Cavanagh and the baby that was coming; Manchester United and City's chances for The Cup; could I fix Hong Kong or Singapore for him next? Eventually the smart Bermudian sentry at Government House was acknowledging our arrival.

"Usual in the morning?"

"That's right; and thank you for the afternoon."

"Okay, sir. Makes a change."

And away he went towards a final run ashore as an A.D.C. greeted me in the hall.

*   *   *

Alone in my bedroom after the dinner at Government House I quickly undressed from Undress and naked threw up the window as the warm night breeze fanned my body. Condemned for so much of my waking life to the restrictions of uniform I have always experienced a physical satisfaction when the moment comes to be rid of it. With one or two exceptions–the padded eiderdown of full regalia, breathing in to accommodate the buckled sword-belt and a tunic collar which verges on restricted breathing; or the smart but unpractical starched white coat of tropical uniform when one blemish means laundering–naval uniform is extremely comfortable and, I submit, smart in its simplicity for both officer and rating.

Both are historic from the days of Anson and when worn correctly have established for their wearers a passport to acceptance in the world. Yet it is uniform which stamps both virtues and shortcomings of personality by a camouflage which can be either a benefit or the reverse. The sailor has long discovered that it endears him to the opposite sex of every colour and creed throughout the ports of the world; and the world has thus accepted his habits, not always for the good of his immortal soul. The honest officer should admit that because of his dress and the respect it has earned through the behaviour of his forebears, he is immediately favourably regarded in most company, particularly mixed company, and treated to flattery which his own accomplishments may not deserve. "When I first put this uniform on . . . ." Gold braid *has* a charm for the fair and what applied to the heavy dragoons of "Patience" has seemed to me to apply equally to the Navy; be that as it may, it is nevertheless delightful even when the fair are not with you, and even more when they are and have shed their trappings too, to be unfettered and seen for what you are. To get out of "The Rig of the Day" is therefore always a joy to officers and man alike, on any pretext. The great advantage of sea to harbour is the laxity which the former allows; so that on the Russian Convoys my Admiral had worn blue corduroy trousers, a feather boa on his anorak and an oak-leaved cap to remind of his authority.

Thus unsheathed I leant out of my window, hypnotised by the orange path of the waning moon, straight as the lines of a race track across the great lagoon which is the centre of the archipelago, gazing across the formal garden beneath me which, had I but known it, was so soon to be the scene of the callous and brutal assassination of Lord Mortonmere's successor as Governor on just such a night as this, and out to the deserted blackness of the old Ireland Island dockyard which the lights of the cruisers used to decorate; across to where I had been that afternoon and where, by premonition, I sensed I would never go again. The restless splashing of the ebb and flow on the rocks at the bottom of the garden was, in the stillness, the treble clef to the bass rumble of the Atlantic. After thousands of uninterrupted miles the ocean meets its first obstacle against the coral ramparts of the reef which guards the islands; maybe the outer lip of the crater at the summit of some hidden volcano which once erupted and from which the depths now fall sheer to thousands of fathoms.

The steaming lights and starboard bow light of a ship emerging from the cut from Hamilton appeared on my left and turned into the Seaward channel which passed beneath me, my own way in *Tiger* on the morrow at the outset of our journey home. The jagged silhouette of the small liner was carved as she crossed the moon's path, the lights from her scuttles dotted like a typewriter in her hull before only her stern light showed as she glided on towards the hole in the reef off St. David's.

No, I did not think I should be likely to return to the love of my childhood, a love which had childishly lured me towards so much. There is too much else on this planet still to see and, while still serving, sailors only can scratch at the periphery of continents. They see the bustle and taste both the stimulus and the sleaziness of ports which sailors themselves create; for time itself and the daily round, the common task of ship's duties generally forbids them penetrating into the inner beauties of a hinterland.

The red and white flashing buoys in the Sound could have continued to wink their hypnotism upon me all night, but a shiver reminded me that I was still naked and the dawn would not be far away. Even now the engine room stoker mechanics of the Morning Watch would be flashing up the additional boilers necessary for sea. The men below start first, as one was to learn during Engine Room training; then after Reveille and Hands-Fall-In at dawn, preparing for sea is continued. Sleepy Officers, who may not have left their last night party ashore all that long before, pull on a pair of trousers and a uniform jacket over their pyjamas, wind a scarf around the neck and cram a cap on the head to appear on deck just before their Commander, who was in all likelihood at that same party. It is a point of discipline that they are there before the Commander . . . just . . . while the sailors, watch aboard, have had a full night in. It is also a point of honour that the Commander,

Second-in-Command, personally directs the sailors' activities at this early hour.

"Prepare for sea. Furl Quarterdeck awning. Hoist boats. Single up wires." The friendly roof over the Quarterdeck which protects from rain and sun in harbour, which allows you to transform the heaving platform at sea into a decorated shrine fit for Kings and Queens in harbour, collapses and is folded away on the shoulders of the Quarterdeck seamen. Many of the wires holding the ship are uncoiled from their bollards to leave the bare minimum for the last moment of connection with the shore. The boats are hoisted to their davits and griped to their sea positions. Radar aerials begin to revolve as all the technological procedure is tested. Watertight doors below are slammed and secured, often to make difficult the navigation of normal passage ways. The hum of the boiler room fans crescendo, and on the messdeck and in cabin alike everything that could move is secured. Your wife and children, your fiancée or mother, go into a drawer. Only the nudes stuck to the lockers stay put. Suddenly from being your home the ship becomes the stark machine for which she was designed; she lifts her attractive frock over her head, shakes her hair and puts on jersey and jeans.

"Hands to breakfast and clean into the rig of the day for leaving harbour", and it is finished. The Captain, recently having been Commander himself, listens to this from his bunk and private breakfast, with comfortable nonchalance; to the bustle overhead and the pipes and the noises of a ship which has found herself. In due course the Commander will simply report "Ready for Sea, sir", which at that stage is all he wants to know.

And so after sincere farewell to my kind and generous hosts, Their Excellencies, I would go on board to be greeted by a smiling Captain and Commander and Flag Lieutenant and quarterdeck staff, a little self-conscious in knowing all that had been happening for many hours beforehand to which I had contributed nothing. Down in the cabin there would be the Press. "Could you give us your impressions?" There would be the Flag Lieutenant: "These are the 'Thank you' signals I suggest you send, sir." There would be the Secretary: "Only five signatures please, sir, to catch Air-Mail. And these two orders for arrest of your fellow Bermudians, please." There would be the Staff Officer Operations with a chart: "We're due to meet the Americans here, sir, tomorrow. I suggest this signal." There would also be a strange crowd of people in the cabin, some of whom one knew and others one did not, but who are always there on the flimsiest pretext. In fact the cabin would be full: full of genuine well-wishers whom one would probably never see again but at that moment must matter.

And doubtless there will be the Mayor. "You'll come back, won't you?", while the Flag Captain whispers, "Excuse me, sir, but I'll be away. We're ready when you are": the definitive moment when small talk must stop and it's time once again to become professional. This helped by the series of bugle calls and the quartermaster's voice through the loudspeakers which announce in turn "Special Sea Dutymen to your stations. Cable party muster on the fo'c's'le. Stand by wires and hawsers. Guard and Band fall in. Hands to stations for leaving harbour." Binoculars put round the neck help to create a professional air, to persuade an animated throng that it is time for them to go; and as the last is shepherded over the side and the gangway slides ashore the Admiral climbs to his Bridge out of the Captain's way.

There is no more relaxed moment for the Flag Officer than this. In company with a squadron or Fleet, particularly if foreign NATO ships are in company, then of course he has the responsibility that they leave harbour in an orderly and safe procession to sea; but as a single Flagship responsibility from the upper Admiral's Bridge is no more than that of a passenger in a liner who watches with interest the procedure of going to sea although, having done it himself, an Admiral may appreciate the niceties of seamanship skill a little more acutely. It is a gay scene. The ship should be looking her best, still to the onlooker in a frock concealing the working jeans; guns all immaculately angled, boats secured, the sailors uniformly dressed fallen in by divisions, all scuttles closed with no inquisitive heads peering out to wave farewell, the Guard paraded on the quarterdeck and, with an imaginative Bandmaster, appropriate tunes being played—"Will ye no come back?", generally some Rogers and Hammerstein current hit ("There's no Business Like Showbusiness", which is just what this is all about), and as the stern fades from earshot, "Auld Lang Syne". Handkerchiefs flutter while the sailors display a stoic calm in the circumstances, standing strictly at ease or at attention, untempted by their temporary female partners of the last few days to be demonstrative to their corny shouts of remembrance. Maudlin pledges are, I am afraid, often more enduring within the female breast than that of the Able Seaman which is already beating to another rhythm; and the Welfare may have some posthumous pregnancies to adjudicate in due course; but now all is laughter and tears at parting in the style of the Navy's reputation.

Although The Flag is standing only twenty feet above, procedure is still adopted by the *Tiger's* Command. Flags asking permission to proceed from the Admiral are run up at the yard arm. "Approved," from the Flag Lieutenant down the voice pipe.

"Let go for'ard. Hold on to the back spring. Let go aft. Slow astern starboard," and the bow swings slowly off the quay.

"All gone for'ard." "All gone aft" from the ends of the ship.

"Very good. Let go the spring. Port 25, slow ahead both. Midships. Starboard 25.". And, nicely done, the stern brushes clear in the faces of a fascinated crowd. "Cable party fall in." while the Cable Officer takes his stance in the eyes of the ship, the men fall in between the cables and the lady makes her final adieu with a curtsey which should say, "Thank you for the dance", fluttering her skirts with the wake of engines now proceeding at half speed.

Down to the Sound with friends of yesterday waving from their balconies and verandahs. Out into the great lagoon, needing to recognise now those buoys by their shape and not by their light. Under the lawns of Government House of memory and official waves; under the swooping salute of American aircraft giving the ship the Big Hullo of Damon Runyon; and out through the hole in the reef to the embrace of the Atlantic.

"Disperse. Fall out Special Sea Dutymen. Close up Cruising Watch," and the scene changes to work-a-day dress, sea routine. The odd remark floats to one's ears, declined with the word which is the staple vocabulary of all sailors from which one gains the general impression that that was Bermuda, that was, epitomised in the words of my Stoker Mechanic of a few days before as the tip of Gibb's Hill lighthouse finally dips below the horizon—"F.....g marvellous." We all have our own way of expressing ourselves.

It is not entirely selfish subterfuge which prompted me to persuade Their Lordships and my C-in-C that it would be appropriate for *Tiger* and me to visit the Caribbean and exercise with the U.S. Navy within that area, thus including my Swan Song at sea to the scene, as it were, of where I began. Shorn of any regular naval presence our loyal (and, in the case of Bermuda itself, oldest) members of the Commonwealth so close to the American coastline now saw the White Ensign spasmodically. NATO works at sea and the more frequently individual ships and their peoples can perform within its auspices the better.

It is perfectly feasible and safe to meet a completely strange international force–Americans, Canadians, Germans, Dutch, Norwegians, Belgians–none of whom have been in company before and form them up in darkness ready for manoeuvres at dawn. No pride of nation: no personality jealousies: rank is rank in all navies, so that it makes not a jot of difference provided the seniority list is known and there is no misunderstanding within the command. When back in harbour those who have sailed together cement their friendships socially during respite from their common antagonist, the sea. Today therefore off San Juan, Puerto Rico was not difficult; only one other nation present whose force was commanded by a charming Commodore with whose family I had just enjoyed a hilarious weekend.

Enough is always enough. "Exercises completed. Proceed independently."

"Thanks, Admiral. Good value. I'll be away now. Have a good leave."

"'Bye, Commodore. Your boys did well. Please convey my congratulations on their performance. Love to Betty, and of course junior."

"Okay. Be seeing you," and off they go in comfortable line ahead.

Alone, *Tiger* is left to set the Great Circle course for the English Channel, Portsmouth and leave. That rare circumstance for the Flagship, alone for ten days while the sea changes from blue to dirty green to a grey flecked foam to brown; from a gentle swell to the angry, cavernous ramparts of a mid-Atlantic gale when the tons of water sluice from the hawse pipes over "A" Turret and the Bridge, and then subside at the Continental shelf.

Occasionally the outline of the navigation lights of a passing ship and the welcome break in monotony by exchange of signal; but in the main the resources of the officers are required to amuse seven hundred men–or rather pretend to amuse them because they do not need it. The facade of quiz competitions, of thinking aloud by "the old man" (as an Admiral of any vintage is invariably called and today, by way of my valedictory, was on the lines of these reflections) of "These you have loved", and other contrived musical divertissements...these are necessary yet unnecessary; they are merely devices to make the clock tick quicker; for everybody knows that every hour endured, be it in the engine room or aloft, is sixteen miles nearer home, nearer to Pompey. And what else matters?

The patience of the married is about to be rewarded by that first long embrace and the young bundles who throw themselves into your arms on the concrete path to the front door in a stampede of affection. The patience of those whose fiancées will be waiting at South Railway Jetty – and there are always many – will also be rewarded; patience is not the word I would use for the third category, though: that of the uncommitted, the stripeys, the characters, the habituals of the knock-shops and the Pompey whores. To them, arrival in Portsmouth is as evocative as to their officers, if in a different way. Each may ask no more than "his Nancy on his knee and his arms around her waist", though I doubt it. Of what I am in no doubt is that be it Captain, Lieutenant, Petty Officer or Able Seaman, that first night at home has a potency which the cynical may decry but which I would still presume to think has a bearing upon the fact that sailors on the whole are happy people.

The first sight of land...Bishop's Rock off the Scillies...The Lizard...Portland Bill...St. Catherine's on the Isle of Wight...the sentinels of the channel...all the familiar landmarks which mean so much when you have been away–these went down the port beam as we made our way to The Nab Tower and up into Spithead...up alongside to the Flagship berth in Portsmouth dockyard. "Fall out Special Sea Dutymen. Finished with main engines." The gangway was quickly out and hundreds were throwing themselves into each others' arms, children milling on the touchlines up and down before the cameras, in a scene of spontaneous and wild affection.

My own was in my sleeping cabin, tactfully interrupted by my Leading Steward in due course with a signal to the effect that the Commander-in-Chief, Portsmouth, with whom I had been shipmates during the Russian Convoys, would receive my farewell call in his Flagship, Nelson's *Victory*, on the morrow and would I bring Rosalind my wife to lunch?

There are some appointments, particularly those which carry

responsibility for planning future appointments of officers, for instance, when a lengthy turn-over may be necessary. In the case of an officer's future, you must know of his domestic problems as well as his professional standing and ability; and hundreds must be considered in detail with your predecessor or successor; but for sea-going Admirals—and how fortunate I had been to be among the now pitifully few—it is little more than a quick piece of ceremonial. Your successor probably has very different ideas from your own on how he wishes to conduct the Fleet and there is an expert staff officer in every technical branch to help embroider the tapestry against which he will make changes or not. A personal letter or two beforehand on the main headaches you will have to bequeath; a single sheet of points to discuss in an hour together in the cabin on the day. You have both been in the Navy a long time and in all likelihood served together at some point. Certainly you will know each other's foibles and idiosyncrasies and, if they don't already, the staff will quickly find them out. The Captain gets one cuckoo out of his nest only for another to fly in. So the signal goes out: "Portsmouth Command General from C-in-C: Info: C-in-C Fleet" (my boss underground in Middlesex with the R.A.F. coastal). "Rear Admiral M. P. Pollock * will succeed Vice Admiral J. O. C. Hayes as Flag Officer Second-in-Command Western Fleet at 1100 tomorrow, Thursday. The Flag of Vice Admiral Hayes will be struck in H.M.S. *Tiger* at sunset and that of Rear Admiral Pollock hoisted at Colours on Friday..."

That's all there is to it. By 10.30 on Thursday the Guard and Band are drawn up on the quarterdeck. The Upper Deck is cleared, the Piping Party is ranged by the gangway, the array of officers is mustered in a semi-circle at its head. It isn't raining. You stand back, for your entrance is not yet. There's no business like show business.

"Sound the Alert," as Michael's car comes into sight.

"Pipe," as he sets foot upon the bottom rung of the gangway.

"Guard... General Salute... Present Arms," as he comes to the top and sets foot on the deck of his Flagship which was once yours.

---

* Michael Pollock, now Admiral of the Fleet, was to become First Sea Lord; but his first duty then was to get out of "our" bunk in favour of the prime Minister who took possession of the ship for the "Tiger Talks" with Mr Smith of Rhodesia at Gibraltar in that Spring of 1966.

All stand still while the band play the Admiral's musi-
cal salute ... Iolanthe ... appropriately (or inappropriately), "When
Britain really ruled the waves in good Queen Bess's time.... Yet
Britain set the world ablaze in good King George's glorious days".
Would that she still did, under the topmasts of *Victory* dominating
the scene.

"Good morning, Michael."

"Good morning, Joc."

"Would you like to inspect your Guard?"   "Thank you." You
follow astern of Michael and the Officer of the Guard as he makes
his perfunctory inspection. In this brief time, though eyes are
steadfastly ahead, he knows he is being scrutinised. The Cavanaghs
are watching.

Down to the cabin, a few awkward words because this is the end;
and then it's your turn. The desk is empty and your pictures have
gone. In no time there will be another girl there and the
Impressionists will be followed by a different taste. Let's get out.
Good-bye to the loyal personal staff who have ministered to your
every need; to Ferraro, the Chef, the valet, your messenger.
Good-bye to those who have carried you on their shoulders and
propped you back on to your pedestal every time your incompetence
made you wobble. If you wear your heart on your sleeve it is hard to
choke back emotion which is untidy; but back up to the
quarterdeck.

"Band ready. Guard, Admiral's salute present arms."

"Good-bye, Michael. Good luck."

"So long, Joc. And to you."

Handshakes to those clustered around you, starting with the
Captain.

"Goodbye, Geoff. Thanks a lot."

"Pipe", as your foot steps onto the gangway. Iolanthe again.
Cavanagh waiting with the car door open. You turn at the salute for
the last time and tuck in your sword as you get in; and as the car
moves away you hear the "Carry On" from the bugle, relaxation on
board, as much as to say, "That was him, that was", while Michael
says, "Now then, Geoffrey...."

Out of the dockyard by the old Navigation School where I had
once qualified; past *Vernon* where I had tried to master the
intricacies of the torpedo and naval electrics; past Whale Island

Gunnery School, where, much to my surprise as a Sub-Lieutenant, I had learnt to say boo to a goose, meaning being taught how to give a command; past the site of the old Hippodrome where many a Sub had misbehaved and suffered in consequence; suddenly away from the sea in command for the last time and on to an unknown different life in an Admiralty House in Scotland which would be the final Swan Song.

"Our Revels" insofar as shared life with that mercurial character, the sailor is identified, "now are ended". They were capricious enough while they lasted.

Chapter 2

Family Forebears—Military and Pacifist

I am aware that my memories of Bermuda, my alpha and omega, the nostalgia and the sentiment, the tiny beginnings and the rather pompous ending to my naval association with the coral atoll have seduced me; for I have left my devoted mother, patiently awaiting her thirteen year old offspring in some bleak vestibule in Tothill Street for forty years. Ejected by the interviewing Admirals I was restored to her via the bemedalled, brown-belted and buckled janitor.

"'Ere y'are Madam. Still in one piece. 'Ope 'e makes it," and we were out on the pavement.

We didn't speak on the way to the restaurant, nothing so immediately trite as "Well, darling, what did they ask you?" To her dying day my mother never asked me an obtrusive question. After lunch we went to look at the death of Nelson in Madam Tussauds.

Conscious of what was uppermost in both our minds, for failure would have been as great a disappointment for her on my behalf, set as I had been on this unlikely goal from the age of seven, my mother was quiet. Indeed of all memories of her, I treasure her reticence and tranquillity, never advancing opinion unless asked and sharing with her future daughter- in-law, the two ladies of my life, that tribute sobbed by the anguished Lear with his dead and adored Cordelia in his arms; "Her voice was ever soft, gentle and low, an excellent thing in woman." So we quietly went out in the tube to Golders Green to see my first Gilbert and Sullivan prior to return to school next day.

24

The double bill of *Trial by Jury* and *Pinafore* was a happy coincidence. The one obviously so, the other to have significance when I married a Judge's daughter. Neither of them, on that night, were to be appreciated by a schoolboy as among the best lampoons of the Law and the Navy ever written. Such appreciation was to come later. Apart from the Judge's song, I was one day to watch my father-in-law, in a moment of relaxation from preparing a judgement on murder when he must have known that the Black Cap was inevitable, crease into smiles at "in the reign of James the Second, it was generally reckoned as a very serious crime to marry two wives at a time".

But in the great days of Henry Lytton and Bertha Lewis, whom the said Judge was to count among his Circuit guests in Judge's Lodgings, *Pinafore*, to an aspiring Cadet was hilarious. The anatomies of my inquisitors of the morning melted from my awe into something insignificant at the very thought of "Stick close to your desks and never go to sea, and you all may be Rulers of the Queen's Navee!" And to think of the daughter of a First Lord of the Admiralty (whom later I was to serve as his Naval Secretary) falling in love with an Able Seaman.... What a caricature! So it was...then.

It isn't, of course, any longer. Ralph Rackstraw to-day is what is known as an Upper Yardman, the cream of Nelson's sailors. It is the name now given to those few hand-picked Able Seamen in their early twenties who are selected on personality and ability to train and become equal in potential and opportunity with their Public School counterparts at the Royal Naval College. I was once privileged to have charge of some of the first of them, amongst whom is the recent Flag Officer, Royal Yacht.

"Art thou troubled? Music will calm thee..." How often that was to be so; and perhaps never more so, on a childish plane, than when I said goodnight to my mother after an introduction to that light operatic world which, to this day, give me at moments as much pleasure musically and by the versifying of our language as on that first occasion.

So to my family forebears; my maternal grandmother was a remarkable lady; when at 8 years old it was time for me to leave Bermuda for school in England, she brought me across the Atlantic in a banana boat to her home in Birmingham, which was to be my home too during my most formative years. Little could I know then of the compass of the life she had led as mountaineer and suffragist–she was just Granny to me . . . .

Although my grandmother was a confirmed pacifist, I always felt she had a special sympathy for my mother, the only one of the family to marry a man who went to war in uniform. My father had just been commissioned into the R.A.M.C., after qualifying in medicine at Birmingham University, when he married his schoolday sweetheart in 1912. A year later, they went to Bermuda, where I was born. When they came home on their first leave, though, they found Europe on the brink of war.

My father's injuries in that war were to influence the rest of his life; I grew up finding a man permanently frustrated by the physical wounds of war but with a mind still rapier sharp, like a well-tuned internal combustion engine set in a fractured chassis, and this led on occasion to a spasmodic but daunting irascibility devoid of any substance. In later years, however, awake in my dormitory bed, aligned with thirty others at the Royal Naval College, or in a hammock in the half-light of a battleship's after cabin flat, I came to understand far better the man who had always hoped that one day he would have the time to write. As we both advanced in years, we became far closer, although I could never reach the peaks upon which his imagination gazed.

Chapter 3

The Very Bottom Rung

January 1927. The Royal Naval College, Dartmouth, D. Block. Frobisher Dormitory. We lay rigid on our backs in our iron beds looking at the ceiling, listening for the next command. The serried ranks, twenty either side, had been dressed like the Guards for the Trooping of the Colour, bedhead to bedhead, chest to chest, twenty of us either side of the bleak dormitory, staggered in alphabetical order. Hayes was to sleep next to Hesselgrave and Hunting for the next four years. One day I was to see Alec Hunting plunge to his death from the Anti-Aircraft Top of *Repulse* while I plummeted off the Flag Deck. So we lay exhausted after our first day in Cadet naval uniform which had begun on Paddington Station that morning. One pillow, two sheets, a blanket and the blue uniform rug folded over the end of the bed with the initials J.O.C.H. uppermost.

"Hayes. Turn out." The Cadet Captain was waiting for me, kindly because this was indoctrination. I was to be taught about my sea-chest, a curious kind of chest-of-drawers which contained my uniform.

"Your cap goes here, at the top in the middle, peak just over-lapping the edge and with lanyard coiled down, so. Your reefer, folded thus, goes on the right of the flap...here. Your vest, folded like a pancake, goes on the left hand side...here. Your two socks, folded thus, cross the vest at either end. Your shirt, pants, tie go here, on this shelf. Your boots go here. This locked drawer is called your Private Till and you can have the key on your lanyard; but of course you mustn't keep anything in it which is against the rules."

(This, I was one day to discover, meant nudes.) "Your slippers go under here at the head of your bed."

At this point we were interrupted. "Dress the chests."

Everybody got out of bed and stood by their chests while two Cadets at either end of the dormitory gave instructions–again like dressing the ranks. "Up in the middle. Back at the far end. Hayes, yours is crooked," until somebody said "Steady". Then the Cadet Captain came back to me. "Now I'll explain the wash-place."We went out to that area where there was a small salt-water swimming bath called The Plunge and a cage above an enamel basin which was my washing pitch.

"Your sponge goes here. Your soap is there and on this mug you will put your toothbrush facing this way and *not* that way. Toothpaste inside the mug. On Reveille you will go through the plunge and then wash. You will have one bath a week and should you slip up on any of these details you will receive a tick. Four ticks means three cuts. Is that clear?"

"Thank you."

"Then turn in and wait for the next order."

Pause while the other thirty in the dormitory were receiving similar instructions. Then:

"Windows half open South. Shut North."

Happily my bed faced South. No time to look then but in fact it commanded that matchless view over Dartmouth and Kingswear harbours and out through the cliffs to the Channel; but right now I was busy getting the sash of my window in line with the other fifteen in the line. As there was a gale from the North my opposite numbers were happy enough to shut theirs.

"Steady! Turn in."

Pause while one wondered what was coming next. You couldn't guess.

"Say your prayers."

Never having been brought up to this habit I didn't know what to think or who to talk to but was grateful for a breather on my knees. Doubtless God, or Whoever may have been the recipient of whatever thoughts tumbled out from us just then, would have understood our final relief at "Turn in. Lights out." Just two pink glows in Frobisher dormitory hanging along the whole distance. Then snoring.

When awakening the dead at the end of a military funeral the Reveille played by a first-class bugler is emotional and enlivening: it is the natural corollary to the Last Post: it is less emotional or enlivening from the Parade Ground at 6.00 a.m. when awakening 500 cadets. One soon got the drill. If you were already awake you could just hear the bugler spit into his instrument before sounding off. This was the moment to get out of bed naked, with the sheet still over your back, and on the first note career to the plunge, wet your hair in the cold salt water and be drying frantically by the time the Cadet Captain appeared to see if you had been through. But this took a day or two to learn; so first days were torture. Cold salt water is sticky and uninvigorating prior to early morning school, and the niceties of "The Rules and Regulations for Preventing Collisions at Sea" as taught by a seemingly very wide-awake Lieutenant, the Term Officer.

Much has been written of the history of that masterpiece of commanding architecture by Sir Aston Webb which still dominates Dartmouth harbour, the Royal Naval College; and if Sir Aston was the professional of works and bricks, bricks which have since seen the kindergarten of thousand upon thousand of embryo naval officers of ever widening background and potential, the great and controversial Admiral of the Fleet, Jacky Fisher, was the visionary who realised that the time had come to supercede the traditional wooden walls of a nineteenth-century man-of-war called Britannia, moored in the river Dart, by a rather more sophisticated method of training.

To judge from the endless controversies which have attended such dramatic decisions concerning the training of either officers or ratings—and I was to be concerned with both in my span of service—the mind boggles at the strength of opinion which must have been mobilised in Wardrooms, Pall Mall, the Admiralty and anywhere the Navy is discussed concerning such a "retrograde" step. To give but a recent example: when it was decided that modern technology in the Fleet demanded rather more than that a boy should be a chip off the old block, a first-class lad with plenty of guts, a damned good sort who would get on with anybody on or off the playing fields, but that he also needed at least two "A"-Level passes in mathematical subjects to be admitted into Dartmouth, the complexions of some naval fathers went deep purple with indignation. The old adage that the fool of the family went to sea and like as not did very well died hard. It is my experience that no two officers ever agree, maybe healthily disagree, on exactly how Cadets or Midshipmen should be trained; and so, because it was long before I was born, I can only guess at the heat which will have been engendered when finally in 1900 the contract for the new College was signed and two years later King Edward VII laid the foundation stone on that hill for what was to become an imposing cradle for those of us who, at the age of twelve, had decided we wanted to lie in it.

Those who wish to probe further into the circumstances which surrounded the replacement of the old Britannia by its more permanent successor, the Britannia Royal Naval College and the history of its early years, and a fascinating story it is, should read the book of that title by Mr. E.A. Hughes. He tells the story of the College from 1903, when the first Cadets joined, to 1948 when postwar and political expediences wrought the next major change in the nature of officer material. Few were better equipped to write that history after thirty-seven years on the staff, finishing as Second Master and Head of the History and English Department. He even managed to teach me that "harass" has one "r" and "embarrass" two; this by bribing with an ice cream boys who could spell fifty such grammatical inconsistencies without a mistake; but he was the first to write about the institution at which the naval officer begins the training that makes him what I believe he is, always was and always will be; and I have always taken it as a compliment, in which Dartmouth must share, that the British public on the whole takes the quality of the Royal Navy for granted. Two World Wars in this century I submit have not been a bad advertisement for that quality; and my parents gave me to understand, when a Midshipman on the China Station in 1931, that the Mutiny at Invergordon (where I now live) had a profound effect upon the British people.

Coming to Dartmouth some twenty-four years after it was first commissioned, I presume only to try to recall some of my more vivid memories of four utterly inconspicuous years. They were neither happy nor unhappy. Nobody was unkind. As I didn't grow until I was seventeen I was always in the middle of the rank, too small to get my Colours for anything in a company which set great store by blazer badges and coloured stockings; and too small ever to be considered for the gold chevron of Cadet Captain, the prefects of the College. In one way this allowed one to find a certain level, if a rather negative one, among others similarly placed: as if we wore a sticker saying "Not wanted on the voyage": in other ways one was too young to understand that physical prowess at that age is the hallmark of puberty. Such attributes as I may have had, a mild ability towards the piano for instance, were no help. Music at Dartmouth in those days was considered, if not actually homosexual, not a necessary part of the make-up. The maximum quota was thirty minutes a week from a dear man with a wounded leg from the last war who taught me in four years to play three little pieces with, still, not many sharps or flats. After the lesson in the evening, exercise for the day had to be made up by running to Ditisham. The pianos for practice were at the end of Frobisher Dormitory. So my repertoire remained fairly static.

Running...running...running....This remains my lasting impression of Dartmouth and happily I was not too bad at it. Why it was necessary to run all day except when eating or sitting in class, the odd system in force at the time and long since changed, seems even odder today.

After the hurdles of interview and exam previously described, fifty Cadets had trudged up the hundreds of steps from the river to the college, in our uniform for the first time and with our initialled Gladstone Bags (now still used by my children) on that January afternoon to become the Anson Term. A term consisted of fifty Cadets, each named after a distinguished Admiral of the past. You stayed in that Term and among that same fifty throughout the four years. Then you went to sea. So it was like standing on a moving staircase, unable to step up or back, until eventually you got to the top; and each term you went up one in seniority, the name of the eleventh Term starting again at the bottom after its three months of God-like stardom. Benbow, Hood, Rodney, Duncan, St. Vincent, Drake, Blake, Hawke, Grenville, Exmouth (I never quite understood why he was included in such company) and Anson—that was the order. Nelson was excluded in case of superiority complex and was the name of the dining hall. Others were relegated to dormitory names. Every Term had a Gunroom, its wooden benched lockered community hall. They were beautiful rooms with superb views, scrubbed and without comfort save for a window seat cushion, and they lined the two vastly long corridors in the two main blocks. You had to run past any gunroom which was senior to yours and so for your first term you ran past the lot, diminishing one every term and were the more ready for your meal because of it.

Class was an oasis in which you could sit down; and concerning this curriculum I have subsequently pondered. Running perpetually, dodging the plunges, endless rifle drill on the parade ground, endless marching, running again to Ditisham to atone for half an hour at the piano, antiquated systems of corporal punishment because you'd misdirected your toothbrush, the rightful scrupulous attention to dress at all times, in fact the whole marshalling of a system whereby the young human material was moulded towards a future purpose in a profession chosen either by itself or by its sponsors. All this has since seemed to me an acceptable pattern of the times to shape for the role of the times. Competition to get into the Navy was colossal from a certain sector and if you were not prepared to take the medicine which was apparently necessary to befit you for it, too bad: or in modern parlance, so what? There was no looking back and no getting out. Your father had signed a contract that you would serve the Navy at Their Lordship's discretion and in my case that lasted for forty two years. Yet there is one aspect of that contract which I have always thought a little one-sided; because in the true sense of the word the Royal Naval College did not give you an education. I do not dwell on this critically but rather through hindsight interest in a mode of upbringing which, discussing it with experienced educationalists today and hideous though the academic gaps within myself have always seemed, may not have been so inhibiting as I then thought it to be.

It was natural enough that the main accent of the curriculum should have been on Maths: you had achieved Scholarship standard in Maths to be there at all: so Maths, Maths and more Maths, the rudiments of Navigation, applied mechanics, chemistry and Seamanship (knots, splices, bends and hitches, parts of a ship rigging, Rule of the Road, anchor work–this latter remaining among the few arts of seamanship together with ship handling in the Navy of today)–this was the staple diet of classroom instruction understandably enough; but for the rest... a little French which reached no higher standard than Noel Coward's "*Parlez vous Francais? Un peu but I never think that's quite enough, do you?*", or Terence

Rattigan's classic remark in *French without tears*–"*Ideés au dessus de sa gare*"–that was French that was.

There was about a period a week for English and two for naval history. During the latter you spent endless time drawing meticulous little pictures of how Lord Howe cut the line from-to-leeward at his battle of the Glorious First of June in 1794 (the date sticks); or how a disobedient Captain called Horatio Nelson defied the orders of his Commander-in-Chief called Admiral Jervis at the battle of Cape St. Vincent in 1797 and gained a knighthood rather than Court Martial for doing so; or how the heroic Nelson with Collingwood pierced the combined French/Spanish lines at Trafalgar; but you were not given a clue why any of them were where they were or why they were doing it. That was left to your later reading and, should you have any, inquisitiveness. Mine subsequently was aroused and so I found out; but not until 1934, when I was sent to the so-called Naval University of the time, the Royal Naval College, Greenwich, and was taught by the most brilliant lecturer in my orbit, Professor Bullock who, when he suddenly switched his remarks from contraceptives to the Battle of the Nile, you realised had perceived that his Head of History department had entered the room. Even then only four hours a week were devoted to English Literature, naval history from the Battle of Lepanto and General history from Bismarck. Professor Bullock and I shared a love of Wagner so that I was able to tap his knowledge on occasions when we together went to The Garden.

That said, the quality of the teaching itself at Dartmouth within the prescribed limits of the syllabus was superb. Our teachers were part of the very structure of the College. Each was a character in his own right, known and certainly revered by us all. I do not think I remember a change in the teaching staff during my four years in their care, unlike today when teachers often seem to me to arrive at a school already looking over their shoulder to see how this rung could take them one higher as quickly as possible. Term by term the originally black gowns went a deeper shade of olive green, a hallmark of seniority like the Club tie of the oldest member. Term by term the idiosyncrasies became more distinct and individual, Cadets either increased or dwindled in their love of escape with what those idiosyncrasies had to offer from the daily philistine curriculum.

There was T.S. Sampson, tremendously tall with black teeth and the warmest smile, a bachelor whose hobby was ancient weapons of war. So he made the most beautiful trebuchets and arbilasts with which you could either sling five–balls or shoot darts into match-box hoards secreted in a fort built above the blackboard of study No. 36. Each hoard contained a sixpence. There was the legendary P.T. Harrison, drier than Tio Pepe, gnarled in his ageing mathematical aegis, outwardly terrifying and inwardly humane, whose gown was perhaps the most mottled green of them all. When you failed to surmount the niceties of differentiation or integration in the calculus or were not paying attention to his illegible hieroglyphics on the blackboard, the sweep of the arm would command "stand out that boy: stand right out where I can see you: now let us look at you", only to be interrupted one day when two cocker spaniels from another Maths master down the corridor somehow got into P.T.H.s study No. 53 to be greeted with, "Get out, you little black bastards", whereupon I sat down again, unnoticed in the turmoil.

They were all personalities like this, part of the Navy list, part of the Navy whom we remember with affection and who together saw thousands of us upon our way and compared notes with our uniformed instructors about our individual progress or otherwise. If old age called one to retirement there was a noticeable gap. They were so fair, so understanding of the physical demands which were also being made upon our small frames.

The system had a normal ingredient in which I was particularly fortunate. Although you may have been taught by T.S.S. for history or P.T.H. for Maths, every Cadet was under the overall guidance of his principle mentor, his tutor. Every master had his tutor set which included a few boys from every Term in the College, the only vertical leveller in the structure of those days.

H.E. Piggott, the Second Master who never in fact became Headmaster, was my mentor. He had known my mother and father previously and was to prove an influence in my young life for which I shall for ever be grateful. Apart from being a brilliant teacher of Maths to whose standards I could never aspire, he was also a brilliant organist and choir teacher, a more than competent pianist, a compelling exciter of interests in the arts, a story teller about those arts to whom you could not fail to pay attention, and a very kind family man. He was to me, and remained so when I got a little bit more senior than a Cadet and corresponded with him to the rest of his days, the oasis in an otherwise artistic desert.

During my early Dartmouth years it was his painful duty to watch my steady decline in the class order. Thanks to Stanley Harris and the teaching at my preparatory school St. Ronans I had entered fairly high; and I suspect I thought I could rest on those laurels. Every term I slipped lower until H.E.P. called a halt and told me that he would no longer stomach such laziness. Nor would he allow his sweet wife to give me the sweet cakes I so much enjoyed in their house overlooking the harbour. This did the trick.

By coincidence, Sir Adrian Boult not only shared a friendship at Westminster School with the Harris family but also with Harry Piggott of whom he writes in his autobiography *My Own Trumpet*:

"In one respect besides my concert-going my musical development was greatly helped while at school by a young master named Piggott. He had joined the staff straight from Cambridge where it had been realised how intensely musical he was, though his main subject was physics. He did not stay long at Westminster but while he was there I had most valuable guidance from him, in a weekly 'private hour', in harmony, counterpoint and analysis, which opened the door for me into the whole idea of structure and formal balance. He showed me how to analyse scores we were about to hear at concerts; he made me write a violin sonata following, bar for bar, Beethoven's F major, and introduced me to Tovey's Meiningen programme, the first annotations, I believe, that he ever wrote. Piggott went on to Dartmouth, where he ultimately became second master, and made the Navy musical."

On reading these words by that great and seemingly ageless Conductor who, in the days of my grandfather, shared with him much of the foundations of the present fame of the City of Birmingham orchestra, I react in two ways. First I wonder what prompted Harry Piggott to forego the excitingly wide horizons which must have been open to him at Westminster and to exchange pupils such as the young Adrian Boult for the likes of me? I cannot guess. Possibly the charisma of Jacky Fisher's vision of the time. Possibly the beauty of Dartmouth compared to the urban majesty of London. Possibly the chance to instil into an otherwise philistine world the seed of the humanities for those with an inborn instinct to clutch at them. I just don't know. Suffice it to say that this dynamic personality who graced Dartmouth College in his ever ageing and flowing gown, who strode around the corridors with a contagious energy, snorting as he went, brought refreshment to many of us and particularly to those who were allowed to attend his General Lecture study of a Monday morning, the only voluntary choice for a Cadet in the week. I need hardly say it was about Music, and having restored my momentum in class, H.E.P. once more included me in his Sunday tea parties; so it was from his fingers that I was first to hear the great sonatas of Beethoven, the Waldstein, the Hamaklavier, the Appassionata and the last great three.

The tandem control of the College under a distinguished naval Captain jointly with a distinguished civilian headmaster must have called for a deal of give-and-take on both sides and mutual tolerance within their respective spheres to achieve the balance of influence and inculcation of essential foundations within their end product, the Cadet: and doubtless still does. For whereas our academic standards under the likes of H.E.P. and T.S.S. (initials have always seemed to be the tag-whereby tutors are known) were the responsibility of the Headmaster, the rest of our training was that of the Captain of the College and his naval staff. Discipline, appearance, moral behaviour, exercise, seamanship in the lecture room or on the river, engineering, navigation, health and general indocrination into the life we were to lead at sea, these were all the responsibilities of the uniformed side of the staff. The Captain answered to Their Lordships and the Headmaster to naval educationalists. Both were outstanding men who had to judge the emphasis put at any one time on any one aspect of the training.

My first Captain in the Navy was a renowned submarine hero, later Admiral Sir Martin Dunbar-Nasmith V.C., who lived in an imposing house overlooking the parade ground. After my second term the Headmaster was the celebrated Mr. E.W.E. Kempson, who had previously left the teaching staff in 1911 to become head of the science department at Rugby, who lived in an equally imposing house a few hundred yards away. Both were God as far as we were concerned, the one wearing four stripes on uniform adorned by that maroon ribbon won while commanding one of the original submarines in the Dardanelles; the other, vastly bigger in bulk, sailing with professional elegance at the head of his academic line of battle, and we lived in awe of them both, meeting them perhaps once or twice during our four years under their joint command.

And what differing staffs they commanded; for if Mr. Kempson had within his Common Room the permanent pillars of the system, the P.T.H.s of what amounted to College history, the Captain had a very different crew in his Wardroom. The Commander, his second-in-command, a few Lieutenant-Commanders; and then the Term Officers, generally Lieutenants, hand-picked for the job, promising in their career so far, athletic, dedicated to the patience which training the very young entails, unquestionably orthodox by standards of behaviour expected of the young officer of those days which included celibacy. You didn't marry a girl. You weren't expected to. You married the Navy; and should an officer, with the single exception of the Captain, have been so misguided as to kick over those traces, his wife was not allowed to live within fifty miles of the college in term time. So as far as their charges were concerned, officer's wives did not exist.

Whatever such sacrifices may have caused them, the Term officers were outstanding people whom we probably remember to this day. If they were not killed in a war they invariably ascended to high rank; and you will read in the columns of *The Times* that when that twenty fifth or fiftieth anniversary dinner of the survivors of the Rodney or the Anson Term is held in some Services Club, the guest of honour is the Term Officer of their uniformed childhood.

The Anson's first was Lieutenant D.P. Evans. "Dippy", throughout his entire and prematurely curtailed life, was the stage example of the clean-cut, straightforward, scarcely scholastic naval officer. He had been among those fortunate few for whom the First World War had dislocated their normal training and so had been sent to Cambridge at the end of it to atone. Dippy had got his rugger Blue, and must have been near international standard in that and most other ball games and anything that needed being able to run. That was his natural means of motivation and whether it was in the long corridor past a senior Gunroom or on the way to Ditisham or on the playing field he shot past like a rocket with "Come on, Hayes: hurry your stumps", accompanied by an encouraging thump between the shoulder blades which half winded. His other endearing habit was to make a frontal approach and as he passed give you a friendly knock on the chest with "Box on". Dippy went on saying

"Box on" even when he was later twice to become my Captain at sea and ashore. The latter time was in Malta shortly after the siege and when, confirmed bachelor as he had always seemed to be, he suddenly announced his engagement to one of the first Wren officers allowed into the stricken island. A mutual friend and fellow Captain of Dippy's came into my Operations Room where I was the Admiral's Staff Officer, plotting some convoy. "Have you heard the news? Dippy's engaged." "Can't believe it. Can she run?" "She'll have to; otherwise he'll hit her on the chest and say 'Box on' and that is really awfully dangerous at her time of life. I must tell him."

So Dippy did marry, very happily; and I remember him as one of the most infectiously enthusiastic livers and lovers of Life. No scholar maybe; but at seven in the morning he could teach you what a steam trawler ought to look like to a Midshipman of the Watch passing at night from port to starboard. He could smile kindly when the Term Cadet Captain had had to report some misdemeanour to him. He was the uncomplicated character you needed when the very speed of the life seemed to make it complicated. He'd have been useless over a sexual problem but then you weren't allowed to have a sexual problem. In any case there could only have been one kind of that, to which my father had presciently alerted me and when it happened I went straight to H.E.P. A bachelor senior Instructor Officer began inviting me to his cabin with embarrassing frequency. That kind of problem was the only one likely to occur as one did not see a young member of the female sex from beginning of term to the end. You danced with each other in the big hall, the Quarterdeck, from time to time, the accolade being to dance with your Term Lieutenant. Dippy regarded that acknowledged perversion much as he would passing the ball backwards down the three-quarter line. It was an odd sensation and I can't imagine anything more painful from the elder's point of view.

A few days before we passed-out (the end of our four-year indoctrination as cadets, the beginning of eight months as sea-going cadets before leaving the bottom-most rungs of the ladder), I was told I was to go to a tough Battleship Gunroom, probably in the Mediterranean, 'the biggest and best fleet today'. My heart sank. It was a sentence I dreaded.

And so the end of Dartmouth neared. The weekly Sunday March Past: the attendant ceremony of Colours for games, the river–gym, swimming for life-saving certificates, running . . . running . . . running, if less for each term: bands, climbing ropes and masts, trying to twist rope into splices and bowlines-on-the-bight: half an hour piano lesson with Mr. Lock followed by more running: the colours of signalling flags and how you signal "Form columns in line ahead": on and on in the remorseless tread-mill of the system which must end one day, and which it did.

July 1930 came at last. Desks were dotted over the big hall of the Quarterdeck, dressed of course, like squares on a chess-board for the passing-out exams which took a day or two. Exams over, there came the final passing-out parade, the last march past around those ramparts, the last of thirteen Sundays per term per year.

Before we finally dispersed, fifty young people who had been together for so long and would only spasmodically rub shoulders again throughout ascending rank in peace and war, we decided to hold a dinner in the Piccadilly Hotel; looking back I suppose it was the first ambrosial dinner I ever attended, though there have been one or two since including one to mark our twenty five years in the Navy and recently to mark our fifty years, attended, alas, by dwindling living members of that Anson Term.

There came the announcement of Their Lordships' appointments of cadets to the Fleet into Gunrooms throughout the world. For the first time my name was in *The Times*, under Naval Appointments: "Cadets Adams, Draper, Haines, Hayes, Mathew, Stallard-Penoyre to *Royal Oak*. September 1930." The *Royal Oak* was a famed battleship in the First Battle Squadron of the Mediterranean Fleet.

Chapter 4

The Gunroom

Only those who experienced the narrow slit in life which comprised endurance in the Gunrooms of the Fleet in the early years of this century, and possibly their parents who may have received some comments about the conditions, can be expected to know that one of our most distinguished men of letters, the late Charles Morgan, wrote his first book, clearly autobiographical, in 1919 called *The Gunroom*. It may not be appreciated by many that the author of *The Fountain*, which won the Hawthornden prize for literature in 1932, to be followed by *Sparkenbrooke*, *The Voyage* and many other notable novels, began life as a Midshipman in the Royal Navy. As an equally distinguished playwright he also presumed to present the first serious naval officer on the stage in *The Flashing Stream* and went on to thrill with *The River Line*.

Charles Morgan was no drop-out as a potential naval officer. He was a Chief Cadet Captain at both Osborne and Dartmouth. He resigned from the Navy in 1913 for the very good reason that he wished to deploy his literary talents unshackled by the philistine limitations of a uniformed service and straightaway volunteered again in the first days of 1914. With the outbreak of the Second World War he again hastened to offer himself to the Admiralty.

The Gunroom was re-published by Chatto & Windus in 1968 with a preface by Eiluned Lewis in which it is said that "During his lifetime the writer never allowed the book to be reprinted. Not because it was anything but deadly true about the Navy as he knew it but because the love story was weak and therefore the novel was not very good as such." With this any critic would agree, it being, by the standards which were to come, a comparatively immature account of a young officer's emotions.

But to the student of naval behaviour and the modes of the upbringing of its recruits the book holds a fascination. *The Gunroom*, wrote Morgan long afterwards, "is, I think, a good book insofar as it gives an account of the lives of midshipmen in the Royal Navy. These parts were written in blood and reflect my own experience"; an experience shared by me and my colleagues identically almost twenty years later. Morgan was interned in Holland during the First World War and from which experience he found copy for *The Fountain*. No such experience overtook me and yet the pattern of my fortunes, first in a Gunroom of a major Fleet (about which Edgar Wallace in his review of *The Gunroom* for *The Sunday Chronicle* headed his notice "The Midshipman's Hell: Amazing Charges in a Remarkable New Naval Novel"), to be followed by the calmer, civilised contrast in a Gunroom on the China Station, bore an uncanny resemblance to those of my famous predecessor. There, of course, the resemblance stops; for I had neither the moral courage nor the prescience, nor indeed the wish, to do what he did. Yet, so identical are our experiences concerning the sadism which seemed to prevail in the creed of "junior snotties must be shaken" upon arrival before they had had time to discover what their new environment was all about, that I shall try to blend the similarity between his reactions and mine. Woefully little change had meanwhile taken place in the habits of a Dickensian situation, not so much through bullying as in a misplaced idea that physical suffering was necessary for maturity in a Service whose traditions, *inter alia*, were once described by Sir Winston Churchill as "rum, sodomy and the lash"; I shall try to endorse the belief held by Charles Morgan that such masochism would be shortlived and which, in fact, was not the case and yet, suddenly in the mid-thirties, for which my own generation can happily claim some credit, it did eventually evaporate. Morgan's was an angry book and rightly so. I suspect that, apart from any inhibitions about it being a frail love story, Their Lordships took strong exception to any reprinting and for obvious reasons. My own observations are sufficiently far removed from the screen that, far from being angry, they just try to recount what extra-ordinarily seemed necessary to have to endure if survival was paramount.

What follows is therefore an amalgam of impressions by Midshipman Morgan in *Good Hope* in 1911 and by Cadet Hayes in the *Royal Oak* in 1930; and if copyright is trespassed by Mr. John Lambert R.N. (by which name I called myself in publishing "Sketches from the Gunroom" for Blackwood's Magazine in 1936) towards Mr. John Lynwood R.N. (by which name Charles Morgan called himself in *The Gunroom*) I would ask to be forgiven.

The gunroom of *Royal Oak* was a narrow compartment off the port after weather deck with a deck-head of about seven feet into which was let a sky-light onto the boat-deck above. As you entered by the only door over a sill there was a long polished table on the right, either covered by a soiled table cloth for meals or a green baize one at other times, surrounded by two benches with the long, hard cushions which must stand up to wear. On the left was a sideboard below the pantry hatch behind which lived the gunroom Maltese stewards, Gauci and Vella, whose sometimes native, sometimes English, expletives could generally be summarised as "Jesu Christ. These bloody midshipmen". When the hatch was thrown open they were generally sweaty and vituperative and uncomplimentary. When they so-called waited upon us it was with an undisguised invitation to be quicker than was possible. But it did not pay to get on the wrong side of these friends because there would be times when, late for your boat over the boom, you had not had time to polish your dirk.

Dividing the main mess (literally) from the sanctum for senior snotties was a wall of lockers, seamanship and navigation books and those magazines which from time to time had their more suggestive pages torn from them to adorn the bulkheads; breasts, black stockings and suspenders. Behind this wall were three dilapidated armchairs, the perks of the Sub-Lieutenant and two Senior Midshipmen, and a piano which had partly survived years of beer to lubricate the hammers, felts and strings. What notes did not play were quite unimportant to the kind of playing to which, on guest nights, it was subjected. One square port aft and one scuttle for'ard provided daylight and two silk-stained shaded lights hung over the long table. Linoleum was the flooring and into this little compartment were crowded about thirty of us in all but not, because of absence on watch or duties in boats, so many at any one time. You ate, scribbled, dozed, discussed, squabbled along those benches behind the one table and you stood up when the Sub-Lieutenant came in. Every now and then a crash from within the pantry would signal that either Gauci had hit Vella or vice versa and then the hatch would fly open to reveal a pelt of black chest hair, one or other would shout "Ow! Signo" and then slam it down again. It was against such background that you wrote up your official Midshipman's Journal in order to encourage powers of observation and these would be scrutinised weekly by the officer in charge of Midshipmen known as "The Snottie's Nurse" and once a month by The Captain.

"The Gunroom. A Chapter without name" describes what were known as Gunroom Evolutions. The Machiavellian preludes, the physical degradation of the victims for the delight of their seniors, began with such ceremonies as "christening". This entailed each junior in turn being forced down on his knees by the cane when a thick ship's biscuit would be smashed over his head followed by a jug of cold water. He was then made to recite a Gunroom parody of the Apostle's Creed. By now fright had generally given way to nausea which was just as well before the staging of the final degradation, "Creeping for Jesus" and which even at this distance in time I would prefer not to describe. Morgan does so in uncomfortable detail which is there for the curious in a setting as accurate in my day as it was in his.

Over the table the electric lights beneath their yellow shades accentuated a pool of blue tobacco smoke that clung in wreaths to the nap of the tablecloth. The next ritual was to gather round the relic of the piano and put lavatorial words to hymn tunes.

"Which of you can play the piano?"

"You can, Hayes" said my most dishevelled messmate. "Go on . . ."

"Please. No . . ."

"Play 'The Church's One Foundation'," came the order; so I banged out what notes would play, something of a respite, while the strings were further lubricated.

It seemed a far cry from "Can you play Chopin?"

The finale to such entertainment was known as the Obstacle Race or Fetch Bumph. This was the name given to the toilet paper supplied to H.M. Ships and was appropriately coloured a dirty brown. Its texture resembled more a light sandpaper than a modern tissue. As time in the Heads was regarded as skulking for

Midshipmen, maybe this added discomfiture was planned. So "Fetch Bumph" was the finale of the evening's entertainment.

Charles Morgan describes it thus:

"'Fall in again" said the senior Midshipman. "Fall in!"

They stood in line awaiting the resumption. It seemed as though more would be unendurable . . . Hitherto they had been called upon only to act singly . . . but now an obstacle race was being planned. It meant fighting with one's own friends in an attempt not to be last.

The course was long and difficult. They were to go out of the Gunroom, aft through the Chest Flat, through a watertight door on the bulkhead, into the Casemate, round the pedestal of the gun, out of the Casemate for'ard through the Chest Flat and into the Gunroom again by the after door. Arrived there, they were to pass between the stove and the wall, over the table from port to starboard, between the settee and the table's edge, under the table from starboard to port, along the deck to the Gunroom's after end, under the table from aft for'ard, over it from for'ard aft, and out of the Gunroom once more. They had then to go by way of the Chest Flat ladder onto the upper deck and to the after twelve-pounder gun in the port battery. Here they would find their quest with which they were to return to the Gunroom and, as the senior Midshipman remarked, the Lord help the hindmost . . .

The six of them started together. They fought at the narrow door of the Gunroom. They sped through the dim light of the Chest Flat, doubled up and with knees bent that they might pass between the hammocks slung there by the Marines. One of the tormentors stood above them as they wriggled through the narrow space, thrusting each other aside, tearing their clothes, hitting their heads and knees and elbows against the projections of brass and steel."

And so on . . . . "They eventually burst back into the Gunroom, thrust their sheets of the filthy paper into the hands of the senior Midshipman and stood there trembling with exhaustion and pain. . . . The last by thirty seconds entered without signs of haste. And they put him over the table, pulled out his shirt and tried to flog the pride out of him. He did not move through it all and when it was over, with his fine mouth set, he turned away from the faces grinning above the canes.

"Fall in again!" said the senior Midshipman. "Fall in, I say!" An affair followed called Torpedoes that consisted essentially in hurling the junior midshipmen's bodies along the table, spread-eagled, into rough hands for'ard and then aft... but there comes a time when resistance, even Mental resistance, disappears. The limbs move as they are told.

At ten o'clock a ship's corporal tapped at the door and announced that it was time to close the Gunroom.

"Last drinks" said the senior midshipman and rang the bell. "Warts fall out!""

So the early tempering on one kind of anvil of a young man who was one day to carve his name on the bark of literary annals within the English language. Suffering may be necessary to sensitivity. There is little comfort at the time apart from the acceptance that the fact of suffering temporarily may have its end reward in ways that cannot be foreseen at the time.

"Stop it!.... Stop it!.... Stop it!.... I can't take any more...." Something was hitting me on the rump.... I opened my eyes to meet those of a friendly Royal Marine, cap immaculate, hitting the underneath of my hammock and saying kindly, "Show a leg, sir. Out you get. You're duty Midshipman. It's five-thirty."

My head swam from the beer of the night before. I groped for the hammock bar at my head and hauled myself up. Somehow I climbed out. "I'll lash it up for you, sir, and the steam is turned on." All the ship's company were the friends of the snotties because they knew we were chased so much harder than they were.

The steam referred to the Gunroom bathroom. This was an old coal bunker down in the bowels and consisted of two baths, one light, a tiled floor and an open tank into which was fed a twisted little copper steam pipe with its nozzle at the top of the water surface. Nothing like a thermostat or the fact that heat generally rises seemed to have crossed the minds of the architects of this contraption. A scribbled chit from the Sub-Lieutenant to the Duty Snotty the night before would say "Shake at six-thirty. Bath at seven" and if the Royal Marine sentry did not turn on the steam when he came on watch at 0400 then the Sub's bath water would be cold and the Duty Snotty was punished.

Climbing out of the hammock to the chest flat and the gear one would need for early morning P.T. on the quarterdeck, thanking the Royal Marine, checking the noisy bubbling of the steam, one then found the Sub-Lieutenant's cabin. "Six-thirty, sir." No movement. "Six-thirty, sir" again. Still no movement from the bunk. "Your bath will be ready, sir." Too bad if he didn't want it; a Senior Midshipman would have it instead. Duty was done and on to the next and much more hazardous chore, calling Lieutenant Glasfurd.

It was an unwritten law that you were not allowed to touch an officer when trying to wake him. Any other trick was permissible; flicking the light, slapping the slippers, calling louder and louder into his ear: but no touching. Rumour further had it that if Charles Glasfurd's pyjamas were the same colour as his sheets—lemon, violet or pea-green—you were all right; but woe betide you if they were different. This morning they were, a nasty clash of violet and green.

I turned on the light. Shouting now: "Mr. Glasfurd, sir, I'm telling you it's six-forty five."

An eye opened and fixed me. "Is it *still* six-forty five? Don't make such a bloody noise." He was there with a reefer and trousers and scarf over those pyjamas when we mustered for P.T. a little later. He was feared by us and loved by us; and ten years later died heroically in command of *Acasta* while escorting the aircraft-carrier *Glorious* who ran into a heavy German battle squadron off Norway and Charles Glasfurd did his utmost to ram them. He is another person I remember with respected affection. He left the ship before we did and was succeeded by another character, a submariner called Lieutenant Jackie Broome, renowned for his caricatures of the gin sodden naval officer in advertising Plymouth Gin and whose path I was one day to cross again later in very different circumstances.

But now the Sub had been called and his bath was going to be ready. The Snottie's Nurse had been called and what he did with the next hour was no concern of mine. Reveille had sounded and the ship was beginning to stir. Into a singlet and shorts and ready for the first routine of midshipmen, early morning P.T. while the quarterdeck-men splashed hoses round your feet, then squeegees to dry up the teak deck, clearly thinking to themselves "rather them than me". Eventually, when the Senior Midshipmen had taken what hot water was left, it was time for Gauci and Vella to administer breakfast. But a description of that stampede, which Blackwood's magazine were kind enough to publish in their "Maga's Log" of 1936, can await its proper setting.

We became aware that the sun was shining, not only from a metallic blue sky above the Greek harbour of Argostoli, the village, the little mountain and upon the three squat battleships smoking their evening pipes, but metaphorically within ourselves. During our few hours ashore, brushing away the butterflies and the other inhabitants of scrub and scree, watching the to-ing and fro-ing of business among the ships below, picket boats and launches plying between ships and shore and each other on the millpond of the bay, listening to the echo of bugles and bosun's pipes, we were suddenly all unreservedly happy.

The awe of the introduction to gunroom life had given way to a sense of relief that we had survived our indoctrination. We had been properly blooded and apparently met with favour for the stoicism of our reactions in the eyes of our seniors.

After that first ordeal everybody had seemed kind. While still having to be careful not to get under their feet, the senior snotties acknowledged us as useful additions to the Mess. We took over the chores hitherto allocated to our immediate seniors. When the Sub or another of those occupants of the armchaired sanctum shouted "Duty Snotty", you dropped whatever you were doing, eating, writing or dozing, and scampered helter-skelter into the narrow opening from the rest of the Gunroom, elbowing and barging as you went. The last to appear got the errand–public school fagging in a different environment and all in the day's work; but there became an attitude towards us which seemed to be trying to say, "You're one of us, however junior". The Wardroom seemed pleased to help us in our ignorance, as indeed they should have been. We had our quick favourites of Officers of the Watch under whom to learn that essential part of our duties: most were understanding, although one or two made life hell: and those senior citizens who did not keep watch, like the Engineer, Paymaster or Surgeon Commanders, would make a point of walking up and down the quarterdeck with us, that perennial occupation of all naval officers who often have no other means of exercise and which by habit generates that certain roll of step, to give us paternal advice. They were indeed old enough to be our fathers.

The Commander himself, the second-in-command, the Executive

Officer, "The Bloke" as he is known to the lower deck, was of
course God as far as we were concerned: or he was the present
semblance of God however you may like to picture Him from the
Book of Revelations, or as painted by Blake, either with a beard or
clean-shaven, kindly or menacing, humorous or austere, omnipotent
or just a human being with three gold braid stripes, an oak-leaved
brass hat and a telescope. The Captain of a battleship in Gunroom
eyes was generally a shadowy figure wearing even more stripes, for
whom one stood aside within sight and remembered the rare
occasions when he spoke to you. There were so many layers of
authority between a sea-going Cadet and his Captain as to raise this
Being who occupied a large part of the after end of the ship into
almost some kind of hallowed influence in harbour, to whom
presumably God too had to answer, and an acknowledged supreme
power on the bridge at sea when he seemed to come into his own.

As already mentioned, part of the training was the weekly entry
into the official Journal for the use of Midshipman: or the S 519 as
known to H.M. Stationery Office. This was no mean scrapbook but
an expensively bound volume of some hundred pages, stiff covered
and with a fly onto which could be stuck the required sketch on any
day it might be forthcoming. I suspect that to this day most of us
proudly keep it in our shelves and protest when our beloveds ask if
they need dust it any more.

Quoting from the instructions they read:
1. The Journal is to be kept for the whole of a Midshipman's sea
time. A second volume may be issued if required. (During three
years most of us filled three as we came to realise that they might
be among our only writings compulsorily bequeathed to our
children.)
2. The officer detailed to supervise instruction of Midshipmen
will see that the journals are kept in accordance with the
instructions hereunder. He will initial the Journals at least once a
month, and will see that they are written up from time to time
during the month, not only immediately before they are called in
for inspection.
3. The Captain will have the journals produced for his inspection
from time to time and will initial them at each inspection.
4. The main lines to be followed in keeping the Journal are:

(a) the power of observation
(b) the power of expression
(c) the habit or orderliness

5. Midshipmen are to record in their own language their observations about all matters of interest or importance in the work which is carried on on their stations, in their Fleet or in their ship.
And so on . . . but here lay the crunch:
6. The letterpress should be illustrated with plans and sketches pasted into the pages of the journals, namely:

(a) Track Charts.
(b) Plans of anchorages. These should show the berths occupied by the Squadron or ship and if a Fleet was anchored the courses steered by the Fleet up to the anchorage.
(c) Sketches of places visited, of coast line, of headlands, of leading marks into harbours, of ships (British or Foreign), of Ports or fittings of ships, or any other object of interest.

7. The Journal is to be produced at the examination in Seamanship for the rank of Lieutenant, when marks to a maximum of 50 will be awarded for it.

It was a stern demand and like a sword of Damocles hung over us perpetually. Officially we were allowed Saturday morning in which to write up our Journals around the Gunroom table; but what with watchkeeping and running boats it never seemed to work out that way. It was generally a scramble of forgotten memory and undrawn sketches to get them into Glasfurd's cabin by the Sunday morning. Being then a Unitarian I could often skip Church and do it that way; but in general we sat bemused at the last minute and wondered what the hell had exactly happened during the last week which was worth recording.

We sailed for that remarkably beautiful harbour of Corfu where, I see from my first accepted sketch of ships present, there were no less than four battleships, one aircraft-carrier, nine cruisers, twenty-eight destroyers and various other support ships such as destroyer depot ships and the Commander-in-Chief's yacht; that part of the

Mediterranean Fleet meeting for what was called the sailing regatta.

Such was the kind of trivia, rightly encouraging powers of observation even if not dramatically expressed, which our Snottie's Nurse had to wade through week after week. Sometimes he put "Good" and sometimes "Inadequate. Better sketch next week." At the time my sympathy for this ritual lay entirely for myself. When ten years later I became Snottie's Nurse of *Repulse* and could hardly get into my cabin on a Sunday morning for the piles of thirty Journals for me to read, I saw that ritual through different lenses. I remembered the desperate searching for something to say which others had not said. I remembered the hours spent with ruler, Indian ink shared, the mapping pen and compasses, copying some intricate piece of machinery which might just get by if Glasfurd was in a rush. I remembered even more how you had not had time to do a sketch at all and so had traded in a boat-trip for somebody else's, secondhand. When the said cartoonist Jackie Broome succeeded Glasfurd I once tried this on: a blotched outline of the paravane outlay on the fo'c's'le, lots of wires and blocks for'ard of a plan view of "A Turret" and drawn by somebody who was no better than me. Back it came with the simulated explosion of a shell from "A Turret" within which was written: "Bang goes another bounce. A sketch of your own by tomorrow."

One may laugh now at what may seem such antiquated practices by modern methods. We cursed then at what seemed such a waste of time. But with hindsight it was quite the reverse. Looking now at the sketches I managed to perpetrate then, I can see over those three years the steady improvement from makeshift charts to reasonably executed mechanical drawing, from sloppiness to tidiness, from evident sloth to the wish to put an arrow into my quiver, from complete disinterest of how an Admiral had to anchor his Fleet to the reasons why he had to be rather careful about it. So that when latterly I had to do just that and realised I had people whose job it was to draw it out for me, at least I could feel less ashamed because I had once had to do it for myself. The navy was not so inexplicable in its methods of training as maybe we embryonics thought at the time.

Chapter 5

A.B. Parks is Introduced to Wagner

Today the island of Malta, awarded the George Cross for the courage of its inhabitants under siege in war, due to the political and isolationist policies and departure from the British Commonwealth wrought by its dominating Prime Minister, aptly named Mr Dom Mintoff, is probably best known as a haven for tourists beckoned by history and climate; but it was not always thus.

Between the wars the Mediterranean Fleet (just one Fleet apart from the Atlantic, the China Station, the East and West Indies squadrons and those ships lent to Australia, New Zealand and South Africa) consisted of five battleships, two aircraft carriers, four modern 8″ gun cruisers and five or six elderly 6″ gun cruisers; Rear Admiral Destroyers in a cruiser (no less than Rear Admiral A.B. Cunningham in 1930) commanding four flotillas of nine modern destroyers each; two submarine flotillas and all the appendages such as destroyer and submarine depot ships, a yacht for the C-in-C and so forth. Nobody lived ashore except possibly the C-in-C himself in Nelson's old house in the Strada Mezzodi. Grand Harbour was full as was every creek which led off it. The Flagship lay at her buoys off the Custom's House with two more battleships astern of her. Two more (of which *Royal Oak* was generally one) moored under the hospital in Bighi Bay together with an aircraft carrier; 8″ cruisers down the middle with the smaller 6″ tucked into Calcara and French creeks; and all the destroyers and submarines berthed in Sliema, stem to stern in permanent review order and all vying with each other for immaculate smartness.

Each large ship owned its own fleet of dghaisas who lay off the after port gangway like a shoal of hungry sharks, waiting to swallow whatever bait would be forthcoming in the shape of officer or libertyman at a small price. Such was the code among them that woe betide the *Royal Sovereign* dghaisa which tried to poach on *Royal Oak's* preserves. The enamel sides were, of course, kept like a mirror by the clandestine generosity of the bosun's parties of the ships themselves. Charlie, our head dghaisaman, was as integral a part of our life as the Chief Bosun's Mate; and the betting on him for the dghaisa race in the Fleet regatta was as relatively heavy as on a Derby favourite. When Midshipmen broke their leave and had to be secreted over the lower boom, it was Charlie who made it possible. When Jolly Jack had unwisely decided to return on board drunk it was again Charlie who somehow got him on board. Officers of the Watch knew all the tricks of these trades because they had done it themselves; and what a healthy code of living.

So we Subordinate Officers began to settle down into some kind of routine. Workwise the two main occupations were Midshipman of the Watch or running either the Picket Boat or Launch. These may be said to have been one's first command and speaking for myself I doubt if any subsequent command cost me more thought. Hoisted in and out by the main derrick upon arrival at any anchorage or between buoys, it was a matter of pride that the P.B. was away and ready for duty within minutes. And it always was.

The seventeen-ton boat could steam at seventeen knots, oil fired. The crew consisted of a Midshipman in command, a Petty Officer coxswain old enough to be his father, a Stoker Petty Officer in the little engine room equally qualified, two senior Able Seamen as bowman and stern-sheetsman, a junior stoker in the little boiler room, and, the only person of Midshipman's vintage, a fender-boy who held the capoc sponge with which to damp the indiscretions of the command when coming alongside. The Launch was a different kind of boat into which a hoard of libertymen would pour at the expiry of their late leave, many the worse for wear and loquacious with it, and who would have to be controlled into some semblance of order before reaching the after gangway. There were differing techniques which, at the age of seventeen, needed differing approach. In each one relied upon the help of one's coxswain.

The Picket Boat was far the most exciting. Here was a little command worth commanding. Every dghaisa in Malta which needed renewal, and there were many, tried to get across your bows at night to claim the insurance. The Grand Harbour was a nightmare of traffic which needed the utmost concentration from the helm. You worked with your crew for twenty four hours on and twenty four hours off round the clock. They taught you everything you needed to know about the lower deck and a great deal you didn't. Heaven help you if you forgot to warn the victuallers that your crew was going to be late for their rum ration. When a gale made it impossible for you to secure to the lower boom for the night and you went in with your crew to lie under a lee shore at anchor, then you learnt how sailors regarded officers and were given a chance to put your side of the relationship from another angle. That was the way you learnt, and there was time to do so. They respected the way in which you had to climb up the Jacob's ladder over the boom in Round Jacket and dirk, provided you respected their conditions. It was the happiest two-way method of communication. These were the people who taught me whatever I may have learnt about the ways of the sailor, one of the most lovable characters of our nation who asks so little and who gives so much, and which experience was to fortify me in the years ahead, in war and in peace.

I grew too self confident. Having tamed my craft, I began to think I knew how to handle her. She kicked to starboard when going full astern and so the port ladders were easier than the starboard and "Stokes" had a little scuttle through which he could judge precisely how much astern power to give me to make a nice manoeuvre of coming alongside; but the rule was that you went Slow before going into reverse. On a flat calm day in Bighi Bay, with the quarterdeck lined with big M-J, the commander, downwards, I tried to show off. From full ahead I rang down Stop and then full astern. "Stokes" did wonders as we pulled up alongside. An egg would have done as well as a fender. I stepped onto the bottom of the gangway ladder full of pride when up shot the cowling of the engine room hatch and a filthy cap-cover appeared above an angry "Stokes" who said in full hearing of the quarterdeck: "I suppose yer f.....g pleased with yerself. So let me tell you, you've f....d up the 'ole f......g show!" and slammed down the hatch again. I crept up the gangway with my dirk between my legs to face the Commander.

"You deserved every word of that," he said. "Most unseamanlike.

If your Stoker Petty Officer hadn't given you the works, you'd have smashed the boats at the port after boom. Leave stopped for a week."

Humiliated, I returned to my wheel. Our next port of call was Naples when Midshipmen were warned to go slow in entering the landing stage because of the expensive yachts moored in the marina. Every time I rang Slow, "Stokes" gave me full and vice versa; so again I was in trouble. At the end of the week a beaming face came up from the engine room. "Well, sir," it said, "That's taught you a lesson. One day you may command bigger boats than this." And so one learnt; and one day I fulfilled the prophecy of "Stokes", including a frigate which had no brakes at all and so when handling her I never ceased to recall his lesson.

Midshipman of the Watch was the other main preoccupation of ship's duties. We dreaded it under certain Officers of the Watch because, whereas in your boat you were away on your own, there was no escape from the quarterdeck; and under the huge canvas spread of the awning which shielded the great 15″ guns of Y Turret, upon that teak stage which was not permitted a cotton thread upon its hallowed planks, among the comings and goings of every controlled activity in the ship for that moment, the nerve centre of the ship was at work. At sea it transferred to the bridge. This was comparatively easy because to some extent a battleship's movements are predictable, ponderous and slow. In harbour, particularly in the Grand Harbour on a busy forenoon with the whole Fleet present, all hell could be let loose. The minute-by-minute routine (and like the B.B.C., the Navy's clock has always worked to seconds) had to be run. "Out pipes. Hands fall in for hoisting the 1st cutter. Away first Picket's Boat crew": only to find that you had forgotten the said Picket Boat was still at Corrodino and earned an expression of your inefficiency from the Officer of the Watch.

A senior officer at the starboard after gangway in his Barge, less senior ones at the port after gangway wanting to visit the wardroom, a launch full of potatoes at the port for'ard gangway wanting either sailors or a crane or both, the Paymaster Commander wanting to know why the rum ration organisation wasn't working, the Engineer Commander wanting to know where he could put the oil lighter alongside, a Padre asking for all Non-Conformists to be piped for a meeting in the port 6″ battery at 1230, some complete stranger saying he was expecting Mr. Hannibal Sclicuna on board and could he be informed of his arrival, the Surgeon Commander asking for a boat to take a cot-case to the hospital steps, the Commander asking why you were adrift in falling in the hands to hoist that cutter–and all the time boats...boats...boats, coming and going. I was once on watch with a charming and moithered Reserve Officer in the midst of such traffic phantasmagoria. He had lost control of the situation as the Midshipman of the Launch reported for further orders. "Oh bugger, bugger man...I've done m'best. Do what you can." "Aye, aye, sir," said the Snotty and went down to his boat. "Shove off for'ard. Half ahead" and happily lost himself until the tumult had subsided.

But it was fun and never a dull moment. The Morning Watch was the most demanding, scampering around all the early morning calls of officers to get them somehow on to the Quarterdeck for Hands Fall In to scrub decks when big M-J would quickly know who was and who was not there. A note from your predecessor of the night before would read "Lt. Cmdr. X still ashore. Will probably need heavy shake. Lt. Y ditto. Treat the Sub gently. He's had a blast from the Bloke. Glasfurd's sheets and pyjamas are the same colour. Good hunting. Will relieve you for the forenoon." When at last you'd go down to that bathroom, clean yourself up and be ready for instruction.

It worked. Well enough. Boats, watchkeeping, technical instruction, navigation from the Schoolies (Instructor Officers), marches to Ghain Tuffehia Camp covered in webbing equipment, Commander's doggie, Captain's doggie, Duty Snotty, a wide variety of adventure which, when pieced together, made the jig-saw puzzle fit into a pattern of training. You had three years in the Gunroom to befit you for the next step. There was no real hurry in the long term; just perpetual movement in the short. Not much leave. No serious conversation. A kind of hectic awareness of being conditioned in a way one had no alternative but to conclude was the right way. Only time could show. That it did work, effectively, is proof of the soundness of the system within the time-scan. The tempo has so increased that now such training would be unthinkable; just as the speed of communications today, the efficacy of weapons, the demanding impact of technology upon war at sea or on land or from the air which has made the manipulators more part of their computers than the slow, human assessors of previous times could not now be tolerated. A few of us were to try to keep step with the revolutionary innovations which overtook our time in senior rank; but for the most part, and certainly for me, experience of the fundamentals of being able to deploy staff expertise to a balanced decision, tactical or strategical, had to camouflage ignorance of much of the language in which that staff was talking. Only the brilliant could effectively tread the rainbow bridge which spanned the pre-and post-War generations.

Privacy was not part of a Midshipman's environs. Your bed was a hammock which was lashed up and stowed away in the netting until slung in the after cabin flat at night. Your clothes had to fit in to a single chest of drawers which lined the hatch of a below decks compartment and through which torpedoes sometimes passed. Your locker in the Gunroom was crammed with the bare necessity of books. You put yourself where you were least in the way of others whenever possible. Most of the time was spent on those Gunroom benches or on the Quarterdeck or in your boat. So it became essential to find *somewhere* in the ship when on occasion you could be alone.

One of my boat's crew had a friend, a three badge Able Seaman, a "stripey" of standing who was the sweeper of the 15" gun spotting top. This was a kind of Wendy House perched on the top of the foremast, full of dials and voice-pipes but with windows which commanded all round visibility and from which, in the event of the main armament opening fire, it could be observed whether the shells were over the target, short or had hit. One day this was to be my job in *Repulse*: but just now, in *Royal Oak*, I had more cause to be grateful for the remoteness of this little sanctuary and the hospitality of the sweeper. The 15" spotting top was rarely occupied except at sea or during harbour exercises and the sweeper was happy to let me escape to its privacy to write my letters home, to write a diary which neither the Snottie's Nurse nor the Captain would see, and most important of all to let me keep the little clockwork portable gramophone I had been given as a sea-going present and the vulcanite records I had begun to collect. I hauled these up the vertical iron ladder and through the hatch in the deck; and could then look down at the funnel fumes and far below me to the guns of A and B turrets stretching out their great barrels towards the cables on the fo'c's'le.

Off duty I loved to sit in this perch at sunset when the baraccas and sandstone cliffs of Bighi and St. Elmo and Lascaris turned slowly through every shade of yellow and ochre and orange to a flame pink as back-cloth to the light grey hulls of the ships at peace beneath them. Activity on board ceased. There was that moment of expectancy as when the curtain of a theatre is about to rise, for instance, upon a classic you know well. The commanding flags were hoisted at the yard-arm of the Flagship. As the sun dipped below the western horizon they jerked down. The quartermasters in every ship shouted "Sunset, sir". Officers and men on the quarterdeck turned aft at salute while the signalmen manned their halyards. Anyone in sight stood to attention. It was a moment in the evening of the Fleet.

The Royal Marine bugler, pre-eminent in his art, sounded the Still from the Flagship; and then, like a martial symphony, every bugler in the Fleet joined in unison. The Call echoed round the cliffs until the dying notes told us of the beginning of the night. The ensigns were very slowly lowered. Anchor lights, quarterdeck lights, switched on with the last note. The buglers turned smartly about with a "Carry on" from the Officer of the Watch and the pipe to the Ship's Company on board, "Shift into night clothing".

But it was on Saturday afternoons, when possible, that I escaped up to my eyrie after the Forenoon watch and prior to the evening Last Dog beginning at 1800. I was thus once contemplating an interlude with myself. The gramophone was playing on the corticene deck when up shot the entrance hatch and the roseate smile of Able Seaman Parks, the sweeper, appeared first above his elbows which then eased his body onto the deck.

Expecting to be alone, A.B. Parks was apologetic. He was under punishment with his leave stopped and instead had been sent up to polish the voice-pipes brightwork. He stood listening.

What in fact I was playing, Wagnerians will agree, is among the supreme moments of *The Ring:* Siegfried (in this case sung by Lauritz Melchior, perhaps the greatest heldentenor of this century), who has never known fear or previously beheld the female form, has braved the fire-girt rock on which the Valkyrie Brunnhilde is still asleep, as her father's punishment at the end of the previous opera, and discovered the woman a wood-bird has told him must become his bride. He can understand its song because he has tasted the blood of the dragon who was guarding The Ring and whom he has just killed. As the sublime music soars, he removes her helmet, then lifts her armour from her bosom and falls back in astonished alarm with, "Das is kein mann", which has been evident to the audience for some time. He stoops to kiss her. She then very slowly awakes, hailing the sun and a deal else, which she has not known for some time, before they launch into an impassioned half-hour love duet.

The record ended. "What was all that about?" asked Parks. Try explaining the story of *The Ring* to a 3 Badge Able Seaman in two minutes starting now.... It's an interesting exercise and I had a shot. Parks reflected.

"Ah, well," he eventually mused, "all I can say is that my Annie down the Ghat wakes up fuckin' side quicker than that: better get on with m' fuckin' brightwork."

Thereafter Parks and I became firm friends. I spared him the Love Duet but he liked *Iolanthe*.

"Nice tuney stuff that. 'Aven't I 'eard it before somewhere?"

"It's what the Band plays when the Admiral comes on board with all that ju-ju."

"Course it is. I'm gettin' on, aren't I?"

Chapter 6

Slow Boats to China

"Great girl, Annie. She's understanding. Tried 'er yerself, Sir?"

I confess to having been sorely tempted by that invitation by AB Parks after our Siegfried discussion. There comes a time when, ready or not, boys yearn to test their masculinity and Annie would doubtless have been as sympathetically instructive as Nessie, "the golden 'earted 'hore" of David Niven's experience in his hilarious *The Moon's a Balloon*. Although at that time a few years older than was Mr. Niven when he had the good fortune to meet Nessie and win his Spurs, if slightly assisted by her in Piccadilly for three quid, I was also clearly less forward for my age.

Lieutenant Niven of the Highland Light Infantry and Cadet Hayes of *Royal Oak* were in fact both in Malta at that time, but I lacked the kind of initiative and nerve which could spill brown olives from a fancy dress goat's scrotum in Carnival at the opera house before my C-in-C. My nerve had in fact been weakened when I had the effrontery to go to a performance of *The Barber of Seville* on a Thursday in plain clothes, when apparently that little architectural gem of an opera house (subsequently demolished by the Germans) demanded uniform in Fleet Orders. I was punished for this lapse of behaviour and have never felt quite the same about the Barber, Figaro (up or down), ever since.

But to return to the possibility of Annie; I was tempted. So was another of my batch. We put on grey flannel trousers, blazer with the naval crown on the pocket, and ventured sober down that disreputable alley, the Strada Stretta: the Ghat. The procuress was

59

charm itself despite our unfledged appearance. Would we come in? Annie was busy just now but would be free shortly. Would we like sherry? (A pale green syrup). Several sailors, happily none of my boat's crew, emerged while we crossed our legs in waiting.

Eventually the moment of confrontation arrived when I was ushered up the stairway to a curtain of beads. It was presumably Annie who lurked behind with a puzzled if kindly expression and an open peignoir which did not completely conceal long, drooping breasts which, today, remind me of those oblong balloons for which Grandfather at Christmas never has quite enough breath to inflate the final nipple. I remember trying to summon up courage to part those beads and enter into that bosom of my first Venusberg: and failed. I fled. Mortified by my cowardice and betrayal of AB Parks I subsequently spent a few hours in Msida gaol with my friend, my only "time" so far, for breaking in frustration the tops of marble tables in a cafe. We were bailed out by *Royal Oak's* Officer of the Middle Watch, returned under escort to our ship and rightly and painfully punished. As I shall confess, I was to have every reason to be glad that I was too timid to be initiated by Annie, kind and instructive as Nessie she would doubtless have been. But at the time it was shaming.

After eight months of being, incredibly, junior even to a Midshipman, we Sea-Going Cadets gained our white patches and our first promotion. It had seemed a long initiation and one wondered how three years of such was to be endured? Had an eager choice of childhood been a dreadful mistake from which there was now no escape? Admittedly, as I have explained, we learnt every hour of every day from the sailors with whom we shared every seamanlike discomfort and from whom in return we received every overt and covert support; but beyond that, more advanced instruction in the profession we had adopted seemed at a premium. Exhausted after twenty four hours at the wheel of a Picket Boat, one was in no mood for the Instructor Lieutenant, fresh from his bunk, or the niceties of spherical trigonometry.

It seemed just to be boats, boats, boats: watch, watch, watch: sea, sea, sea; although that sea took us to fascinating places. Journals every Saturday, provided one kept to the matter-of-fact doings of ship or fleet. Run, run, run: sleep, haphazard sleep; but where was the kindly encouragement to make us feel that we mattered, or might matter one day? We had been in the battleship a year; and although, like Peter Pan, it was all "an awfully big adventure", the impetuosity of youth to scratch at more than material superficialities doubtless warped perspective. In fact I know it did; for looking back at my journal over that first year of adventure I see that in the Mediterranean alone I was given to see what most people have to await decades to pay to see. Cephalonia and the Greek Islands several times: Malta, of course, for months on end: the Riviera ports and their seductions: Sicily, Naples, Capri, and Gibraltar filled to capacity by the Combined Fleets with every inch of the miles of moles occupied by battleships or battlecruisers; heavy and light cruisers at every buoy; scores of destroyers filling the pens like a tightly parked garage; and towering above them all, that great Rock impregnable, and still so, as one of the few literal bastions of a fading Empire. In retrospect, little did I grasp what was in fact being showered upon me at the age of seventeen.

Nothing is permanent but change; and it happened when we were least expecting it. A signal arrived from Admiralty, a year to the day after our appointment to *Royal Oak* that our section of five were to be sent to *Cumberland* of the Fifth Cruiser Squadron on the China Station forthwith. We happily packed our trunk preparatory to starting for Port Said in a sister battleship *Resolution*. AB Parks helped me down from the 15″ Spotting Top with my gramophone. "Best o' luck, Sir. Annie was sorry you didn't feel inclined. I'll remember that Wagner chap"—and with no crocodile tears we left our first cradle. Had I known it, my naval footsteps were again following Charles Morgan's to the mystique of the Far East. I had seldom felt happier. Gone in a moment were any doubts that life was for living: even a Midshipman's!

The next four weeks in the luxury of a first class cabin in the old three funnel P & O Liner *Naldera*, after a hammock and one chest of drawers, did nothing to detract from this impression; and there was no Senior Officer on board to mar the delights of the taffrail behind the lifeboats. The historic China Run from Port Said to Shanghai, seduced as one must surely be by first slow introduction to the Far East, nothing to do but enjoy the lifting of curtains upon new scenes, new peoples and new smells. Aden, Bombay, Colombo, Penang, Singapore, Hong Kong, all their monuments to the heyday of the British Raj, apparently so secure that they cast a ridiculous feeling of propriety as, on landing, every native instantly sensing our ignorance threw their offerings at us from bric-a-brac to rickshaws; and even at this distance in time the luxuriant beauty of Penang, later to have with Singapore such tragic associations for me, sticks photographically in my mind.

Sitting underneath the punkahs in the Taj, The Galle Face, the Runneymede, or Raffles Hotel, served by immaculate coloured waiters in spotless white and cummerbunds of the rainbow, there was then clearly no doubt, in the words of the recent Flanders and Swann lampooning song, that "The British, the British, the British are best..."! The first breath-taking sight of Hong Kong, the Peak, the Sampan population each with its family of grandmother, children, baby grandchildren and chickens—Boat People in a different setting to that of today: a battle through the Formosa Strait into the ferocity of the NE. Monsoon and so, on an October morning into the vast estuary of the great Yang-tsze and the muddied flow of the Whangpoo river to a Shanghai wharf below The Bund with its majestic silhouette dominated by the Cathay, the great domes of Bank and Shipping headquarters, maybe commonplace today but rivetting then to the newcomer. Flags of all nations seem to flutter from the masts in this centre of gravity for East-West trade while floating homesteads of the Chinese drifted downstream perilously close to ships at anchor.

Our journey was not yet over for *Cumberland* was apparently at Wei-hei-wei, the northern exercise anchorage of the British Squadron up in the Yellow Sea in the same latitude as central Korea; so with no white ensign ship to take us and after exchanging vows to write to those whose hands we had held across the Indian Ocean and the Bay of Bengal, two of us found ourselves sharing Stateroom No.6 in S.S. *Ting Sang*, a little Jardine Northern Coaster on the Hong Kong-Tien-tsin run, a tenth the size of *Naldera*. A stateroom consisted of two bunks one above the other, a collapsible wash basin, a seat of sorts, a dashboard of switches for fans, just room to stand up together and, most useful, a candlestick mounted on gimbles which already showed the permanent list from the deck cargo of petrol drums on what we were told proudly was her 220th voyage: but nevertheless still palatial compared to *Royal Oak*.

Our fellow passengers were Chinese, a mattress and food basin each under an awning over the hold between the oil drums and separated, sometimes of necessity, from the Staterooms by iron bars; and so for a few days we butted our way, the gimbled candlestick active at all times from the little ship's antics–far more so than the Chinese who lay resigned as corpses–until one midnight we glided quietly among the anchor lights of the cruisers to our journey's end and *Cumberland's* pinnace waiting to grab her new charges.

Chapter 7

The China Station

The British Far East naval force then consisted of five or six 8″ County Class cruisers of the Fifth Cruiser Squadron, an aircraft carrier, a flotilla of eight destroyers, a flotilla of submarines and their depot ship *Medway*, several sloops (or what are now called frigates), one of which was the personal despatch vessel for the C-in-C, and the little gunboats for the Upper Yang-tsze and the West River from Hong Kong to Canton. The comparatively new 10,000 ton cruisers–*Kent, Cumberland, Cornwall, Suffolk, Berwick, Devonshire*–had been built for trade protection with high speed (some thirty knots), long endurance, a main armament of four twin 8″ turrets with a newly designed high rate of fire, admirable all weather accommodation and no armour. White elephants to their critics because of the latter, they were perhaps among the most successful class ever to grace the Royal Navy: and their war record bears testimony to this. Cool in tropics because of their high freeboard of thirty feet and therefore two decks with scuttles, unique at the time; superb seakeeping qualities for the same reason, they acquitted themselves on the equator or in the Arctic alike, with high morale among their crews even if an imposing silhouette to the enemy. Two only were sunk in the war: by the Japanese off Ceylon. *Cumberland* herself was ready to be in at the kill of *Graaf Spee* had she not been scuttled, ran many a Russian Convoy and was still useful into the sixties as a gunnery trials ship.

I was fortunate enough to serve in four of them from Midshipman to Commander and my first acquaintance in Wei-hei-wei that night laid the foundations of deep affection for them. For it was hard to believe that the contrast from the "accommodation" for Subordinate Officers we had previously endured could be true. What I find so impressed me at the time was that the Gunroom itself for only the Sub-Lieutenant and twelve of us had three scuttles looking out to the sea instead of a weather deck; a high deckhead, an electric fire and a fan which worked and, to crown it all, a locker which actually locked. Our chest flat on the deck below also had scuttles, was not in a gangway and with room actually to stand and dress by open drawers without giving way to passers-by. We were allowed camp beds here, or on deck when hot, instead of hammocks; but perhaps the greatest joy of all was our own bathroom. Instead of the converted bunker in *The Oak* with the steam pipe bubbling into the top of an open tank, here was a tiled deck and two baths with taps which really did run H and C as marked! A proper school room with yet another locker each completed these five-star quarters.

During the first twenty four hours when one is given time to what is called "slinging hammocks" (camp beds or not), time to find your way around the ship, discover who's who in the Wardroom and the Stars of the Lower Deck, stow your gear and from questions also discover what are the idiosyncracies of those on whom your life will chiefly depend, it was clear that in this ship the Snotties, instead of being something of an encumbrance to have to train, were part of her complement and life. For the first time in mine, I felt needed; hardly professionally but with a contribution to be offered. Morale soared.

As before, the three most important people in my life were to be the Commander, the Snottie's Nurse and the Sub-Lieutenant. The Captain himself, as ever being God and therefore traditionally in his elevated world apart, presumably controlled our eventual destiny. But in this case he was to take a sometimes uncomfortably detailed interest in our progress.

The name of Commander Russell Grenfell was something of a byword in the Fleet. Renowned as a martinet, a bachelor married only to the Navy, obsessed by the immaculate appearance of every detail, human or material, capable of severity at the smallest lapse, he had therefore established a ship in whose reputation every man who served her was proud. No such rubbish as cotton waste with which to clean the quarterdeck brightwork; he paid his own Chinese boy to use only calico for this task alone. The strand of yarn on the deck caught his eye. The enamelled white hull and three grey funnels reflected sunlight. You could safely have eaten a meal from the deck of any compartment; and in consequence the old adage applied that a clean ship was a happy one.

It was therefore with some alarm that I learnt I was to be his Doggie, the Commander's messenger and shadow who in working hours, from dawn muster of the hands until he had finished with you, kept station a few paces behind his every movement. How I got to know that back! But in retrospect I know that whatever I may have learnt about the running of a ship—and twenty years later I too was to have my Doggie behind me when trying to run an Aircraft Carrier—I owed to this remarkable man, latterly a minor naval historian.

The Navy, though liberal in extreme with its judgements, is stern whenever there is a shortfall of its self-imposed standards, often a sole reason for denying promotion in the cut-throat competition which in so small a Service must always exist. There can be no wider gulf in rank within any of the Services than that between the Midshipman's lapel white patch and that first single gold stripe of the Sub-Lieutenant who must rule the Gunroom officers as he thinks fit, eat with them, sit with them, everything in fact except sleep with them! As I was later to find, that sleeved embellishment for the first time weighs heavy: and as I have described could then lead to uncivilised measures of authority. For a brief time one is cock of a roost, then with the advent of a second stripe in the big ship, the junior member of the Wardroom. Progress in the Navy is therefore forever being pulled down to size whenever there is the feeling of misguidedly seeming important.

We were again fortunate; labelled aristocrats are rare and, although granted every licence by the sailor who is at least something of a snob (a drunk Viscount was given particular assistance after a run ashore, provided he showed no after effects on taking his ship to sea next day), officers could be suspicious: but in Lord Hugh Beresford we had the perfect Sub. Apparently lethargic, relaxed and humorous, he camouflaged his complete awareness of all our activities by a combination of fair discipline and that essential quality of knowing when to look the other way. He allowed our spirits full rein, presided over our Guest Nights with a whimsical tolerance and utterly forbade any of that nonsensical sadism still so prevalent in some of his generation. He made you try to please and so we were happy. Such measures as the cane were not in his compass. To be on watch with him was to learn and not to be frightened. So then, I began to learn.

At sea I also began to learn the particular aspect of my trade which as a school boy I had told those Admirals I wanted to follow: for I found myself the Navigator's Assistant, "Tanky" as he is known for reasons I am unsure, and which excused sea watchkeeping. The duties consisted of predicting what stars or planets a Navigator could expect to see in his sextant at dawn or evening twilight and at what altitude on what bearing: keeping his charts up to date and supplying him with them: in fact satisfying his every demand and thereby seeing a part of one's profession at close hand. Navigators could be fussy and finicky and until war some worked under the misguided impression that theirs was a full-time job which excused them from other mundane ship's duties. Those who properly regarded the job as part of the whole were promoted. Isolationists were not. Again I found a patient teacher who finally convinced me that this was the tributary of the Navy up which I intended if possible to sail: for the sextant was about the zenith of my technical grasp.

There was therefore only one aspect of this new-found paradise which for me fell short of the battleship: *Cumberland's* power boats. They were no substitute for that first proud command and of course, with no Maltese dghaisas, one sometimes waited interminably along-side jetty steps, for officers to finish their evening's blandishments into the small hours. The single screw motor boats were unimpressive and hard to handle with the wheel in a cockpit right for'ard; so that I had every sympathy, if not excuse, for a wartime Midshipman in the Mediterranean cruiser in which I was then serving who tried to take a similar boat alongside steps at a port in the South of France during the landings for Operation "Dragoon" which took an axe to cut a pat of butter. In H.M. Ships boats hoisted at starboard davits are given odd numbers–first or third motor boat–and those at port davits even numbers. As Damon Runyan would have put it, the Snottie was making no kind of a fist of it, watched by an American G.I. leaning over the jetty rail above. After watching the steps rammed twice, the G.I. slowly took the cigarette out of his mouth and drawled: "Say, Ensign, what d'you call that gasoline gig o' yours down there?"

Stung, the Midshipman drew himself up to his full 5 ft 4 in and said rather pompously:

"It's the first motor boat."

"I'll say it is!"

"It's such a pity," a friend said to my wife on putting down the newspaper shortly after the war, "that China's shut now. How lucky John was to see something of it before its early closing day"; as indeed I was. There followed a year which took me not only to those ports to be expected from Hong Kong to Shanghai, but also to the less often visited by large ships, such as Wei-hei-wei and 500 miles up the Yang-tsze to Hankow. Routine and commonplace to the Navy of that day, later to be on the lips and screens of the world by the heroic performance of the frigate *Amethyst*, her exploit under siege conditions was more vividly understood by those of us who had sailed the river in normal times. Even then, in the climate of permanent pre-war Sino-Japanese tension and scrapping, a cruiser was kept as guardship for the safety of our nationals in Hankow. During the Summer months, as the Himalayan thaw raised the level so as to be navigable by the County Class thus far, it was one of us; and in the Winter, when the river fell, a smaller cruiser took our place. Above Hankow, the upper river was patrolled by our shallow draft gunboats as far as Chungking, a thousand miles from Shanghai and the mouth.

So, after a "Winter" in Hong Kong when our ship docked and refitted, during which stagnant time the Midshipmen were decanted into the small aircraft carrier for an Air Course, to a destroyer for a month or two to see something of life in the terriers of the Navy, to a submarine to be bewildered yet enthralled by the contrast of motion and diesel noise when surfaced and the stable quietness when submerged, it became *Cumberland's* Summer turn for The River, preceded by Shanghai where the Ship's company could find more recreation, particularly at night, prior to a month's incarceration at Hankow.

It took five days because, *Amethyst* excepted, navigation by night was impractical even for that celebrated character and sage Mr. Pote Hunt, the Admiralty Yang-tsze pilot for over thirty years, then over seventy, bald and bearded beneath his wide-brimmed felt hat which presumably he removed only for sleep. Seated in a high chair before the compass, now *de rigueur* but then exceptional, for the 100 miles a day, he never once stopped talking or looked at a chart, for he knew every mark, every change of depth among mud banks, every quirk of the current, tidal to Nanking.

"Starboard 10–that pagoda over there–midships–I'll tell you a story–meet her–last year when *Kent* came up–port 10–there was a junk coming down–midships: as you go–with the channel shifting–watch your steering, starboard a little–I couldn't alter–keep her there–but on she came, like that one ahead now–give four short blasts–starboard a little..." and so on; Woosung, Chinkiang, Nanking (the capital of the country and so a twenty one gun salute returned by a Chinese cruiser), Wuhu, Anking, Kiukang, and so, to our achorage off the small Bund of Hankow and that area of the town known as the British concession, where the river is still a mile wide. Our predecessor, once Mr. Pote Hunt was aboard, with a new audience for the same stories, could not wait to start downstream. And so for a month we would lie here under awnings and side screens to give what shade was possible to messdeck and cabin scuttles, temperature in the nineties, the chocolate stream running at five knots, the only movement of the screws to steam up to our anchors every few days lest they become too embedded in mud to weigh, static harbour gunnery drills and evolutions and the overriding problem of keeping occupied. For us, boat running in these conditions had its hazards. A year ago the river had flooded to the extent that our predecessors had comfortably gone alongside the golf club steps, normally a mile inland from the bank; but on this occasion, although hardly the ideal climate in which to train, the obsession throughout the ship, from the Captain to the youngest, was the forthcoming Fleet Pulling Regatta when we would rejoin the squadron at Wei-hei-wei.

The hallmarks of a ship's efficiency, the yardsticks by which she was judged by the Fleet, were her cleanliness, her gunnery proficiency and her performance in the annual regatta. To win this was obsessional and taken desperately seriously: and although called rowing, it bore scant resemblance to what is known to the public in the University boat race. Ratings pulled in crews of twelve in double-banked clinker built cutters, built for their sea worthiness and weighing two tons, or half that number in whalers weighing only one. Officers or Chief and Petty Officers pulled in a six-oared carvel-built gig, streamlined by comparison but still weighing a ton.

The boats were principally intended for sailing and Captain Bligh would have considered himself luxuriously equipped. To pull in any seaway they were hell.

To train to win the Midshipman's gig race was therefore our main preoccupation at Hankow. Twice a day, at dawn and dusk, the Snottie's Nurse took us away; and although hardly comparable to gaining a Blue, the anatomy on fixed thwarts, trying to manipulate an unbalanced oar was tested. Bottoms were soaped, blisters had to be hardened, and the pain suffered for a moment's transient glory; and against a five knot stream to achieve a ship's length ahead in that temperature was sufficient for one outing. Small, I was given the responsibility of cox, spared the pain but open to the abuse of my colleagues. The day came at last after a month of artificial ubiquity when Mr. Pote Hunt took us back down the river, once more into blue waters to rejoin the squadron for the great event at Wei-hei-wei.

This anchorage, perfect for Fleet requirements because of its ease of access from the open sea exercise grounds, was sheltered by the Chinese mainland to the West and South and from the North by the Brtitish concessional island of Lin Kung Tao of two square miles. It boasted a tiny emergency dockyard, a golf course and recreation ground, a ratings canteen, a church and the Island Hotel. It also boasted a perfect Summer climate; and as a very *avant garde* privilege the new diesel-powered submarine depot ship *Medway* was annually allowed to make one of its rare excursions to sea from the heat of Hong Kong to Wei-hei-wei, carrying the wives of such officers as could afford to have their beloveds on the station. The peace of Hong Kong harbour was shattered by the starting-up of her engines, rivalled it was said by the squabbling chatter of rank-conscious wives concerning their, accommodation, which they continued among the flimsy partitions of the Island Hotel on arrival. Many were stage caricatures; and on the occasion when Mrs. Surgeon Commander had kept me waiting an hour alongside the iron pier, to arrive without apology to say "Carry On, Snottie," I vowed that if ever I acquired a wife she would hopefully be different from Mrs. Surgeon Commander. She is.

Came Regatta Days with the ships moored to form their own grandstands on either side of the course. Each ship ran its own tote and the betting was fierce. Like horses which had not been seen on the training gallops, *Cumberland*'s crews went to the post as unknown factors which made the betting more interesting. It is the only time I have ever carried odds and because of our endeavours at Hankow our own ship's company had us favourites.

Never having had the chance to experience what the world knows as rowing, I am still reminded of that day as I annually watch the struggle from Putney to Mortlake. The moment when the sweaters come off and are passed down the boat, in this case revealing the Cumberland rose on a white singlet. The horrid juggling to straighten for the start: and at last the relief of the gun. Astern of us came the ship's pinnace, her bow almost submerged by dangerous overcrowding of the supporters yelling their encouragement. At times the gig seemed to stop dead in the water as a short sea soaked the thwarts. At the last grandstand cruiser we drew ahead to win by a length. The training up the river had been rewarded. We had covered the course in twelve minutes, well over half the average time it takes Oxbridge to cover over four times the distance! But no less feeling of accomplished glory.

We were towed back to our gangway and reached the quarterdeck to the Royal Marine Band and the ship's company cheering their heads off, for a lot of money had been put on us; and so down to the Wardroom to break training after so many weeks, cox included, not because weight mattered in that kind of contest but so as to keep my authority with my exhausted colleagues.

We were among few *Cumberland* winners, for the Yang-tsze Summer had taken its toll. The ship had acquitted herself but we were among her heroes. Captain, Commander, Snottie's Nurse, Lord Hugh, beamed upon us; we could do no wrong–anyway for the moment. A silver cup and a few dollars each may have been visible rewards; but the invisible assets were what mattered, the blind eye to our over-indulgence in night leave which was to follow.

If it seems absurd that I should dwell upon such trivial detail as this incident there is reason; for in some ridiculous way even at a range of some sixty years I remember it as a watershed, a moment when we crested the mound of apologia and saw beyond that we were accepted not only by the Wardroom but, far more important, by the ship's company. We could now hold our head high and, such as they were, our chests out. In a few minutes we had become accepted.

Chapter 8

The End of a Beginning

"The Captain will have Midshipmen's Journals produced for his inspection from time to time", reads the instruction in the fly-leaf; and this week included mine.

As the ship was in dry dock at Hong Kong with one day as ordinary as the next, it had become even more difficult to make the official diary less boring than usual; moreover my dodge had become to await Sunday Matins on the quarterdeck, virtually compulsory for officers and thus claiming the Snotties Nurse to set us a good example, excuse myself as a Unitarian and then scribble my entries for the week by the deadline of the Sabbath noon when they had to be in his cabin.

This week I had enjoyed a performance by Heifetz of the Beethoven Violin Concerto and had managed to fill a whole page by extolling his virtuosity and explaining the necessity for complete cough-free silence in the audience, so that those four opening beats on the timpani can be heard. The concert had been my only oasis in otherwise a desert of inactivity.

I see that the Captain's red-inked comment on this subterfuge was: "Much as I appreciate your interest in music, remember that your aim in life is to become a Captain R.N. and not a drummer." Fair comment, depending on the accent you place upon "cultivating a power of observation".

Various divertissements were found to keep us occupied, two of us for instance to each destroyer of the Fleet for a few weeks where such attention was devoted to our training, and such the antics of the

Navy's terriers in any sea, a wet discomfort which seemed to weld
the spirit of their company from Captain to Able Seaman into an
entity so intimate, compared to a battleship or cruiser, that I never
forgot, particularly when watching their heroic achievements from a
cruiser in those horrific conditions of the Winter Arctic Russian
convoys. They were the testing ground for young command which
produced a high percentage of the Navy's finest seamen and leaders
of this century such as Lord Cunningham; men of initiative, courage
and flair so difficult to display in these days of tight control from
underground shore headquarters; names like Warburton-Lee of the
Hardy in that first battle in Narvik Fiord (the first V.C. of the war):
Vian of *Cossack*, *The Navy's Here* in cutting out the Altmark
prisoners; Sherbrook of *Onslow* off North Cape, another V.C.: and
so on. I have always regarded them, together with the best
submariners and aviators as the First Eleven of the Navy.

So on until the day came to hoist the paying-off pendant for the
first time, that long white streamer of bunting from the mainmast, a
foot for every day of the commission of over two years; a golden orb
at the end which bobbed in the wake astern, as *Cumberland* sailed
for home. Our idiosyncratic Commander Grenfell had been replaced
some months before but his hallmark remained in the white
enamelled hull contrasting the dark grey funnels and the gleaming
brightwork, not a detail out of place for critical eyes, the epitomy of
what was meant and held dear as a taut ship and which mattered so
supremely.

The China Run in reverse, only this time no philandering on the
moonlit boat decks of P & O liners. With the Navigator in his
element and Jupiter in his, there was fascination in every changing
mood of a generally empty horizon. Rare not to be in company,
hurling ourselves about in some exercise; there was also time to face
up to the fact that we Midshipmen were about to look down that
flight of hurdles from the starting line which comprised a series of
examinations in those technical subjects which together determined
suitability for promotion to the dizzy heights of Lieutenant.

And so on one cold December morning in 1932 with storm clouds
hurtling across a proscenium of apparently nothing but flecked
chocolate water studded by buoys, the paying-off pendant frayed,
gallant, and unseen we entered the Thames estuary and the Medway
to drop anchor off Sheerness. The sailor has an unprintable

description of this bleak spot, justified now after the glamour of past months with the entry and departure of Fleet bases abroad, reciprocal bands and bugles welcoming us in and out, to end in barely discernable drab flatness of land either side of the river, not even a handkerchief to be seen.

We were home; and if it seemed an anticlimax to most of us, Petty Officer Broadmore, the captain of the Fo'c's'le who had taught us anything we knew about cable work, was happy. A native of Sheerness he had not set foot ashore since *Cumberland* had commissioned at Chatham over two years before and was proud of it. His work, his tot, his prick of tobacco and his letters to and from his wife (I fancy in that order) had apparently satisfied his life. A vast hairy man, not for him the temptations of the knock-shops of Shanghai or the geishas of Nakasaki or even a respectable run ashore; he had been content to watch the effect of those on others, to smoke his pipe in leisure hours on the Petty Officers' deck, to direct the operations at his end of the ship from his caboosh or lifting cable as if it was rope, and teaching his art to others generally with patient kindness and expletives paraphrased for his audience. Incredible as it may now seem, this monastic existence was not then uncommon. Now to keep a sailor in the Navy he must be guaranteed that he is never separated from his wife, wherever he is serving, for more than nine months; and although this may smack of gynaecological coincidence, it makes it infernally difficult for the Vice Chief of the Naval Staff and manning authorities to operate the Fleet.

Cumberland herself was to outstrip all others of her, so-called, white elephant County Class which were to play such a conspicuously successful role in the war to come. As I have said, only two were sunk—she herself only missed the end of the Battle of the River Plate because *Graaf Spee* scuttled herself. I was to be with her again on the Russian Convoys and as a Gunnery trials ship in the sixties; but lest any sentiment should have been beginning to prevail at now leaving her, a final buff envelope in my Gunroom letter rack pulled me down to size. It was from that same Mr. O. Murray who informed Mr. J.O.C. Hayes that their Lordships hereby appointed him Midshipman of H.M.S. *Renown* and directed him to repair on board that Battle Cruiser at Sheerness on 7 January 1933. So, after two and a quarter years abroad, I was to have sixteen days' leave from Chatham to the dreaded Sheerness again; and this was further

reduced for me "at home", which had become Switzerland where
my parents had gone to be in the same country as my younger
brother, smitten by chronic asthma and thus confined for four years
at school in the High Engadine at 6,000 feet.

Christmas looking across the Lake of Geneva from above
Montreux, up the Rhone Valley to the Dents du Midi and Grand
Combin, watching the light change on Gramont, climbing it and the
Roches de Naye, descending over the Col du Jaman at sunrise; it
passed in a moment during which I sensed my parents found it hard
to adjust to the change in the Cadet to whom they had bidden
farewell it seemed an age ago; and before I could give thought to
that, I was once again on my way back via the Gare de Lyon for the
last lap in the Navy's subordinate ranks.

Sheerness again on a gale-swept January night to comply with Mr.
O. Murray's directive to join the Battle Cruiser *Renown*. Basking
still in the charisma won for them by Beatty in his *Lion*, during his
sorties with his Battle Cruisers into such actions as The Dogger
Bank, and culminating in the historically controversial role they
played in the last major British confrontation of heavyweight
proportions to dispute our enemy's sea power off Jutland, perhaps
their successors still enjoyed a glamorous epitomy of the accepted
invincibility of the Royal Navy into the second world conflict. There
were now three of them. The "mighty" *Hood* of over 800 ft and
40,000 tons; *Renown* and *Repulse* only marginally less. Together
they blended power with grace, speed with formidable armament of
15″ guns; admittedly unarmoured, nevertheless with their staggered
funnels and their yet graceful silhouette they combined an aggressive
presence with the essential elegance suitable to take Kings and
Queens, Princes and their Princesses when visiting the Empire's
wide dominions. *Renown* in fact still had the squash court on a
weather deck specially built to keep the Prince of Wales exercised on
some such mission. But when it came to the last war to which they
brought such potential of British might, *Hood* was to be destroyed
by the *Bismarck*'s guns, to blow up and disappear in a few moments
leaving only wreckage and three survivors upon the Atlantic;
Repulse, not far away at the time, was to disappear herself in eight
minutes later that year from the calm of the South China Sea at the
hands of Japanese torpedo bombers; only *Renown* who by then had
been fortunate enough to be modernised, achieved more happy fame

by her countless contributions, particularly when flying the flag of Admiral Sir James Somerville.

All that was to come, right now it was back to the Gunroom and a hammock with a jolt, or rather on that first night at a drunken angle as slung by a hammock boy even younger than the Midshipmen, who paid him one penny a day for this and to lash up and stow the sausage in the nettings each morning. But we were on the last lap of the three years in the kindergarten now as Senior Midshipmen which meant that we could enjoy the curtained seclusion of an armchair or an electric fire and juniors to "fag" for our every want. Good intentions in this respect evaporated as quickly as those made every New Year and although we abolished those dreaded, sadistic "games" for our juniors, other memories were still vivid enough, perhaps shamefully, to want our pound of flesh.

There was probably never a time in one's naval career when one's head was more full of information, much of which was useless for the future, than for the coming examination, a first class in which (85 per cent) carried ridiculously the same kind of charisma as first class university honours in other walks of life; and, age for age, maybe one had to work as hard, the fundamental difference being that whereas the one depends on flair ours depended on blotting paper memory for detail; from how often a Petty Officer's Mess was allowed a new tablecloth to the size and breaking strain of every hawser in the ship. Duties of Officer of the Watch, Anchor Work, Rigging, Victualling, Boatwork, Signals, marks for previous day to day performance and even our Journals, they were all covered by verbal interrogation from strangers in other ships, fairly, of which probably an apochryphal example is:

"You are Officer of the Watch in harbour and it comes on to blow. What d'you do?"

"Let go the other anchor, sir."

"It's blowing harder still . . . . "

"Let go the sheet anchor, sir."

"And harder still to storm force . . . . "

"Let go the other anchor, sir."

"Where are you getting all these bloody anchors from?"

"Same place as you're getting all your wind from, sir."

As inevitably it eventually had to, the day dawned for our ordeal preceded by what I imagine is the kind of sick-making apprehension felt by even experienced artists before a first night. Endless trouble had been taken to groom us like young colts to the starting gate; for how we ran on the day brought credit or failure to the training stable. Dressed in Round Jackets and dirks we were inspected for the creases in our trousers, shine on our shoes, clean white Midshipmen's patches on lapels (hopefully nearing their end), brushed, dusted, everything save looking at our teeth, and finally passed fit to appear before the examining board in *Valiant*, at Sheerness, of course.

Unlike those original interrogators of a twelve-year-old, these were at least in their frock coats so that you knew the level you were up against. A morning beginning with over anxious strain, dwindling to almost carefree relaxation before kindness from those (who of course one forgot to credit) had all been through it themselves: then out for an agonising wait before the final curtain fell on . . . applause or not?

Three firsts and three seconds. I had scraped home by six marks among the former. We were welcomed back to the unsaddling enclosure and fêted by *Renown*'s Wardroom. Perhaps that's how artists do feel when the tension snaps? Yet behave more sensibly with the morrow's performance in mind; for I shall never know who ladled me into my hammock for the last time that night.

The Naval Appointments published in *The Times* of 13 September 1933 carried the promotion of the fifty of us Midshipmen of the Anson Term, or nearly the original fifty, to the rank of Acting Sub-Lieutenant: the second rung.

Chapter 9

The Second Rung

The tram clanked its way through the cobbles of the Old Kent Road. Past the New Cross Empire where I hoped my new-found status would allow me many an evening, along the railings which guard the domes of the Royal Naval College, Greenwich, and so to its iron gates on a wet September evening in 1933. The naval police were waiting.

"Name? Sign the book. Over there. King William block."

So to a dim lit, cell-like lobby where the porters, all naval pensioners with generations of Sub-Lieutenants through their hands, were waiting.

"Name? Sign the book. Right. Cabin No. 10 Third Floor. 'Ere y'are, Sir. Book o' the rules. Mess regulations. Supper at 7 in the Painted 'all. Call at same time in the morning'. Up in the lift." and I was bundled out into a long, stone corridor. The door of No. 10 slammed behind me.

It was palatial: wallpapered; the first room of my own in the Royal Navy after a hammock and one chest of drawers. Below me the gas lamps threw shadows among the pillars of neighbouring blocks. The glow above London to the West silhouetted those famous domes of Christopher Wren and Inigo Jones, frowning above the black flow of the Thames as it muddied its way towards its estuary. As I stood captivated at the little window I felt privacy for the first time.

A truckle bed with nobody to see me get into it. A table, a cupboard with nobody to share it. An armchair. Mine; all mine! Somebody had been here before me. My luggage was unpacked;

treasures from China, previously hidden away from deft fingers, were arranged on a dressing table. Snapshots in her bathing dress at Wei-hei-Wei watched my every movement. Clearly I was to put on uniform for supper and clean pyjamas afterwards. I dawdled, savouring such luxury. No running water but presumably that was somewhere. Ready at last I went back to the lift shaft and pressed Button A. The porters greeted me at the bottom.

"You can't do that, sir. Seen the notice? For use of the staff and sick." As I wasn't either I didn't argue, even wearing that single gold stripe on the sleeve for the first time. Nothing since has ever weighed more heavily than that replacement of Midshipman's patches on the lapel, albeit that these are reputed to be the oldest remaining unchanged insignia dating from the days of our own Admiral Anson in the mid-eighteenth century. They may not have changed to this day; but the way in which those who now wear them is regarded as indicative of the release from traditional shackles.

This is a story about that gradual social change and not very much about battles. Partly because as fate decreed when war came, I never seemed to be on the winning side; and partly because the former has occupied my thinking more than the latter. The one is an on-going evolution, the other is a flash in the pan: often some flash! When it came, the kaleidoscope twirled quickly enough and that will have its place: but for the moment I was immersed in that slow indoctrination of acceptance of tradition which, with hindsight, made it possible to focus on patterns which were to come. I made my way down to the Sub-Lieutenants' Ante Room.

Within this architectural gem it resembled a suburban station waiting room; stark and practically unfurnished. Padded hair seats between stone pillars, a metal counter serving as a bar, an upright piano which continued to defy the abuses of its felts, oleographs of old wooden walls with their cracked canvases bearing the scars of dart matches. This is no criticism, for it would have been crazy to provide us in that particular space with anything better. Important though we may have considered ourselves, as is the cycle of naval rank, we were in fact again the most insignificant form of life compared to Commanders or Captains, students of the Staff College or War College also within this famous campus. They had got beyond smashing things after dinner. Sub-Lieutenants hadn't: even after the surroundings of Thornhill's unique Painted Hall where, among the magical vignettes of his art on ceiling and walls, the butcher Cumberland of Culloden is shown as an innocent, be-wigged, ruddy cheeked little child behind the High Table, beside the artist himself holding out his hand behind his back for the payment from those who had commissioned his genius and who were slow to reward. If we wanted to bask in the glories of this public monument with the Queen's House across the way and the observatory on Longitude 0, the Greenwich meridian, they were there for us to do so. If we wanted to smash up our ante room there was really nothing left to smash. A perfectly equitable arrangement.

It was a curious reunion. The same fifty of us who had toiled up that hill to the naval college seven years before; the same herd who had been orginally stabled together, then scattered among the battleships, battle cruisers and cruisers of the world, now again brought back to the same pasture. Hardly one of those little boys of the Anson Term, now aged twenty, had dropped out. We met again, some strikingly matured, a little self-conscious in discovering how each of us had changed. Little squeaky boys like me, too small and undeveloped to become a Cadet Captain at college or get into any team, lost in the middle of the front or rear rank, had grown to be at the tall ends of those ranks. Others, who had seemed to be so manly then, seemed now to have stood still. The hail-fellow-well-met was the same. Some of the shy were still so: a polyglot assortment of human instruments, making those discordant noises to each other like an orchestra tuning up after a lapse together and trying to recapture the right harmonies of a score they used to know.

"Hullo, Joc. Nice to see you again. Where were you?"

"*Royal Oak* in the Med, then *Cumberland* in China."

"What was the Sub like? Bastard or human?"

"First one, then the other. Where were you?"

"Home Fleet Battle Cruiser. *Repulse*. Hell."

"Good Snotties Nurse? Did he take any interest in you?"

"All right when he wasn't having promotionitis. Got married which helped. She took his mind off us. Specially at night."

Then, of course, girls. Girls in Malta. Girls in the East and West Indies. Girls in Shanghai...and also, more recently, girls in Greenwich.

As luck would have it, the recent summer had seen the pageant staged in the College precincts by Sir Arthur Bryant. Our immediate predecessors had contributed to the males in the crowd scenes. Rehearsals and performance over, they had not needed to rehearse their subsequent performance with the local female extras underneath the scaffolding. The Captain of the College was a serious gunnery officer. His Commander was an ex-physical training specialist who better understood the boxing ring. Both lacked humour. The spin-off for us was that instead of enjoying the freedom to London we had expected, our clocking-in after dark was made more difficult than that lower boom in Wei-hei-wei. This was inhibiting but developed initiative along undergraduate lines.

And so to Portsmouth for a series of short technical professional courses in gunnery, navigation, signals, torpedoes in their various specialised schools, all part of what, with that Seamanship ordeal and Greenwich, were termed examinations for promotion to the rank of Lieutenant. Depending on the classes achieved, so you scored points and subsequent seniority could differ by two to three years. In the end of course that didn't make the slightest difference to a career; but at the same time, as I suppose in any real University tripos, personal decision alone dictated the balance between work and play and the latter generally won, save for the most dedicated embryonic admirals.

The band of the Gunnery School on Portsmouth's Whale Island (rightly known as H.M.S. *Excellent*) took a lot of stopping. The big drum tended to drown the inexperienced word of command of Sub-Lieutenant under training on that renowned parade ground; but on this Friday morning, the day of battalion drill, it suddenly did stop and a black-gaitered Staff Officer from somewhere shouted:

"Battalion at the halt on the left form close column of companies in line retiring."

It took me a moment or two to realise that this gobbledegook was apparently directed at me. Paralysis. My Christian Soldiers marched onward, onward—not to war but towards a bank lined with Gunners' Mates and the historic squawking peacocks on The Island. It seemed that from every quarter somebody was converging on me and shouting. "Do something A Company Commander. Pay attention to orders. You're asleep. Wake up." Everybody seemed to have something to say. Everybody that is except me. Moithered I remained mute. Then they started to run at me. I could see them coming out of every corner of the eye. This stung me into action. I emptied my lungs with "A Company–Halt!" Some of them did but by no means all. B Company certainly did not and piled into the rear of A. ("See how the fates their gifts allot: for A is happy, B is not.") A fair question was to come next. "What exactly are you doing A Company Commander?" I was doing nothing. This seemed to be the trouble. So to help matters the big drum started up again. In the *post mortem* it was judged that my general idea had been right but poorly executed.

This is called Field Training.

One may smile. It was something of a vogue to smile at the behaviour of the gunnery world, particularly among those of us who had no pretensions of trying to join it–in fact only two of us Ansons did, most of us electing for the Fleet Air Arm, Submarines or Navigation, the first two claiming a high proportion of casualties in the war which was to come.

It was a misplaced suspicion, possibly bred of inverted jealousy because in those days the gunnery specialisation undoubtedly achieved the highest promotion among Executive Officers over that first hurdle to Commander. And rightly; because although they certainly needed navigating or communications or torpedoes, what was the main role of warships before the missile age if it was not to carry and fire guns? Wasn't one grateful that there were those who actually wanted to know how to aim them and fire them . . . and shout!

But more than that in retrospect; where did one first learn to say boo to a goose or even a fellow being (except to a Gunner's Mate) if not on Whale Island's parade ground? Where did one first learn the niceties of ceremonial, so essential an arrow in every naval officer's quiver throughout his career? "Who taught me to nestle in a buttercup?" asks that ample Fairy Queen of Iolanthe; and equally conversely, who taught me to understand how to this day the world is impressed by the precision achieved by British Sailors in that art of ceremonial which had originally so flummoxed me? The London crowds stand in admiration of that gun-carriage's crew whose honour it has become to draw the Sovereign's coffin towards its final resting place; and who trains them in a few days for such an impeccable performance? In many ways the role of the naval gunner, as his army counterpart, is the centre of gravity of his Service. They are the very kernel of its armoury.

Such was I later to understand. Right now I had to learn that a simple T-spanner was called a tool-removing-and-inserting-ring-protecting-seat-of-obduration for use with the 6″ gun. I was remembering such nomenclature quite well during the final whole week of examinations, parade ground or desk; but then the Thursday guest-night beat me to it. Two trivial orals on the following morning could be no bother; but a lethal hang-over is no whip with which to hold on during that last furlong to the winning post and I failed a first class by 10 marks out of 1000. So mortified was I that I decided play should replace work in the torpedo and electrics course (neither of which have I ever been able to understand) in their school, H.M.S. *Vernon*, where I only just missed bottom of my batch by the same margin. I felt *much* better after that. There remained only six weeks of the navigation course, the specialisation on which I had my eye. Hayes must do better.

The examination came. With no home in England for weekends, I had been forced to work and achieved my aim. All I can remember about that was trying to help an Indian friend who was similarly placed, if less daunted by competition in his navy. The paper on Tides was allowed two and a half hours. These days you look up in a book what to expect off any port in the world. Then you had dreadful arithmetical calculations for some places called Harmonics. After the exam I asked him how he'd coped? He admitted that his only contribution had been in answer to the question on ocean currents: "Onyway there is the Golf Stream". This in fact was very good sense because that warm flow, which originates in the Gulf of Mexico and meanders across the mid-Atlantic to meet the egress of the English Channel, dominates the climate of the Western British Isles. But he failed.

The appointments of our batch were announced. To my joy I was to go in charge of the Gunroom of H.M.S. *Danae* on the America and West Indies Station, a 6″ light cruiser with only a handful of Midshipmen; and join her in Bermuda after passage from Liverpool in R.M.S. *Orbita* of the Pacific Line, sailing in December 1934.

Chapter 10

Towards Maturity

"When the cabin port-holes are dark and green
Because of the seas outside....
.... Why, then you will know (if you haven't guessed)
You're 'Fifty North and Forty West!'"

Once again, December in The Bay (there is only one for the minds
and stomachs of those prone to sea-sickness) was living up to its
reputation. Luckily I was apparently born with mine on gimbals and
thus, according to my parents, was able to win my first prize of a
teddy bear, which I treasured for years, in a crawling race at the age
of one on first crossing the Atlantic. Going the other way after
twenty one years via northern Spanish ports and the Azores was a
miserable voyage; and not only nannies were prostrate. Tempers
were frail among passengers and crew alike as we buffeted our slow
course across that cruel sea. But eventually, a few days before
Christmas, the clouds lifted enough to allow the glare of Gibb's Hill
Lighthouse to be sighted.

Next day I joined H.M.S. *Danae* of the Eighth Cruiser Squadron,
a 6″ cruiser of the "D" Class. The fact that in Greek legend she was
daughter of Acrisius, King of Argos and gave birth to Perseus—who,
the oracle had warned, would kill her father so that the latter placed
her and her infant in a wooden box and threw them into the sea,
later to be picked up by someone called Dictys—mattered little to the
sailors who manned her. The various irreverent pronunciations of
her name in the canteen would shock classical scholars; but today her
successor survives, not because the lady begins with D but because

the Leander class of modern frigate bears mythological names such as *Ariadne*, *Dido*, *Andromeda*, and other better known maidens (to the sailor anyway) than the lady in question.

And so, having decided to join the Navy because I so enjoyed children's parties in a C Class Cruiser, I now found myself as Sub-Lieutenant of the Gunroom of one of her successors, not much younger and very similar. There was my old schoolroom in the dockyard, no more changed that the bollards which held our hawsers. My father's Army bungalow and laboratory now belonged to navy ordnance, but the crane on the little jetty was just as rusty; the angel fish, pink squirrels and the yellow and black striped sergeant-majors, the little octopus for luring by dough on a bent pin, the wall which had prevented me from being blown among them in my first hurricane–they were still there; and so were the wives of married officers in Somerset, who were now the kindly, attractive young hostesses of bachelors instead of the lead ladies of my parents' charades who used to kiss me goodnight clandestinely when I ought to have been asleep.

It is now nearly sixty years since my main duty became strutting the quarter deck of *Danae* as junior watchkeeper in frock coat and sword-belt: that and looking after the small gunroom of two converted cabins: sharing a tiny double bunk cabin with Lieutenant Hubert Fox and being the general dogsbody of the Executive branch of the Wardroom. In the New Year we sailed alone for what was then called British Guiana on what was called the Spring Cruise to Central and South American States. We were light in oil so as to be able to get over the bar to the Demarara river and anchor of Georgetown. We were light and so we rolled. This made one of my early duties of Sub of the Gunroom interesting: administering punishment by cane in the only possible site for this undignified performance, the cramped Gunroom bathroom, was not only ludicrous but hilarious when the ship goes wop with a wiggle between. Henceforth I refused to be a party to such antics.

The next eighteen months of my so-called career were entirely trivial; trivial that is from gaining much professional expertise other than in public relations. Although when war came the old cruisers like *Danae* acquitted themselves from reserve all over the world from the Northern Patrol to the Far East, their fighting potential was limited; but they had the classical features of beautiful ladies and, as beautiful ladies do, wooed their way into personal situations which commanded attention from admirers, black or white, Commonwealth or Foreign, in unlikely places. The admission that there were really only two evolutions in which the ship had regular practice, rig quarterdeck for reception and dance or Open to Visitors, is no stigma; for that was virtually her task in the Caribbean Sea and on the seaboards of America. Showing the Flag, diplomatic relations, worthy ambassadors of Britian was, and is, an essential role of the Navy; a role which indirectly has brought substantial trade benefits to her but which I have yet to hear admitted by a Trade Minister when his Cabinet colleague is advocating money for the Navy to perform its "uneconomic" nuclear role. Understandably today the weapon punch is predominant; in those days *Danae*'s punch was negligible but her reputation among the thousands she entertained was not.

"Open to Visitors". This is a dreaded commitment which has to be observed in any goodwill visit. His or Her Majesty's Ships belong to their Sovereign. It is therefore their subjects' right (particularly a British tax payer) to see what they pay for whenever opportunity permits. I imagine that for those whose ship is to be invaded it is much the same sensation at Stately Homes today, with the difference that in the Navy's case there is no profit. Thousands come to see their ships; and rightly. It can be great fun to show them off to their "owners". It can also be hellish.

Generally on a Saturday afternoon, every officer goes ashore who is not on duty. You screw tight your cabin scuttle, lock your door and put away anything valuable in sight; but for those left on board my experience is that the general behaviour and respect for H.M. Ships by the hoards of every colour in every part of the world who have come to see us is on the whole impeccable. They are genuinely thrilled just to see the odd conditions in which we live, to hear of our funny ways, to tell us of their relations who are, or were, anything to do with the sea. They are litter-conscious and well behaved. The sailor has a touch with children. Having locked my cabin I have generally preferred to be proud of what we have to show rather than escape. On balance, even when overwhelmed by thousands in a British Summer holiday resort, I have found my own people easier. Numerically dwindling in numbers as it is, the White Ensign still seems to command respect even if only symbolic of the sea-power it once signified; and never does Open to Visitors go by without meeting families either whose son is thinking of the Navy or who have some connection with it. I was one day to fly my Flag in a cruiser leading a squadron around many of our own Island's ports–Operation Jack Tar–specifically to show our people their navy of the time. At Newcastle I received the six-year-old great-great-great grandson of Nelson's cabin boy at Trafalgar. We still correspond, Christopher and I. Such meetings are worthwhile and are why I did not always shrink from remaining on board when not on duty.

To rejoin *Danae*, our next port of call was Puerto Barrios, Guatemala's only outlet to the Caribbean and therefore for her banana crop to the western world. Our visit was to do more with diplomacy than fruit. Recently (1981) in the presence of Royalty the Union Jack was hauled down for the last time in Belize. A detachment of British troops are still stationed there to ensure such independence against the demands of neighbouring Guatemala with designs on what used to be called British Honduras, its mahogany jungle and capital. Fifty years ago the situation was much the same. I was to sit next to a ravishing Guatemalian film star called Bianca in Hollywood's Twentieth Century Fox Studios. Although her cleavage interested me more than her politics, she nevertheless laughed to me that peace only occasionally broke out in Guatemala.

In a Texan port I lost my Captain at his own reception. Having arranged a fair programme for him, when it came to his dance with the mayor's wife there was no sign. He had changed his uniform for that of her husband who was a cowboy and arrived on his own quarter deck with pistols at the hip. Happily the mayor had resisted the invitation to don naval uniform which might have invoked another clause in the King's Regulations. Nor had I yet learnt that part of every reception at American ports was a ladies' uniformed "Red Hussars" band on the quay. In Port Arthur (and we were the first H.M. ship ever to visit) they were to have medals of some sort pinned on their breasts by my Captain. I failed to brief him adequately so that when it came to circumnavigating the big drum with a safety pin, one protuberance balanced on others, the squeak of pain was audible on the quarterdeck. And so to Jamaica.

"Welcome, glad welcome! The Blue Mountains ring it–

Hills of this leal land which Nelson has known,
Welcome, yes welcome! the tropic winds sing it
Where proudly and long England's fair flag has flown,
Welcome, ten thousand times, Son of our King!"

This euphoria was the overture to the official programme in 1935 to welcome the Duke of Gloucester. It was announced from Government House that he would shake hands with the first thousand in the queue. On this occasion I did better after a late start and *Danae* was properly represented–just. South through the Panama Canal and then at twelve knots the three thousand miles north to California with never a ship in sight. It wasn't easy to keep a ship's company efficient under such undemanding conditions; but somehow they were and the ship was spotless always.

Hollywood. Miss Shirley Temple aged seven (off the set of Fox studios) as the gunroom guest: and then one Sunday afternoon alongside at Los Angeles; a hot, still moment with nobody on board save those on duty, the ship gently cavorting against her hawsers to the scend, when a huge figure appeared at the bottom of the gangway.

"Permission to come on board, Sir?"

"Of course."

He came and near dislocated my arm with his handshake. His gnarled, craggy features were familiar.

"Say! I'm Vic. Always pleased to meet the Royal Navy."

Victor McGlaghen had just won an Oscar for his performance in *The Informer*. It was no penance to entertain him for many hours. On leaving he said "Would you care to come up to my ranch?" I have not subsequently ever spent so many hours by a swimming pool with so many high-balls pressed into my hands by so many half-clad beautiful girls. This, on nine shillings a day, was what I felt was meant by public relations. Vic remains in my memory as among the warmest, most outgoing, patriotic, irresistibly sudden of men I have ever met.

Santa Barbara, San Diego, San Francisco, Vancouver, Vancouver Island and up to those enchanting outposts of British Columbia with such names as Cowichan, Chemainos and Comox–paid to have such experience among such friendship and such beauty, paid to accept the outgiving American hospitality, paid to represent a country which others seemed to want to know about; small wonder that one was spoilt: small wonder that one could be forgiven for forgetting that a man-of-war was designed, *in extremis*, for that purpose; that although life is for living it was an artificial life which began to pall. So that I longed for some kind of professional jolt. It was to come: as jolts do when least expected.

The Cayman Islands lie some two hundred miles north west of Jamaica and south of central Cuba: Grand Cayman with its "capital" like so many others called Georgetown, Little Cayman and Cayman Brac, a little trio emcompassing a mid-sea circle of some hundred miles diameter. Today, and understandably because of its superb climate and beaches albeit in the hurricane zone, Grand Cayman is a resort and tax haven with the consequent ritzy hotels, tinsel tourist attractions, bikinis by day and not much more before bed by night. In 1935 it was scarcely known save to the Governor of Jamaica whose dependency it was; mariners whose charts showed that they existed, unlighted, and therefore deserving of a wide berth; philatelists whose collections of stamps from the more remote parts of the British Empire the Caymans enhanced; and turtles.

On a February morning *Danae* sighted a low strip of land. The highest point of the scrub cannot be more than a hundred feet above sea level. This low plateau of coral rises from unsounded depths, a tiny shelf in mid Caribbean, and thus provides only a fringe of sand to which an anchor will reach before a ship of any draft is aground. A Union Jack flying from every roof suggested that this *must* be another Georgetown. With an escort of natives under oars singing "God Save The King", the Commissioner, a florid Somerset Maugham fictional character, was received with honours on the quarterdeck. The social niceties were arranged for our short stay. I was to be on duty in the evening when there was to be the naval reception ashore which the Captain was to attend.

The sun set to its bugle call upon a scene calm enough and after dark just an off-shore breeze started from the north-west, from windward so that the ship swung to a lee shore. Moonless, the purple clouds were invisible. Within minutes it had freshened to a gale so that the quarter-deck awning was fretting at its stanchions and boats were tugging at their booms like frightened horses in a fire. Hardly any sailors were ashore because there were no fleshpots. Happily the senior officer on board, one of a few of us, was the First Lieutenant, a superb seaman. There was no dearth of Engine Room people who began to raise steam. We blew the sirens and waved searchlights to the sky to attract attention ashore. The awning came down like a recalcitrant dragon. The boats cavorted on their tackles and falls as the sea steepened. One was sent inshore in the hopes of fetching the Captain before such landing there became untenable. It was all happening at once.

This is what I meant when I said that on that Station it was not always easy to keep a ship's company efficient. This was the kind of moment, against the elements, when proof will come or not. Every music-hall song, every girl in any port, will tell you that there is something about a sailor.... There is: and indefinable. At one moment apparently, historically often drunkenly, happy-go-lucky and irresponsible; but next, given a challenge, be it a gale at sea or rescuing children from an earthquake, he displays an individual initiative I have yet to see bettered. So it was tonight.

There is only one thing to do with a ship anchored on a shelf off a lee shore with a full gale now threatening to drag her anchors on to it: and that is to go to sea. Sea room to ride it out is the only hope. You don't choose to go to sea in any ship without your Captain. The question was, in the mind of the First Lieutenant and those few officers on board, could we get him on board? We had raised steam, shortened in the cable to the verge of weighing, and were ready for sea. The Navigator was stranded ashore with the rest of those attending the Commissioner's reception; so I went to the Bridge to assume his responsibilities. There was nobody else to do so.

Just before even a rope ladder could safely embark anybody, we got the Captain on board, sending back the boat because conditions were too dangerous to try to hoist her. The First Lieutenant reported "Ready for sea, Sir." The Captain said "Who's on the Bridge?" The First Lieutenant said "The Sub-Lieutenant." The Captain said "Oh" and came straight up. With him came the Gunnery Officer who whispered to me "He's been navigating since before you were born. Keep your end up."

I tried desperately to remember what I had been taught at the Navigation School when I ought to have been paying attention. There was nothing difficult; but the wind was now severe gale and the gyro compass had not had time to wind up its revolutions and settle down. Magnetic compasses are capricious when rolling.

We hove-to, facing the sea, for the night. Dawn brought little change; but by noon my Captain Knox-Little (a Destroyer officer of World War I in the classic mould and what we used to be able to call a "character") was tiring of hanging about and determined to anchor if even to rescue the wardroom still in Mess Dress from the night before. He was in one of his more puckish moods.

"How d'you think our Commander bedded down with the Commissioner's wife? Now then, Sub; we'll run in and anchor somehow."

Just as there is a norm for any precise professional performance, so there is an easy, straightforward way in which to anchor a ship on a sixpence given normal aids. All you need is some church spire ashore, some lighthouse, anything conspicuously plotted on the chart on which you point your line of approach; but you also need something abeam to tell you how far along that line you have progressed before reducing speed and letting go the anchor. Normally the Navigator crouches over his compass with his pre-determined bearings in a notebook in one hand while he manipulates the azimuth mirror with the other. Easy.

But today it was not normal. A doubtfully charted caswarina tree was all there was ahead and nothing but a storm-tossed sea abeam. This is the moment when you pray the echo-sounding machine will work: and in those days they too were capricious.

"Are we nearly there, Sub?"

"No bottom" from the depth operator in the chart house.

"Not quite, sir."

"Aren't we getting a bit close? I can see a bedraggled Commander still in Mess Dress."

Then suddenly from the chart house–at about this speed–"Bottom at Fifty fathoms, sir: twenty: ten ..."

We had hit the coral shelf. "Stop engines, please, Sir. Will you go astern?"–all very politely.

"Five fathoms, sir," and the Captain dropped his flag: quite calm while the wind howled. The clatter of the cable was music.

"Are you happy, Sub?" he said as the astern wash from the propellors surged up the side.

"Yes, sir." Whether I was or not was not the point.

"Thank you," he said "well done. We got on quite well, didn't we, when left to it?"–and disappeared with, "We'll quit here as soon as the night castaways are on board."

And the lesson for me? That the instinctive professionalism in K-L, in any real sailor, was only camouflaged by his reputation for libertine behaviour ashore. Characters, as I have said, are necessary to the colour of life. How I changed my opinion of him from that moment! He didn't harass or bully me: simply put me through my paces to assess if there was any future for me as a naval officer. He sent for me at sea next day in the gale which had not abated.

"What kind of branch of the Navy were you thinking of pursuing, Sub?"

"I had thought about navigation, sir."

"Well, you got away with it yesterday, quite creditably. But be careful. There's no magic about navigation. Some specialists try to pretend there is. If you simply want to take ships from A to B and try to pull the wool over the eyes of destroyer officers like me, you'll never make high rank. Any bloody fool can do that. If you just regard it as an arrow in your sailor's quiver and are useful to your Captain when things are happening fast in close company at night, then that's another story. Do you want a recommendation for N?"

"I think so, Sir. I'm no good at guns or torpedoes. The sextant is about my mechanical ceiling."

"You may be right. I wasn't considered clever enough to specialise. I just fought the enemy in destroyers. Hopefully you won't have to."

At St. Petersburg in Florida and Charleston in South Carolina we were back on the beat; there to show our little cruiser to the might of the U.S. Navy and to cope with swamping hospitality, our last duty of the commission before setting sail for Plymouth and Christmas at home.

After our social meanderings it was not unnatural that our C-in-C in Bermuda should wish to put us through our paces before allowing such. This meant an Admiral's harbour and sea inspection, in which all officers hoping for promotion in the fierce competition of the day sought to demonstrate their individual efficiency by whatsoever means presented. Guns and torpedoes must work. Targets must be hit. The ship must be spotless and all unlikely evolutions, in the unlikely event of real necessity, had to be performed. Bower anchors must be slung under boats. Kedge anchors must be laid out in any direction. Lower booms must be exchanged. Everybody must run fast in every direction and speaking personally, not quite sure in what direction or why. Awnings were furled and spread. Pipe followed pipe while the C-in-C and his staff strolled about in nonchalant passivity. The sailors regarded it as something of a joke; not so those Lieutenant Commanders knocking on their brass hats. They rushed to hoist whalers at their davits or anything else to be hoisted which came their way. I do not write cynically for I was not in contention; but such was realistically what had to be performed on stage, like an actor in audition trying to secure a future part in the face of stern competition.

The C-in-C in question was rather a daunting little gunnery specialist. "But don't be frightened of father" said our friend, his daughter, "you should see him in bed with a green eye shade and without his teeth. you wouldn't be then." Perhaps, like our American friends, "Not in this uniform" was again pertinent. *Danae*, to the surprise of us all, acquitted herself on all counts. K-L charmed his C-in-C and kept his cool with more ease than I had seen him in other circumstances. I was sorry, years later, to learn that he had run his battleship into the boom on entering Scapa Flow in war, which did not enhance future promotion. You needed more than character to get away with such indiscretions. I remember him with affection and he taught me so much more than probably he, and certainly I, were aware. Such characters are for preserving in the memory. Relieved on station by another cruiser, *Danae* sailed for Plymouth. The Atlantic was its usual self for that time of year and we were battened down for many of the twelve days. Lieutenant Hubert Fox, my friend and senior, and I were thrown together more literally than ever in our tiny double cabin no bigger than the average larder. Hubert was a bachelor and loved horses. I was a bachelor and loved pretty girls. Our tiny shared desk had room only for two large framed photographs. His was of a beautiful quadruped, mine of a beautiful biped called Imogen with whom it then seemed possible marriage might materialise when I got home. Rightly it didn't; but meanwhile the said photographs, Imogen all attractively blurred with her contrastingly dark hair upon cream shoulders by Lenare, and the horse, had to carry our drying socks on occasion. I felt that she might have demurred more than Hubert's hunter. How we remained fast friends must be to the credit of us both.

A naval homecoming from a long commission abroad was an emotional moment to be savoured. Sodden handkerchiefs waved in the rain. On his lawn of Admiralty House overlooking our approach, a kindly C-in-C had collected all the families: not Imogen of course: she was hardly family but I knew she had come to Plymouth to meet me. They cheered K-L ashore. He was well liked for all his eccentricities. Indeed they were the very reason for such affection. "Thank you, Sub," he said "for trying to look after me. I hope you get your Navigation Course, and remember what I said about never trying to make magic out of a sailor's fundamental trade." I never saw him again. But he secured my promotion to two whole stripes, a fully fledged Lieutenant for the next eight years, before he said goodbye.

Home had become a Cotswold old mill-house nestling between Nafford lock on the Avon east of Tewkesbury and the northern slopes of Bredon hill. The front looked up to Grafton firs and the back sloped down to the river and the heavy wooden lock gates. The sound of running water reached the drawing room. To walk alone up the hill which was the scene of my father's and grandfather's youth, up past the eerie emptiness and warm Cotswold stone of Woollas Hall, to overlook the thatched cottages of the Combertons, these were the illustrations which decorate perhaps my grandfather's best poetry, The Vale of Arden; this was the antidote for the past year of tinsel and motley, for thousands of ebullient acquaintances however hospitable, for being perpetually artificially tired, for the little romantic trauma which had recently been so good for my immortal soul. I looked and thought and came to the conclusion that it was about time I put away childish things and began to grow up.

I finished the book about the Gunroom I had begun through weekend boredom as a Sub-Lieutenant when, during those Courses and when my parents lived in Switzerland, I was invariably alone in near-empty training establishments. I gave it to my father to read, who rightly pronounced it appalling. "You know about the life of a Midshipman, my boy. You know little about anything else. Quite right to have a try. You might doctor bits when you have lived a little longer. Don't burn it. Just lock it away." I did.

Chapter 11

Persian Gulf Patrol 1936-1938

Today I fancy that there must be more sophisticated methods of determining exactly where you are within a yard or two on the surface of this planet, should you really want to know, than existed in 1936; and in this nuclear, satellite age there are those who must know for obvious reasons: but when appointed to undergo what was called The Long Navigation Course in H.M.S. *Dryad*, then within Portsmouth dockyard, I was confronted with a less advanced means of determining exactly where I was. This consisted of a tiny rectangular bowl of mercury under its roof of refraction-free glass like a mini green-house, called an artificial horizon. You placed this contraption on the ground between your legs, let it settle and then tried to find a star reflected into your sextant telescope. "When you wish upon a star, makes no matter where you are ..." precisely described my ineptitude in this performance.

Lieutenants Hogg and Hayes, partners for this hot summer night on Portsdown Hill whose latitude we were to determine, approached our task with initial zeal. Our selected star–Vega, Arcturus, Betelgeuse, Sirius–I can't remember and doubt if I even knew– apparently had to be approaching the meridian. We were then to gaze into the mercury bath through the sextant, tell the time by deck watch while reading the altitude and then, we knew, spend hours of spherical trigonometrical calculations on Friday afternoon with the weekend looming to determine just how far north of "The Coach and Horses" pub we were. But there were other couples in the grass around us that night preoccupied in less scientific pursuits and whose erotic communion we found distracting. So we abandoned Betel-geuse in his twinkling Orion constellation to his inevitable orbits, together with our copulating neighbours, and spent until closing time in "The Coach and Horses". When challenged about our blank observations next day we protested about other activities on the hill provoking too much vibration on the surface of the mercury. This was not well received and from that moment it was likely that Hogg and Hayes, should we ever qualify, would be sent to the Persian Gulf to navigate frigates in what was then regarded as a penal assignment for young naval officers. We were.

Despite our lack of enthusiasm to establish the exact latitude of Portsdown Hill, our instructors unwisely put us together again when it came to the week's practical hydrographic surveying of Dartmouth harbour. Having previously spent four years in that college overlooking the Kingswear Golf Club on the opposite down, I knew roughly where it was. Ian Hogg didn't because he had entered the R.N. from Cheltenham. We were now given a theodolite and told to help to establish a main survey triangulation by angles to various salient features, such as the college flagstaff under which I had previously suffered tortures of rifle drill. We began well enough but again enthusiasm waned and we succumbed to the temptations of the nineteenth hole.

Hoo Down was the final nail in our respective coffins. Although we tried in vain to make amends back in *Dryad* we had overstepped the mark in the eyes of authority. We passed, Ian well and me just; but both of course sent to the Persian Gulf; Ian to *Bideford* and me to *Fowey*, two of the four little ships who then comprised the Gulf element of the East Indies Fleet.

Until the war the Persian Gulf squadron, an off-shoot of the command of a C-in-C based in Ceylon who came to see this remote corner of his parish when the climate cooled and the snipe over the Euphrates were to be shot, consisted of four little ships called sloops. They were commanded by a captain in *Shoreham* who rejoiced in the name of Snopgee (Senior Naval Officer Persian Gulf). The fourth was *Deptford*; altogether a wide range of English sea or riverside environments. Snopgee occupied the only civilised billet in the river off Basra, it seemed almost permanently. He was an old sea-dog who liked people and entertaining people. As the only white ones (apart from a few elderly exceptions in other ports, so for us youngsters the absence of any white girls anywhere promoted an artificial sexual anaesthetic) lived in Basra as the diplomatic and consular families in Iraq, he was tethered to that buoy in the Euphrates most of the time while his junior Commanders roamed around the Arab coasts, controlling the illicit traffic in slave pearl-divers and disputes between sheikhs.

Those four little sloops were scarcely bigger than Onassis's yacht: pretty, as comfortable as conditions then made possible, a pop-gun forward and mighty little else to class them as warships. As navigator I had no Gyro compass, no radar and frequently at sea would dangle my feet from the bottom of a harbour accommodation ladder in order to achieve a height-of-eye of nought, thereby minimising the effects of refraction and a mirage horizon in trying to get my sextant to help me find out roughly where I was. We had a ship's company of eighty white and thirty Somali ratings, who were the only people who could stand the afternoon humidity on the Trucial Coast without air-conditioning. The quarter-deck was virtually the wardroom's verandah under double awnings. Our maximum speed was less than twenty knots. My Captain, Commander Evelegh, was one of the most charming of men. There were four or five others of us, including a young doctor and two Warrant Officers. That was H.M.S. *Fowey*: and we were a very happy, tiny little cog within what was then one of the more remote areas of the world in which the White Ensign seemed to matter. It seemed to matter not because of any armament but because the likes of Arnold Wilson and Gertrude Bell had previously inculcated, through years of patient diplomacy and trusted friendship among the primitive Arab sheiks of tiny desert domains, that Britain *was* to be trusted and that the flag fluttering above our quarter-deck symbolised that trust. The post-war Wind of Change has long blown it another way.

Where today stands the Hilton Hotel of Abu Dhabi, the rich air-conditioned accommodation for countless dabblers in every Emirate, who court the colossal wealth of sheikhs whose forebears of no time ago were nomad tribemen, then consisted of one long sand beach from the Mussandam mountains overlooking the Straits of Hormuz to Doha in the south-west corner of the Gulf, called the Trucial Coast. The sand swept in an unbroken stretch for hundreds of miles to form the southern boundary of the Gulf: a fort, some mud huts, the odd scrub bush, nothing else to be seen from seaward.

Nothing else... which sometimes provoked its problems for me in exercising our gun-boat diplomacy. It happened like this.

In 1937 Imperial Airways, as they were then known, ran an air service to the Far East via the Gulf in land-aeroplanes named Hannibals. The desert strip on the Trucial Coast they used was within the Sheikhdom of Sharjah, who therefore coined the royalties. The airline then decided to replace the Hannibal by a flying boat. The Navy were called upon to survey possible landing sea areas for this alternative. Ian Hogg in *Bideford* was detailed to undertake this and I to help him. We wished we had not taken our week of survey instruction so lightly. We bought needles and coloured inks in the Bahrain bazaar. Ian began by hiring a dhow in a lagoon in Umm-el-Qwain. He acquired it from the Sheikh as his work base and paddled about in appalling heat doing his topography. He suffered such sunburn of the legs that he had to lie with them suspended from the deck-head while I found him the necessary alcohol to help him to endure the pain. He eventually recommended to Their Lordships that the best bet was off Dubai, adjoining Sharjah. This they accepted and one day rightly awarded Ian the Shadwell Testimonial Prize for the best survey undertaken by an unqualified hydrographer. (On a later day he was to become Vice Chief of the Defence Staff). So Imperial Airways moved their landing ground from Sharjah to Dubai. Royalties were transferred from one desert neighbour to another. They went to war.

The political British set-up was simple. We had a Political Resident in Bushire on the coast of Persia who communicated with London and Tehran and whom we seldom visited. He had two underlings, Political Agents in Bahrain (who looked after the Gulf within the Hormuz Strait) and in Muscat (who looked after the Batineh Coast down to Muscat and its Sultan). *Fowey* was ordered to embark the Bahrain P.A. and sort out the war. I was told to anchor exactly off the frontier to Sharjah and Dubai. As there was not even a fort to guide me, I had to resort to first principles. So we steamed along the beach until eventually we found six cannon, three each side pointing towards each other. This we felt must be the frontier and we anchored with the compass bearing nicely dividing the opposing armaments.

The P.A. went ashore. An hour later he returned with the two sheikhs, one of whom came up the starboard ladder and the other up the port on to the quarter-deck. With their retinues of brigands they sat in our wicker chairs confronting each other. Sherbet was served and quinine tablets, our doctor's diplomatic cure for cataract, from which all sheikhs suffered. With the P.A. in the middle under the ensign they talked for several hours. Then the sheikhs went over the side by the same gangways, the cannon were turned away from each other and the war was over. We weighed the anchor and went back to Bahrain.

I am not suggesting that this was in any way contributory to the Imperial Airways decision, for disaster invariably overtakes the best measures taken to prevent it: but in the previous year such had struck a Hannibal which had disappeared over the desert on its way to Sharjah, nobody knew exactly where. Helicopters or emergency direction-finding wireless transmissions from crashed aircraft did not then exist and so for such air searches as were available it was something of a needle in a haystack. There were two R.A.F. squadrons based in Basra, one of flying boats (203) and one of limited-range fighters (231). To the latter fell the task. Near the end of its range one of them happened upon the stricken machine in the nick of time. Subsequent rescue found most dead and a few survivors near the end of their tether under what shade the wings could still provide. The heroine proved to be an attractive young American nurse who had tended to the injured and had stripped herself virtually naked to use her clothes as bandages. Such as she had left, her silk bra and panties, she autographed in gratitude and presented to the R.A.F. squadron, who had such trophies framed and hung in the Officers' Mess of their own desert outpost of a base.

Such was our celibate life that it became a fetish of wardrooms to mount raids on the R.A.F. in the hope of capturing the trophy. We never succeeded, because whenever the White Ensign appeared in the river the duty R.A.F. officer slept beneath their treasure. I have often wondered if that Florence Nightingale knew of the pleasure and perpetual interest to so many starved young officers her "smalls" had provoked; and whether now she is still alive to read this?

When our Captain, who was a horseman, had to return the call of the Sheikh of Ajman he asked the doctor and me (who were not) to accompany him. Naval uniform then still endorsed Noel Coward's "Mad Dogs and Englishmen" by demanding its wearers to go out in the midday sun. An enormous white dome of a topee above a throttling tunic collar on a white starched jacket comprised what was called No. 10s, and thus you called on the Sheikh of Ajman. We landed on the beach and were confronted by three snorting white Arab chargers. Our Captain leaped gracefully into his saddle. The doctor and I had to be helped. The worry was that, whereas I had been given to understand you were generally allowed two reins to a bridle, this one only had one, on the starboard side. My steed and I looked at each other, as well we might have done, sizing each other up until clearly he had formed his own conclusions. An Arab hoisted me into the saddle and the horse promptly bolted. We went through the market of attap huts at John Gilpin's Speed, scattering the vendors. I came off underneath a stall selling ghee and other sticky delicacies. The vendors and onlookers were more solicitous than my mount, who left me to continue the rest of my journey to the Sheikh's fort on foot. There I learnt that you must go on sipping coffee until you turn your cup upside-down.

As previously mentioned, during those Sub-Lieutenants' Courses at Portsmouth and with no home in Britain, I had to spend many a lonely weekend in an empty Gunnery or Torpedo School. To while away the time I had the conceit to write a book and further to submit it to several distinguished publishing houses, who returned this classic in polite terms which need only one guess: with one exception–Blackwood's historic monthly magazine which graced every Service Mess and Sahib's Club throughout the Empire and whose recent death is mourned by all who loved it. Blackwoods to my astonishment had accepted a few rewritten chapters true to one of their principles in encouraging amateur authors; and so again from *Fowey* they accepted "A Persian Gulf Patrol".

In the Persian Gulf, there had to be *some* fun, some kind of traditional recreation and relaxation for the Ship's Company to offset the miles of steaming in very hot nothingness with no runs ashore. As the junior ship in the squadron we were rarely granted a taste of Basra or the Abadan Oil refinery for white social company. We therefore had to create our own fun.

All very well for the romantic hypnosis of the desert, the near mediaeval habits of its nomads, the picture-postcard views of mud forts and date palms to fascinate those whom they seduced: but the sailor was not among them even though morale was cheerfully high in our happy little company, despite the odds with no air-conditioning and the humidity of the Trucial Sheikhdoms at 99 per cent. Again all very well for the Captain and his six Wardroom officers: we had our little upper deck mess which gave out to the verandah of the quarter-deck under double awning, and our bar; but the sailors had their mess-decks below (often untenable), the fo'c's'le, and to save their lives their tot of rum. The sailor's epithets are never quite for ladies' drawing-rooms, with every noun prefixed and every verb declined by sheer habit with a word they only paraphrase when talking seriously among themselves about making love; and such language in those conditions was often justified. Our base at Bahrain was well removed from the village and airfield of Manama in a huge coral lagoon called Jufair, with a tiny cut as its only entrance. In the desert ashore there were three little buildings: the officers' club, the ratings' canteen and their beer store. Those, and mercifully a swimming-pool, were all. So something had to be done in the way of recreation.

It began with enthusiasm from the lower deck that we should publish the *Fowey* monthly magazine, and would I be editor? Certainly; on condition that it really was a ship's chronicle and not just by the officers. Of course: a locked contribution box would be put on the mess-deck and the editor's decision would be final. I badgered the Captain and Wardroom to subscribe to the first instalment, contributed an introduction myself and weekly opened the box. After exhortation and three weeks there was one submission, a poem. It began:

"Roll along, old ship, through the sun or the rain,
　And don't ever go near that there Persian Gulf again...."

—natural sentiments as far as they went, and they went in similar metre for quite a long time; signed "Anon".

And that was all. The first edition, with that one exception, written entirely by the officers, was well received but alas failed to provoke further contribution. "*Fowey*'s Follies" died a mournful and early death. Then the Sub-Lieutenant—a cheerful extrovert whose talent for histrionics possibly exceeded that for his profession—and I had hopefully a better idea. We would form a concert party: the inevitable sailors' concert party. This again was greeted with acclaim and a committee was formed consisting of the two of us, the Chief

Stoker and Able Seaman Bullock, who was well named. Assuming that these follies would founder as quickly as their predecessor, to our surprise support flamed through the mess-decks like a bush fire; surprise became tinged with dismay when we realised how much we had bitten off to chew, and the Sub said "I have a horrible feeling that this is going to be great success." It was, culminating in "*Les Folies Jufère*, Christmas 1937" when we played a two-hour show to packed houses in Abadan and Basra; but there was a lot of literal sweating before the curtain went up.

Sailors can sing and with a little lubrication are uninhibited; so of course censored sea-shanties for a start. Again of course one or two of those dreaded monologues "The Pigtail of Liu-Fang-Fu" or "The Green Eye of the Little Yellow God" from the Chief Stoker. We persuaded our charming and love-lorn First Lieutenant to interrupt his daily letter home to his fiancée and to play the judge in that clever little triologue "In Port"; and the *pièce de résistance* of a finale was "Their Lordships have always under consideration the dress of those serving in His Majesty's Fleet...", which was translated into the evolution of fashion for both sexes through the ages. With garish coloured materials from the Bahrain bazaars, the creations from Adam and Eve to the present day were the preoccupation in every caboosh on board–no green room seamstress for us–and AB Bullock had elected to open the charade as Eve. Practically naked with his thick black chest pelt he found me with his pair of conical metal breasts made from condensed milk tins and joined by spun yarn. "What d'you think o' these, sir? Thought I'd give the tips a touch o' red lead: more realistic like. Bosun's party is doin' my serpent. Stuffed number six canvas and Putty the Painter's makin' a great job." Alas I now only have the picture of Bullock's Garden of Eden in my mind's eye, particularly on reading Genesis from our local lectern.

Rehearsing might have been a problem but was solved simply. As half the ship's company, even including our devoted Goanese wardroom steward Socrates, were in the cast, they were the starboard watch; those not participating formed the port watch, and thus we could rehearse ashore in Jufair when starboard were the leave watch ashore. We had no piano, so the squeeze-box, the Admiralty-pattern harmonium–"collapsible–portable–Divine Service for the use of", to give its full naval store book description–had to do. I could conjure enough from it to get the shanty soloists into the right key when they were duty on board, and we knew we'd have a pianist from the oil company on the day. When that day came, *Fowey* was vociferously applauded for a hitherto unique achievement by every white family in the refinery, starved of any live theatre, however amateur; and not even Bullock, who of course brought the house down, got drunk.

The end of our commission was heralded one day by an unexpected signal from Admiralty to say that instead of turning over to successors on the East Indies Station, we were to go to Malta for a refit to include the fitting of Asdic, which was then, as I have mentioned, still the Cinderella of naval weaponry within a year or so of the outbreak of war (then those few who had had the foresight to specialise in it, such as Captain Walker and his famous *Starling*, became heroes). So on April 4th 1938 we made our final exit from Jufair for the 4000-mile voyage to Malta, through that coral cut where I had originally touched bottom with the bilge keel during my first few minutes as Navigator without causing more than scratches. In his recent book *The Story of H.M.S. Dryad*, my "alma mater", Admiral Schofield, one of its most distinguished graduates, included the following in his section entitled "Experiences of young Navigating Officers":

"Those who know Bahrain Lagoon and the 90° turn into a tiny coral cut to gain the outer channel, the ultramarine race falling off the ramparts to form a river current, can picture the scene with only a crude beacon to tell the moment of helm over which was starboard 25. When the rudder action first listed the ship in its own direction, before opposing momentum took over, there was a nasty crunch and a tell-tale thickening in the wake. No doubt but that the bilge keel had touched and no moment to stop for divers to examine. So in the first five cables of my navigating career I fulfilled what all who have never felt that feeling in the stomach say you should in order to become fully-fledged; 'take ground' but preferably without damage!

"The Lieutenant of the time also reminds us that in those days the Navigator of a sloop was also the Paymaster which meant that in addition to a basic pay of 13/6d a day and 2/6d (N) allowance, I was given another 2/6 a day for the privilege of being court-martialled should my accounts be in error. It was said that more Navigators suffered in this respect than for grounding of their ships and certainly, having been given just a week's course in accounting and victualling, it cost one more anxiety. It was a cheap bargain for Their Lordships; and although when errors in the cash account or rum return became apparent, the letter from the Director of Navy Accounts was probably more polite than had you been wearing white between your stripes (then the distinguishing mark of Paymasters)—"The Accountant Officer of H.M.S. *Fowey* is requested to explain how he arrived at the following conclusions"—nevertheless the mailed fist was there. Star sights were mathematics one understood; the victualling account in favour of Mr Sorabji Prestonji of Bombay was something only Supply Petty Officer Venables understood and in whose hands of loyalty or otherwise one sank or swam. You quickly learned the technique of pouring out the baskets of so-called chickens onto the quarter-deck to reveal a residue of plucked sparrows; but the ship's ledger and victualling account shared my dawn chart table with Polaris, Capella and Betelgeuse. The latter were reliable and familiar; the former were neither."

So we could not feel sorry to be going. We could not have forecast into what world importance and prominence our remote patrol area would leap in the second half of this century. We could only anticipate civilisation, a temperate climate, seeing a white girl at last and even dancing with her in the Sliema Club—only dancing for orthodox naval officers in those days!—and what would separately happen to us all after that.

So, our lives were entirely self-centered, utterly absorbed by our own activities. The world without his wife went by without our knowledge or particular interest, save in letters from home. As an example of this isolation and aloof mental attitude, when Britain was convulsed in the traumatic drama of the Abdication, *Fowey* was being thrown about by the south-west monsoon while crossing the Arabian Sea on her way to Bombay for a quick docking. One dawn I staggered up to the open bridge to see if any star was visible under the scudding low cloud in a gale-force wind. The Officer of the Watch had his head in the chart table and otherwise only the Signalman was visible in his oilskins.

"Morning, sir; bloody awful, isn't it? See from a signal we're getting' a new boss."

"What d'you mean? Surely our Captain is not leaving us?"

"Naow, sir: not the Captain: we've got a new King. 'Nother George. Proper rumpus going on, my old woman wrote, over some American fancy-lady called Simpson."

The stars did not twinkle for me that morning any more than they did in London, in that other world I had virtually forgotten.

The passage to Malta was to be my last lethargic voyage in the Navy: round Ras-al-Hadd, down to Aden to refuel, up the Red Sea at a kind time of year and into the Canal. I had time to experiment with stars less frequently used in the sextant. Though of course the pilot was compulsory at Suez, the Frenchman considered our size scarcely worth his attention apart from explaining to me the signals and time-checks at intermittent stations. Only when some oncoming large tanker might not notice us did he show interest; then, leaving the Port Said gully-gully men and the children diving for hundreds of rupees or annas thrown from the fo'c's'le, we entered the Mediterranean for the last leg. On May day the little stranger of different colouring, a white hull and an ochre funnel, crept between the breakwaters of Grand Harbour, past the great light grey battleships in Bighi Bay including *Royal Oak* of my nursery days, under the baracca from where one could almost hear the usual onlookers saying "What *is* that?", the "still" piped to the C-in-C himself on the quarter-deck of his flagship, peering critically through a telescope at our appearance, and at last safely alongside among the destroyers in French Creek.

"Ring off main engines," said the Captain for the last time. "Secure. Fall out special sea dutymen. Thank you, Pilot," as he held out his hand to me. And from the passage log in my Navigator's Work Book (still with me) I see that after that near-disastrous first half-mile a year and a half before, I had managed to add another 20,078 without further mishap. My successor was waiting for me, happily an old friend from the 13-year-old Dartmouth days to whom I bequeathed my trust. "Over to you, Peter."

Chapter 12

...And The Personal Aftermath

My introduction to Shakespeare began at the age of eleven when *A Midsummer Night's Dream* was chosen as the annual school play and I was cast as that love-sick virgin Helena ("I am a right maid for my cowardice"), anathema in itself to a male child who had just got his football colours and made worse by having to play opposite a boy called Pope, whom I detested, as Demetrius. The following four years at Dartmouth were, shall we say, limited in this field of literature and consisted of one reading of *King Richard III* around the English class under an elderly bachelor, omitting those passages considered in any way risqué and thus unsuitable for Cadets. It was as well for him that we were then unaware of the existence of *Titus Andronicus*, containing one of the Bard's more succinct stage directions, when another Demetrius enters "with Lavinia, ravished; her hands cut off and her tongue cut out".

Nevertheless, my home while a Cadet had been not far from Stratford where my parents had taken me to see many of the plays, including an uncensored *Richard III*; and so, by the time I was sent to the Gulf, my interest had been kindled. Having been warned that reading matter out there would be virtually unobtainable, on a whim I took with me to *Fowey* the entire New Temple edition of little scarlet volumes, together with as many classic works for students of Shakespeare, plus a glossary, as my luggage could hold. By the end of the commission I had managed to make my own marginal notes for each play, and have since been eternally grateful for that whim which gave me a chance for which it was to be long before either the time or the quiet for such study recurred. This filled a vacuum as far as it went which was not far enough. I wrote home once a month but had no correspondence other than my mother's devoted replies, and "O that this too, too solid flesh would melt" became near to reality on the Trucial Coast during summer. I therefore needed what is now called a Pen-Pal, and the direction of my Cupid's arrow was clear; the strength with which I dared fire it was less so.

During my week-end motoring between home under Bredon Hill and Portsmouth I had met a young lady whom I subsequently discovered to be the daughter of a Judge. Alarmed I had nevertheless presumed to ask her down to the Navigation School dance at the end of our Long Course, by which time I knew of my forthcoming banishment, and she had accepted. Next day I had met her mother and father, whose gentle contrast from that stern image of the Bench dissolved all apprehension, reinforced by the quiet, shrewd kindness of his wife. It was a very happy Sunday; my attention was not focussed on the pulpit.

Just as fiction and the stage must of course include the sociable Adonis of a Flag Lieutenant to covet his admiral's daughter, so could I be forgiven for comparing this to those young aspiring barristers who in the same way look after their master's well-being on Circuit, and doubtless his daughter's too. Somehow I had to find an ally who might further my impertinent objective *in absentia*; I found two in Mr. Killick, the judge's family retainer, and Mrs. Tosh, cook and wife to their gardener. "Mischief, thou art afoot...".

To spend time in dwelling on the bliss of homecoming to the Cotswolds in May after so long at sea off the desert would be discourteous to the imagination. To my relief the judge's daughter was not engaged. I must have been an inconvenient and pretentious nuisance, even managing to get tacked on to her party for the Caledonian Ball by borrowing Ball Dress uniform from a kilted friend of Anson days: and I was rich! What could I have spent in *Fowey* beyond a monthly £3 messing and £5 wine bill? So I booked two stalls for the whole of a *Ring* cycle and made sure that it was the one she was attending with her mother close by. I took my mother and father to two each and we dined *à quatre* during those long intervals which then separated Acts I and II. There is only one permitted laugh in the *Ring* when Siegfried tries to copy the Woodbird on a reed plucked from under his linden tree and makes a mess of it – fun too for the instrumentalist in question. My knowledge of German stretches no further than Siegfried's puzzlement. *"Voglein, mich dunkt, ich bleibe dumm . . . ."*

That decided me. I too had been dumb and could risk it no longer. That was a Friday and I had been invited down to Wiltshire for the week-end before a final *Götterdämmerung* on the Monday. Next night, when her parents had left the drawing-room hearth to us alone, and praying that it would not herald a twilight for me as well as the Gods, I summoned up courage.

Normal progress after navigating your first little ship alone, preferably without mishap, was to be sent as assistant to a senior (N) officer in some impersonal colossus such as an aircraft carrier for a year prior to what was known as "The Big Ship Course" back at *Dryad*, when you became qualified to navigate "ships even of the first class" – cruisers and above. Such time was dreaded: second string to a master instead of being your own: yet Fate was kind; possibly for having expiated my sins of Portsdown Hill but probably because Captain Jackie Spooner, who had then been my Captain and one with a sense of humour, now commanded H.M.S. *Vindictive*, an elderly cruiser converted to the sole purpose of training ex-Dartmouth cadets at sea for the first time. The seamen who would normally man her were, save for a few hand-picked Chief and Petty Officers, replaced by the Cadets who worked the ship while continuing classroom studies of naval flavour and taking turns to be trained in the engine room, victualling department, indeed in all aspects of what makes a cohesive ship's company. The officers chosen for this "one-off" appointment were expected to know their onions and previously to have kept their noses reasonably clean. Jackie Spooner was an accomplished pianist and married to Megan Foster, a professional singer; so that when he had had to give a duty invitation to each student to share his personal table once during their time under him, he may have been glad to find one who at least knew that the *Waldstein* or *Hammerklavier* were nothing to do with artificial horizons! Having been offered names from which to select his second (N) officer and a junior Cadet training officer he had evidently chosen a devil he knew.

June 1938 was bursting out all over while I bit my nails on leave at Nafford. Then I received an invitation from Mr. Justice Finlay to come for a weekend to Judge's Lodgings in Wells, where he was that term's Assize Judge on the South-Western Circuit. By the time I arrived her father had already gone to dine with the Bishop. We dined *à deux* after she had lowered the drawbridge. On his return, and as was the custom, I formally asked her father for his blessing. I was not to know of his affection for a naval brother-in-law, mined off the African coast in the Great War while in command of his destroyer; and after the cathedral service next morning, when my thoughts were not with "M'dear Bishop's" sermon, he invited me to stroll down the Cheddar Gorge with him. Eventually coming to the kernel of the hour he said: "Forgive my asking, John, but what exactly are your financial prospects?" This took thirty seconds to explain. "17/10d a day, sir, rising to a guinea in three years' time and a bit more in 1943 when I add my half stripe. I'm afraid that's all, sir."

He stopped. "Well," he smiled, "the Royal Navy is an honourable profession if not a well-paid one. Selfishly I shall miss Rosalind. Look after her. I've only got the one. Have you read any Jane Austen?"

"I'm afraid not, sir."

"I suggest you begin with *Persuasion*. You'll soon see why."

I found in my future father-in-law, from the outset of our all too occasional meetings, everything in such a relationship for which I had previously groped. Admittedly the one had suffered from the trenches and the other had not, and they were to respect each other's mutual knowledge of literature; but there was not the irascibility, the uncertain reception of success or failure which tarnished true ease with my father and which I found instinctive towards my new-found sponsor. Here was somebody to whom to confess mistakes instead of concealing them was relief; somebody moreover who seemed willing to bequeath to me the greatest trust he had to give; alas, the war to come, and his premature death as the active man he was to the end just before V.J. Day, denied to me and to my generation any long benefit of his affection and wisdom.

It would have needed a twisted mind to dislike Will Finlay; for he seemed to love everybody and if he couldn't find something nice to say of them he said nothing. He loved too the majesty and panoply and traditions of the Law in general and of the Middle Temple in particular, Jane Austen, Mozart, claret and his golden retriever called Fudge who, he said, was too beautiful to need brain and once went straight from the garden to win all his classes at Crufts and then back to the garden again. He was the most unselfconscious man I ever knew and would hum during *Figaro* at Glyndebourne which was to him a shrine. He couldn't whisper and was in no way perturbed when the row in front, to his wife's shame, turned round with "Sssh!" at his "perfectly beautiful aria" during *"Voi Che Sapete"*. At a Temple wedding when the groom promised "with all my worldly goods I thee endow", his whisper of "Poor dear, and she's got *so* much the most," was hardly *sotto voce*. I write now of this much loved and respected judge–admired not only by laymen but alike by aspiring nervous young barristers, struggling before him in their first case, by Sir Norman Birkett and Sir Patrick Hastings themselves who opposed each other several times before him and who both pay him tribute in their memoirs–because I was to be denied meeting him for longer than the occasional hour or two during the war years. He was elevated to the Court of Appeal and following his work there was, I understand, being briefed to become the British Judge at Nuremberg when he suddenly died. Never having flown before, the sudden sights within a recently liberated Belsen by the British shattered not only his faith in humanity but also a tired heart.

The annual cycle of cruises for *Vindictive* to train her Cadets was to the Mediterranean in September and home for Christmas: the West Indies in January and home for Easter: Scandinavia or France and the west coast of Scotland in May and home for summer leave: a curriculum combining sunshine and storm in the best ratio for her purpose and one for which those who love sea and sun would have paid the earth. But joining at Plymouth that September coincided with the Munich crisis; instead of sailing for Gibraltar I found myself in charge of the draft of a ship's complement I had not met, on a train to Chatham on mobilisation of the Fleet for war. Euphoria was in the air on every station platform. Ladies shook the sailors' hands. There was cheering like scenes from Noël Coward's *Cavalcade*. The machine-like procedure was tested in the barracks while we wondered, in expectant anticipation of . . . . what? Then Mr. Chamberlain returned from his meeting with Hitler, waving that umbrella with "Peace In Our Time", and we all went back again. The Senior Cadets who had completed one cruise had been sent to help win the war in old cruisers of the Reserve Fleet. They returned desperately disappointed, which Their Lordships were not. The next year is history. Despite the critics of appeasement, the Navy as one part of our shield was made to realise what a collection of rusting hulls comprised an unready Reserve Fleet before the days of mothballing ships when not in commission. We were given a vital year of breathing space to put this as near right as possible, and the lesson had been learned; so now I was back at sea in more temperate conditions, teaching our charges, trying to remember what I had been taught myself and forgotten, the details of Midshipmen's behaviour one had learned the hard way oneself; as for instance, when bringing lady guests to dine on board in your motor boat and it had been forgotten to rig the canvas screen underneath the steps of the open ladder to the quarter-deck, to avert the eyes as they climbed it. Coupled with the discovery of Cadets' mimicry of my habit of telling them "nothing looks worse" than (say) leaving fenders over the side on leaving the lower boom, I found light doggerel effective:

"It's a simple code of decency that training must impress
Not to gaze from under ladders up a lady's evening dress.
What may appear 'the thing to do' is really the reverse;
And ladies will endorse the fact that *nothing* looks worse."

The first of countless partings, of indefinite time and which never got any better, took place in a bitter January night gale in one of Britain's least romantic surroundings, Bincleaves Pier at Portland. The Cadets' crew of the motor boat tossing alongside discreetly averted their eyes in polite deference to our kisses and with "Let go aft. Shove off for'ard," headed into the darkness and towards the cruiser straining at her bridle from her buoy under that inhospitable Bill. Sunburn camouflaged my blushes on return from the Caribbean at Easter a fortnight before our wedding for having contributed practically nothing towards the arrangements except, she teased, to suggest what may have been left out! So the day came for uniform to be blended into legal surroundings founded centuries before even the Navy, the Round Church of The Temple and the ancient sublime hall of the Middle Temple, counting among its contributions to our heritage the first performance of *Twelfth Night*, and where I now facetiously ended my bridegroom's speech before such judicial company in adding one more vow to those we had just undertaken;

by promising that I would strive to further that natural understanding which had always existed between the Navy and the bar.

After the Cadets' summer cruise to Iceland, Argyllshire, Ireland and Brittany, we made August leave an extension of our honeymoon. Tyn Gors was a tiny shepherd's croft let into the Welsh hillside high above the Rhayader Valley of the River Elan and commanded a magical view over the still waters of the lowest dammed reservoir, which supplied Birmingham's soft water. Oblivious to the world beyond our own, with no radio or newspaper for a fortnight, newly married, headlines like "WAR CLOUDS GATHERING .... HITLER THREATENS POLAND .... MOBILISATION LIKELY ...." had not troubled Tyn Gors, though of course one was aware of those clouds on the horizon before our seclusion. But then there had been Munich...sufficient unto the day...and that day came with an early-morning visit by a sheepdog sniffing under the door and a knock by a boy from the farm in the valley below with a little yellow envelope in his hand. "Lovely mornin', sir. Sorry to disturb. 'Ere's a telegram. Come out o' there, Pickles! Any reply I can take down again?" Still in my pyjamas I read **"RING DUTY OFFICER *VINDICTIVE* FORTHWITH"**.

A helpful operator got me through from the Elan Valley to Chatham dockyard and the ship. The Duty Officer told me I was appointed to join *Cairo* as her Navigator—tomorrow. "They're mobilising the Fleet. There's a bit going on. 'Bye." And I was left only to the sound of running water.

It would be surprising if each individual of the millions involved did not in some detail remember their first call to the War; sometimes heart-rending, sometimes jolly, sometimes flattered as departing hero or heroine, sometimes with feigned hearty laughter, but not forgotten if chosen to be remembered. For us it was August 23rd 1939, with "this little world, this England" flaunting her beauty at us in summer frock as we drove all day in quiet speculation. Farewells at Nafford and the collection of some personal memorabilia, a first understanding of the gravity on the European stage from my father, a nostalgic moment by the lock which baseless intuition told me I would never see again. (Nor have I.) Farewells to her parents in London and on to Chatham to pack such uniform as time allowed, hating to have to scamper in such a way from the ship which had given me nothing but professional and private happiness. It seemed so ungrateful to her. Nearly midnight now, and after a final wardroom drink with the dwindling few on board—for *Vindictive* was not designed for war in her present costume—over the brow and a "Good luck, sir" from the quarter-deck watchman. Tyn Gors seemed a long time ago. It had been a taxing day, the kind of strained experience which mixes the cement of understanding for the foundations of marriage.

At least *Cairo* transpired to be only at Portsmouth, a quick train journey while Rosalind went back to my cabin to bring on the trunks. The 6,000-ton cruiser was a hive of activity, suddenly coming to life after an extensive refit and conversion to a floating anti-aircraft battery. Not having been at sea for years from the Reserve Fleet, there was understandably nothing at all in my department, not a single chart; so when she arrived with the car it seemed a good idea to get some. After a visit to the Chart Depot the back springs of the little car sank under the folios of The World with three chronometers perched on top of them. It had been drummed into us that these gymballed special clocks (which didn't tell the time as you and I know it, but went fast or slow at constant rate so that navigational watches could) were

"An instrument rare
To be handled with care
And ought to be treated as such ...."

as I had had cause to tell cadets when their elbows upset the magnetic compass; but no time for ceremony; who minded now what time it was?

Yet it had come—time for her to go home to Wiltshire. Dame Vera Lynn had not yet immortalised, "We'll meet again, don't know how, don't know when...."; but as I lingered to watch the car disappear, one emotion at least was clear: the music now to be faced was written in another key.

FACE THE MUSIC

A SAILOR'S STORY

PART TWO 1939–1945

WAR AT SEA

"Suppose you go to war, you cannot fight always; and when, after much loss on both sides, and no gain on either, you cease fighting, the identical old questions as to terms of intercourse are again upon you."
(Abraham Lincoln, Inaugural Address, 4th March 1861)

"Death and sorrow will be the companions of our journey: hardship our garment: constancy and valour our only shield. We must be united, we must be undaunted, we must be inflexible."
(Winston Churchill to the House of Commons, 8th October 1940)

Chapter 13

The Curtain Quickly Rises

Although the gathered war clouds were to break in a few hours' time, the dawn of Sunday 3rd September 1939 smiled serenely enough upon the ships in harbour under Portland Bill. Funnels smoking their morning pipe, they were outwardly like any other sabbatarian doze in the fleet about to conform to Article I of the King's Regulations and Admiralty Instructions, which commanded that divine service should be performed compulsorily, like it or not.

A few days before, having embarked everything available which anybody could think of from oil and ammunition to food, clothing and those charts for we knew not where, we had managed to wrench *Cairo* from her Portsmouth mooring. Of an older vintage than *Danae*, though similar as originally a 6" cruiser, she had been in the reserve fleet for years before going into dockyard hands for conversion to a floating, mobile 4" anti-aircraft battery. Only she herself could remember when she last went to sea and, as we had shyly crept past Nelson's *Victory* and the modern giants beside her, every gyro-compass alarm bell had rung to warn me of this fact, together with the unadjusted magnetic compass spinning round in protest at the idea of being used instead. But I could see and knew the way to Portland, whence we had been ordered.

Idle the old lady may have been but not the hands which had fashioned her for war. Somebody with imagination had foreseen a particular requirement for the A-A protection of convoys and so four of these old C-Class cruisers had had their original surface armament thus replaced: *Calcutta* of my early children's party days in Bermuda, *Curlew*, *Coventry* and ourselves, none of whom were to survive the war, so much were they at once in demand in hot seats.

Imagination had gone further. Four divisions of the peace-time R.N.V.R., that heroic band of civilians who gave of their leisure time to train to help the kernel of us regulars in the event of war, had been trained to embark as a unit in each of these cruisers. The London Division had come to *Cairo* led by a publisher, a solicitor, a tea-taster and one of the Moss Bros. Their ratings were all highly intelligent, educated volunteers who quickly gained their commissions. Today therefore, the first day of the war, in addition to our Captain Oram, one of the few survivors from the *Thetis* disaster off Liverpool that summer, there were only three regular R.N. officers among us: the Gunnery Lieutenant Horace Law–to become Admiral Sir Horace and a distinguished Controller of the Navy–myself, and a Sub-Lieutenant. The rest were either reservists or retired R.N. recalled from their chicken farms. We were strangers to ourselves and our ship, the blind leading the blind. (My assistant navigator had been one of my Snotties' Nurses). This sudden strange assortment of young and old, professions past and present, doctors straight from their large London practices, were thrown into quite a small healthy ship's company, civilians now permanently uniformed no matter what their real place in life, who like each other or not had no time to wonder–this jerked us into meeting our challenge perhaps quicker than had we been acclimatised. There had been a few hours exercising at sea to blow away the last vestiges of dockyard control, to discover if and how she worked (which included her compasses); but work she did, and had to, from the outset–to the credit of those who had transformed her in recent years.

The Prime Minister was to address the nation at 1100. That voice which only a year ago had told us of "Peace in our time" came now from a man at bay, tired, frustrated, disillusioned, an amalgam of savage despair and defiance. Scarcely before anybody had broken that shocked silence which follows the reality of the inevitable, there was a sailor at my side. "Captain wants to see you, sir." Alone in his cabin he handed me a signal with a half-smile. "Take a look at this, Pilot."

CAIRO FROM ADMIRALTY IMMEDIATE
BEING IN ALL RESPECTS READY FOR WAR PROCEED

FORTHWITH TO JOIN MINELAYERS IN SOLENT. ESCORT
TO STRAITS OF DOVER AND COVER WHILE BARRAGE IS
LAID.

"That, sir, must be the greatest over-statement and compliment
ever paid to this old lady."

"She'll meet it. We'll sail as soon as the engineers can raise
steam."

England may not have looked ready, but navigationally she was.
No longer the sweeping glare of the lighthouses such as St.
Catherine's. Either extinguished or dimmed, for obvious reasons,
reliance had to be placed on light buoys which as students we had
been taught never to trust lest they had dragged from their charted
positions. Now there was no alternative as we crept up a moonless
Solent to join the darkened shapes of our charges, *Adventure*–the
Navy's only minelayer built as such–and two converted train ferries.
Reaching Dover to embark a different cargo, for several days they
plied their normal cross-channel run laying their nasty eggs over the
stern. Every now and then one impatiently exploded in their wake.
Unmolested by the enemy, it was a good overture to war in weather
helpful for settling us to begin to work in unison before the onset of
that first brutal winter for those at sea. The mine barrage laid,
leaving only narrow safe channels under the white cliffs and the
French coast, we were ordered to the Humber.

"Dirty British coaster with a salt-caked smoke stack"–these
blackened, humble little servants of local trade suddenly found
themselves in the front line of war at sea about which there was
nothing "phoney", whatever what was not happening on land at the
outset: a situation not of course analogous to the mud of the trenches
in that first holocaust–there was nothing static in their wallowing in
North Sea gales at seven knots from the Thames estuary to the Firth
of Forth–they soon became first focus of enemy attention.

London held only a fortnight's stock of coal failing regular supply
by coastal collier from Scotland and the north. The east coast
convoys were therefore at once established to run in each direction
every other day, protected and shepherded throughout mainly by
those little "V"and "W" destroyers whose design was conceived in
the early months of 1916. The youngest of them was now fifteen
years old, the senior of these veterans of the Kaiser's war was twenty
three, and they fought from the Arctic Circle to the Far East, many

still in service in 1945 as the sheepdogs of their flocks.

But these east coast flocks were not like the huge, rectangularly-shaped convoys of the Atlantic battle; they strung out as best they could to wend their way in the narrow swept channels between the shoals off East Anglia. From Methil or Orfordness where they assembled, the destroyers gave them what protection they could from U-boats, *Calcutta* and ourselves against aircraft.

Our duty seemed easy enough on paper: every other day one of us was to be with the south-bound convoy when during daylight hours it was between Whitby and Orfordness, the other vice versa for the north-bound. Both of us were therefore present for the protracted cross-over. In fact from our anchorage in the Humber this meant sailing in the middle of one night to reach our flock at dawn, staying with it until dark before returning to the river in the middle of the next night, and off again in the opposite direction the night after that: and so on. Every other day at anchor meant preparing for the next at sea, which in my own case entailed bringing daily wartime measures up to date on the charts I was using, together with some trivial correction to a buoy's position in Valetta harbour, since we carried those charts of the world and it was then still my personal responsibility to keep them up to date: just in case...!

Would that the North Sea weather of that first winter had been as tame as that experienced by Valetta; yet its ferocity may have been partly responsible for the sparseness of such enemy air activity as there was, while the efforts of all escorts was mainly directed towards encouraging the gallant little colliers to try to keep some vestige of station in the line. Then came the first of Hitler's so-called secret weapons, the air-dropped magnetic mine, concentrated naturally first in the shallow waters of our route. Hour by hour, it seemed, the latest victim sank in a channel ahead. An immediate signal would suggest an alternative, if such was even practicable for what was scarcely a huddle of sheep controlled by "one man and his dog". It was like trying to drive along a road one knew only to find a road-block and police diversion every few miles. On one occasion we had to pick our way among new wrecks in order to skirt the Thames estuary from the north and eventually enter from the south. It was anxious work, until eventually the Germans made the mistake of dropping a mine on the mud-flats of Shoeburyness, exposed at low water. In cold blood two officers from the mining school *Vernon* extracted the firing mechanism, one telephoning to the other beyond explosion distance what his next move was going to be, and thus gave to the scientists the vital knowledge that the Navy so desperately needed. Among those scientists who quickly produced the simple remedy of de-polarising a ship's inherent magnetic field was my uncle the owner of Tyn Gors. We breathed again, but not before suffering major damage to the Fleet.

Following the daring night exploit by U47 in breaching the supposedly impenetrable defences of the main Fleet anchorage in Scapa Flow, when her captain, Prien, was unfortunate in finding only my first ship, the ageing *Royal Oak*, to torpedo, an alternative was found in Loch Ewe among the high hills of Wester Ross, big enough and deep enough for temporary use although undefended. Quick to learn of this, one of Prien's colleagues had laid his cluster of magnetic eggs in the narrow entrance, one of which had blown a hole in the bottom of the C-in-C's flagship *Nelson*. Thus incapacitated, she had only her own anti-aircraft guns in self-defence. *Cairo* was released from our convoys and ordered to act as an additional floating battery at anchor close to the 16″ battleship. We stopped steaming and for the first time could relax. Boilers could be cleaned as well as the ship, we could actually sleep at night and stretch our legs in superb country by day.

So this was Scotland. Why had I never seen it before? Still, crisp, sunlit snow-capped mountains around us under wide skies as blue as the shell of a robin's egg. Day by day minesweepers swept the entrance channel to explode the rest of the German mines. We minded not how long they took for Christmas was upon us. They were, as I have hinted, a very special company of R.N.V.R. sailors, able to relax for the first time. Prompted by the navigator's yeoman who helped me with charts of Loch Ewe or the world, I once more commissioned that portable gramophone and in some corner which was not a gangway played my Desert Island Discs to anyone interested in my brief notice-board programme notes. They were more discerning than A.B. Parks as they propped themselves against bulkheads, writing their letters home. When it became a case of standing room only, we borrowed an empty magazine from my friend "Guns". I quickly found that the *Andantes* were most to their liking as they scribbled to their loved ones, the slow movements of Beecham's lollipops; nothing boisterous, thank you very much, for there was enough of that in real life. The needle scratched deeper into the Beethoven concertos and symphonies, the *Jupiter*, "What Is Life?", "I know that my Redeemer liveth" (and during those moments for some of us He clearly did). Music was indeed providing the food of love being expressed by those scribbling pencils. Even if it could not play on for very long, it served a purpose.

In normal circumstances Christmas in the Fleet is a hollow feast for those who have to remain on board. Not even the image of that Bethlehem manger seems to be able to penetrate or even camouflage the stark surroundings of metal and guns, the enforced camaraderie engendered by rum during the traditional rounds of the messdecks, brave substitute though it may be for the family stockings, paper hats and the excitement of children which all are missing. But today held no forced hilarity, with the duty watch closed up at air defence stations, a Christmas so still that only the gulls and the sheep on nearby hills broke the silence. The drifter detailed for our needs, appropriately named *Christmas Morn*, brought off her little cargo of offerings from our families which had given the one-man railway staff of Achnasheen, miles away across the mountains, more than he was accustomed to handle.

This respite couldn't last, and eventually sufficient mines had been accounted for to make the risk of *Nelson's* exit and passage to the nearest dock acceptable. We made a strange procession led by the little sweepers. A German prize merchantman captured by our northern patrol cruisers was brought to play her part. Manned by a volunteer naval crew and ballasted to the same draft as the battleship, this potential scapegoat led her safely out. I could not then know that one day I would come to be identified with the Highlands and Loch Ewe in a very different appointment.

Back to the east coast convoys, night after night peering through the rain for the next red flashing buoy which intermittently marked the searched channel. For the first time in life an inner sense of foreboding engulfed me which I could neither shrug off nor explain to myself. To be confident needed daily more effort. As I have previously written about my time in *Fowey*, trust between Captain and his Pilot is paramount and once betrayed is beyond redemption; but this was war and no time for personal apprehension, jaded as everybody was. It would pass. Then one stormy night off Flamborough head the Captain asked:

"When are we going to alter course, Pilot?"

"By my reckoning, sir, when we reach the next flashing buoy—which ought to be any moment now."

"It's going down the starboard side."

And I couldn't see it.

The aftermath was quick and inevitable. The opthalmologist diagnosed defects which are only caused by severe strain and commented that I should never have been allowed into the Navy, let alone have been made a bridge officer. It seemed a little late for that. Today, behind windscreens and their wipers, enclosed bridges where not even an oilskin is necessary, spectacles might be tolerated: but not then. The sudden collapse of all that one thought oneself capable of doing is a challenge which probably overtakes us all at some time or other, earlier or later in life; but such philosophy in hindsight made it no easier to bear at the time, as though I had been sailing under false colours. But you can't expect Captains to put up with navigators who can't see!

My friend Paul was luckily available to succeed me and we travelled up to the Humber together for the necessary turn-over. Freshets of ice were floating down the river as mini-icebergs in the muddied flow as we took the little train from Grimsby to Immingham where *Cairo* had anchored in my absence.

"Isn't she a little high in the water?" Paul wondered on first sight of her.

"Probably the illusion from her trawler bow," I hedged—but she was indeed a little high.

In fact she was aground, having dragged her anchor in the shifting mud-bed in so severe an ebb current. Not many navigators can have transferred their charges when actually aground, if not for long. The kindness and sympathy of my messmates alone mitigated my feeling on leaving a lady to whose early face-lift in war I had perhaps contributed, if denied a final embrace. Paul was sadly to see her to her brave end.

Chapter 14

A Battle Cruiser and her Captain

1940. Taken off the sea for as rewarding a shore appointment as they could have given me, Dunkirk was nevertheless happening.

Hitler's blitzkrieg was over-running France. Dunkirk had somehow turned rout back upon itself into a Pyrrhic victory. Of course we weren't going to lose the war but sometimes it was hard to see how not. Then on my twenty-seventh birthday Winston Churchill became Prime Minister. Those words—throaty, grating, defiant, uplifting, emotional words of great oratory—began to engulf us. Suddenly we became different people within ourselves. Still unable just then to see how we *could* win, it was crystal clear we wouldn't lose.

Then one day the telephone rang. It was the Appointments Officer of the Navigation School. "The Admiralty have now agreed you may go back to sea. You are required to be in Scapa Flow on the 26th December. Appointment follows."

As the final hours of historic 1940 drew to their close, I joined the battle-cruiser *Repulse*.

I now face a dilemma; for whatever may have been her achievements since her first commissioning at the time of Jutland, and they were considerable, modern history must link her name with catastrophe. The sinking of *Prince of Wales* and *Repulse* by Japanese torpedo-bombers in the South China Sea on December 10th 1941, three days after Pearl Harbour, will for ever remain a rebuff, a defeat for British sea power analysed, debated, dissected, condemned strategically and tactically, described again and again by those who were present and those who were not. Churchill gambled against undeclared odds and lost.

124

Inevitably, as now among the oldest survivors of *Repulse*, I have been drawn into this web of subsequent conjecture through considerable correspondence. As a junior officer at the time I had recollections but no judgement. As I have grown older, the focus has become sharper and enabled me to see personal loss in tragic circumstances as part of the kaleidoscope of sudden war against an underestimated enemy. But, having been besieged by many, some of whom have printed my contributions in their research, what may now be left for me to say with any originality has consequently dwindled. As I see it—for I cannot shirk it—I must therefore confine myself to factual personal experience, omit unsubstantiated opinion and try to convey how *Repulse* will for ever remain the centre of gravity of my naval life, even in that one year; above all attempt a personal tribute to a magnificent ship and her company, so many of whom died that day (in fact twice as many of my shipmates as the number of British dead throughout the whole Falklands conflict); an epitaph by somebody who had cause to love the distinguished old lady.

"*Repulse*. Battle Cruiser. 32,000 tons. Shaft Horse Power 112,000. Guns—6 15": 12 4" . 4 4" High Angle. 4 3-Pdr."—is how a contemporary Navy List describes her, heading a list of 50 Wardroom and Warrant officers and some 30 Midshipmen. The only part of that armament potentially effective against airborne torpedo attack were the four antiquated high-angle guns together with two multi-barrelled pom-poms and six single oerlikons. She was a determined old lady with no more than an umbrella to shake at her muggers, eventually overcome but not without resistance. When the final rain of blows hit her, she died in eight minutes: a death throe only minutes longer than her sister battle-cruiser, the mighty *Hood*, who had disintegrated seven months before in the North Atlantic, hit by a *Bismarck* shell plunging into her magazines. The third sister, the face-lifted *Renown*, lived to tell the tale.

Among the qualities of those battle-cruisers which perhaps most impressed was their dignified grace. Fast, unarmoured and powerful as they were, they evoked more the feminine presence than that of the cruising battleship. Because of their lines, 800 feet from low quarterdeck to gently sweeping bow, the staggered funnels, the superstructure uncluttered by angular excrescences of radar, the slender high main mast lending proportion to the turrets beneath, they had seemed the most appropriate of Britain's capital-ship might in which Royalty should visit their Empire. Kings and Queens, Heirs to the Throne, all circumnavigated the world in one of them—never in a battleship—and indeed this *Repulse* company had been originally selected to take the King and Queen to Canada in 1939, prevented only by war clouds. Not me. I merely inherited a cabin designed for a lady-in-waiting, with fitted wardrobe, corner fire and suitable bedstead: even a switch still labelled "Hair-curler" (it was a pity to say good-bye to that): but the majority of the ship's company were still hand-picked.

Despite her looks, in every other respect she was ill-equipped, as old ladies are, to face the perils of those days. That is why, when Force Z was despatched to the Far East, her name was never mentioned among the "heavy units" for obvious reasons. *Prince of Wales* was an unsinkable armoured modern battleship: her colleague was not: and her name would have not impressed a potential enemy. She was pathetically inadequate for what was to come. Marine engineers will understand what I mean when I say that she still had 42 Babcock & Wilcox fire-tube boilers. The first Japanese bomb was to penetrate and explode in "F" Boiler Room.

Ships, be they battle-cruisers or deep-sea trawlers, are historically feminine. "She" has beautiful lines. "She" obediently answers her helm in all weathers. "She's" a brute to handle. Maybe the custom springs because on the whole most sailors are men and, whoever their fellow crew, they love their ship for herself, be she slim of attractive figure or dumpy without outward appeal—provided she behaves! Statistically, most men love the opposite sex more than their own and therefore ships may be said to anticipate the protestations of Women's Lib: they just are the dominant sex at sea, and man would not have it otherwise.

Yet I do not surrender my own sex unreservedly, for ships on the whole are commanded by men; and be she ever so graceful, so obedient, so accommodating to the guiles or whims of he who handles her, a ship takes her character from her Captain, whether he is dressed in fishermen's jerseys or with naval rank on his arm. She can have all the attributes of armament, construction, speed, technical equipment, purpose, comfort, or even beauty; but, as Kipling describes in *The Ship That Found Herself* when he makes even the rivets chatter in their agonies, she will not be a character without the man to discover and conjure these attributes. There is a naval adage that there is no such thing as a bad ship's company, only a bad wardroom. True: and I would add that the wardroom in turn must be able unreservedly to look to their Captain for the respect and confidence in which they are entitled to hold him. We in *Repulse* did not find that difficult.

Of the many questions I have been asked by those who wished to write about Force Z, the most common request was for my impressions of my Captain Bill Tennant—the late Admiral Sir William. This is presumably because the finest sea captain I have known was reserved, let you discover his qualities gradually and by example, disdained any artificial admiration for rank's sake. I am not surprised that his modesty was an enigma to those who had never met him, let alone come to understand him. As a countryman, an ornithologist, and a profound practising Christian, he would not have wished otherwise. He was then the senior Captain in the navy at sea. This meant that when *Repulse* was with a big convoy and large destroyer escort, he had an admiral's job to perform without an admiral's staff. Having previously been navigator of *Repulse* herself for royal world tours, nothing held fear for him as her Captain except the sheer physical demands of command—the limit to which he could drive himself and remain efficient.

Quietly, almost surreptitiously, however, despite our initial awe of him, this Captain was to appear as the *"pater familias"*. Men realised that when their case was genuine they had no more staunch advocate. Awe became an undisguised affection and respect for someone in whom they saw a power of discernment and command, someone who would meet in war whatever was asked of *Repulse*. How right we all were when the day came to see that feeling proved. So on going to sea from Freetown on our journey east, it was not as surprising to us as it was to Bill Tennant that a vase of flowers appeared on the desk of his sea-cabin "from the stokers".

They were dull days in that inland Orkney sea of Scapa Flow: grey, just the outline of the surrounding cordon of islands, the Fleet at air-defence stations, the gulls swooping on the offal from the gash chutes, occasional stretching of the legs around the one moorland path on Flotta before a drink in the Nissen hut Officers' Club and the boat back to the ship: the unpleasant task at the wardroom table of censoring our sailors' letters home ("Well, pet, I hope you're not too sold on him that's taking you to the Odeon in my absence ... "–the loving mistrust of understandable jealousy): and then mercifully and suddenly jolted by, "Raise steam with all despatch" for a sweep into the Atlantic, such as for *Hipper* the previous Christmas. So the days passed: superficially monotonous, inwardly tense and exacting.

It was 7.15 p.m. on May 23rd 1941 when Able Seaman Newell, look-out on the starboard side of the bridge of *Suffolk*, a County Class cruiser on patrol in the Denmark Strait between Iceland and Greenland, saw the black shape of *Bismarck*, one of Germany's Goliaths, not more than seven miles away in fickle, ice-conditioned fog, moving at speed to force the narrows between the Arctic and Atlantic wastes, with the intention of devastating our vital convoys and western sea communications. A few seconds later he sighted another ship, the German cruiser *Prinz Eugen*. *Suffolk* was not far from her sister *Norfolk*, which was flying the flag of Admiral Wake-Walker. *Norfolk* was commanded by Captain Ellis, himself one of the original devotees of the new-fangled radar still in its operational infancy. The two cruisers, in appallingly difficult weather conditions, hung on to their prey, shadowed them at maximum radar and visibility range during their headlong flight southwards along the Greenland pack-ice limit, signalling every enemy movement and, like two hounds on the scent of their quarry, refusing to be shaken off. Should they get too close, *Bismarck's* huge guns would quickly demolish them. Should they fall too far astern they would lose contact and thus deny the information on the basis of which Admiralty were deploying every warship from the east coast of America to the western Mediterranean theatre–a considerable part of Britain's available naval strength–to deal with the threat. The hounds held on until the small hours of 25th May, thirty six hours since first sighting, when *Bismarck* and *Prinz Eugen* disappeared–"And like this insubstantial pageant faded, leave not a rack behind," so to speak; for before vanishing into the winds and darkness of the Atlantic as suddenly as they had appeared, *Bismarck* had destroyed Britain's "mighty *Hood*", for long the biggest warship in the world at 42,000 tons, and injured *Prince of Wales*. This is now, of course, history.

When the two cruisers found *Bismarck* against Greenland's ice, *Repulse* had already been at sea for a few days and was about to rendezvous with the brand-new aircraft carrier *Victorious* which was carrying forty eight crated Hurricane fighters for Malta, and to escort a valuable Middle East troop convoy (WS8B – a "Winnie Special") to the Cape and beyond, together with a score of cruisers and destroyers. We were therefore already short of full fuel capacity, a fact which was to play its part in our destiny. With no time to top up we were off the Clyde and ordered to join the C-in-C, Admiral Sir John Tovey in *King George V*, off the Hebrides next morning. We took station astern of the flagship and plunged westwards into an unkind sea for May, surrounded by cruisers and destroyers. Admiral Holland in *Hood* with *Prince of Wales* were to the north on an exact converging course to *Bismarck* as she was shadowed south. So throughout May 23rd, while we read by signal of the net prepared by Admiralty. Assuming the cruisers held their prey, action would be joined by heavy ships at dawn on 24th May, first by *Hood* and *Prince of Wales* and, should *Bismarck* survive that, by *King George V* and *Repulse* next day with air strikes from *Victorious* in-between. At 6.00 a.m. on 24th May *Hood* blew up under *Bismarck*'s salvoes, leaving three survivors. *Prince of Wales* was damaged but, as was not known at the time, had hit *Bismarck* in a bow fuel tank. Air strikes from *Victorious* were unsuccessful. The enemy still careered south during the night of 24th-25th. Immediate confrontation at dawn on that day could only be from the powerful *King George V* and her elderly battle-cruiser consort. There could be little doubt about which target, following her success over *Hood,* the German ship would pick first. So we steamed on, south-west. As the converging range as reported by the cruisers decreased, so our nerves tautened. Contact was due at 8.00 a.m. on May 25th: if only we had enough oil! We hadn't: not comfortably or confidently to endure action between capital ships. Those forty two boilers drank oil inordinately. The old lady could pant along up to a point: but, like old ladies, her endurance was limited. Admiral Tovey suggested we should consider turning back. Bill Tennant implied that, even if we subsequently drifted as a fort, nothing would induce him to do so. There was always Newfoundland to the west. The range closed minute by minute. A few more hours and this great ship and her crew must prove their mettle.

It's a sensation that presumably we all interpret differently: when you become aware that, on balance, you may shortly die, that fact doesn't seem to worry you all that much. Sitting up in that 15″ spotting top–a replica of *Royal Oak*'s, in which ten years before I had endeavoured to explain Brünnhilde's Awakening to Able Seaman Parks–while the darkened bow below belched the plunged waves over the fo'c's'le to empty down the plugs of the hawsepipes, there was little doubt that our adversary might well pick off *Repulse* as quickly as she had *Hood* a few hours before; and yet a quiet calm of the inevitable pervaded all more material thought. Like Peter Pan, "to die would be an awfully big adventure". But on that day none of us did: for at 3.00 a.m. on May 25th *Bismarck* and her cruiser consort gave their pursuers the slip. The heavy gale-ridden dawn revealed an empty northern horizon save for our own destroyer escort. The anticlimax for *Repulse* was debilitating. Keyed-up for action, hopefully to have been an actor on the stage, we must now vanish into the wings. We crept away at economical speed to Conception Bay in Newfoundland where we arrived with only a bucket of oil remaining.

The rest of that story in which we were denied a real part is one of the naval annals of the war. Admiral Tovey *had* to sink that ship. The reputation of the Navy was at stake. The wastes of the Atlantic are terrifyingly big. Where had she gone? He wasn't to know that in fact a 14″ shell from *Prince of Wales* had penetrated one of *Bismarck*'s port bow fuel tanks. He wasn't to know that this prevented her foray further southwards into the Atlantic, that somehow she must reach German-occupied France. Fickle visibility in the Atlantic didn't help. An agonising period of uncertainty ensued until that Catalina found the quarry steering south-east for Brest at 1030 on May 26th. The "dogs of war" were then closing around her. Guns couldn't and didn't sink her. A torpedo from a gallant obsolescent naval Swordfish aircraft from *Ark Royal* hit her rudder. She then steamed in circles, a battered hulk, still enduring enormous shells from *King George V* and *Rodney*. *Dorsetshire*'s torpedoes finally despatched her. The reputation of the Navy, at risk had we failed, was redeemed–just. It's easy to wonder why so much had to be flung into the chase. Only those who have known the vast emptiness of the Atlantic in bad visibility can understand its capacity to hide even one of the biggest warships ever built. In the event the Navy didn't fail–again, just!

Chapter 15

Prelude to War With Japan

Among my other duties was that of Signals Officer. A few months later a Petty Officer Telegraphist appeared at my cabin curtain with "I think you ought to see this, sir. Nobody else has seen it." It was a signal from Admiralty in the low code, addressed to *Repulse*, which simply asked "DO YOU HOLD CONFIDENTIAL BOOK NO.....?" The said C.B. referred to the South Atlantic and the Far East. I took it straight to my Captain who said "Burn it"; but the damage was done. The buzz was round. We were off... somewhere. A few days later we were ordered to the Clyde.

As I have already said, Captain Bill Tennant was the senior Captain afloat. He was therefore conveniently used to take command of the huge troop convoys destined, via the Cape, for the build-up of the 8th Army which was poised for Alamein. Apart from the tens of thousands of army troops in converted merchant liners, protected by a pack of destroyers, he therefore had to undertake operations generally awarded to admirals with staffs. Fuelling at sea, logistic support to Task Forces such as in the recent Falklands operation, was in its infancy. Had it not been so, the Second World War at sea would have been a less complicated business. *Repulse* had no staff to lift such considerations from our Captain's shoulders. I was therefore seconded during one middle watch to become his Operations Officer. This was to have subsequent repercussions on my professional life.

I should now recount what is left to me that I have previously witheld from questing authors or historians; a factual recitation as I saw it with no ifs or buts: as a poor player who fretted and strutted his hour upon an uncomfortable stage while its very boards disintegrated beneath his feet.

Churchill's insistence began to take shape in November 1941. By then, the new aircraft carrier *Indomitable* had gone aground off Jamaica. But still overruling the protestations of Their Lordships the Prime Minister had continued with his plan that the sudden presence of a "heavy force" in Singapore–despite the absence of any air cover which was to have been provided by *Indomitable*–would deter the Japanese from any Far East offensive. *Repulse* discarded her Eighth Army convoy at Mombasa and was directed to Colombo via the Seychelles. There we were subjected to a sea inspection under a C-in-C of the time, and were not found wanting. So we were allowed to proceed eastwards across the Bay of Bengal and into the Straits of Malacca. There we were joined by *Prince of Wales*. She had been sailed east under full coverage from the British Press. The name of *Repulse* had been withheld because she was so old. Nevertheless, because the new C-in-C Eastern Fleet, Admiral Sir Tom Phillips (straight from his Admiralty desk as Vice Chief of the Naval Staff), had not yet arrived and Captain Tennant was senior to the Captain of *Prince of Wales*, *Repulse* led the newly formed Eastern Fleet up the Johore Strait to the Singapore naval base on December 4th. That brief moment was to be the only time the old lady was allowed to assert her dignity on such a modern stage.

It was therefore to be an unbalanced force of six ships that set out from the Singapore base into the sunset of 8th December to presume to intercept such Japanese effrontery: out to skirt south of the Anamba Islands in the South China Sea. The weather was cloudy, visibility poor, as the force turned northwards in the small hours of the 9th. Ensconced in my box on top of the foremast I felt grateful for a similar shroud with which Loge had protected Brünnhilde for different reasons. No Tarnhelm for me now. No Loge. No Tarnhelm for any of us. Inevitably we were sighted on December 9th by enemy reconnaissance aircraft hovering on the horizon when the sky cussedly cleared just before dark. We were still steaming north. After dark at 1855 Phillips altered course north-west towards the Gulf of Siam, still clinging to the hope that our mission might not prove abortive, a hope which operationally had dwindled, if not evaporated, in view of his knowledge that the element of surprise had gone.

Events during the next hour when Force Z was still steering westwards have provoked disagreement and puzzlement among those many who have subsequently dissected and re-dissected conflicting evidence about those flares in the sky to the north. Let me first establish what is true.

Unknown to us in the darkness and beyond surface radar range of *Prince of Wales* (that of *Repulse* was in its infancy), at 1920 hours there were four heavy Japanese cruisers twenty two miles away and steaming towards us. This force became embarrassed by their own aircraft who, mistakenly thinking them to be British, dropped flares and began to shadow them. In vain did the Japanese admiral try to tell them of their error (remember they had only been at war for forty eight hours, with only peacetime training beforehand); and so, infuriated, he reversed his course at 1920 to the north-east. Had he continued to the south, a night action would have been joined between Force Z and the four heavy cruisers under Admiral Kurita with his supporting destroyers. Before conjecture as to what the outcome of such an action might have been –"The Battle of the Siam Gulf"?–I continue with the facts.

Concerning the loss of the two ships, Martin Middlebrook and Patrick Mahoney, in their book *Battleship*, attribute Phillip's decision finally to abandon the venture westwards and alter course back to the south-east, to his reactions of the reported sighting of a flare by *Electra*, one of our destroyer screen, five miles ahead. In fact the flares dropped in error to illuminate Admiral Kurita's force would have been about twenty five miles to the north, and visibility was then by no means that distance. From my eyrie on top of *Repulse*'s foremast, as high above sea level as anybody in the Force at that moment and straining into the darkness as I was, I would have had to have seen any such flares: and if I hadn't, one of my sharper-eyed sailors would have done. Moreover, a most experienced member of Phillip's staff, Captain F.S. Bell of River Plate fame when in command of his gallant *Exeter* testifies that to the best of his belief there was no flare seen or reported to the flagship, and that his Admiral's decision at 2015 to retire to the south-east was, after full discussion with his staff, taken because clearly the element of surprise had gone and he had received no information that Japanese forces were as close to him as in fact they were. With whatever Phillips may subsequently have been blamed, he was not a man to shirk action with the enemy he had sailed to seek. Of course if he had been aware of those flares–which incidentally are not mentioned by *Electra*'s officers–he would have turned his Force towards them and not away. The evidence would seem to be that those aircraft flares over the Japanese force were not in fact sighted by the British; but so infuriated with his own forces was Admiral Kurita that, shortly before Phillips turned south, he reversed course to the north at 1920. And so we missed each other.

Alpha and Omega:
My birthplace "Southcote",
Bermuda 1913;

Revisited 1966, when Second-in-Command of the Western Fleet, with the
current owner of the Smith family from whom my father rented it in 1912;

My last voyage under the White Ensign. H.M.S. *Tiger*, my Flagship, passes 'Two Rock Passage', Bermuda, for home.

Lieutenant Hayes, R.A.M.C.
and my mother;

On becoming a member of the Anson Term
at R.N. College, Dartmouth, 1926
"... because I so enjoyed the children's parties in
H.M.S. *Calcutta* in Bermuda, Sir.";

R.N. College, Dartmouth, 1927: Cadets at Sunday Divisions Parade.

15th April, 1939. The best day of my life, when I married Rosalind Finlay.

Repulse at peace;

Formerly beloved Captain Bill of *Repulse*, the late Admiral Sir William Tennant as a C-in-C: his memorial bust in Upton-on- Severn reads,
"Lives of great men all remind us
We can make our lives sublime,
And, departing, leave behind us
Footprints in the sands of time."

December 10th, 1941 Last defiance by *Repulse* as seen from *Prince of Wales*.

The Argyll and Sutherland Highlanders, "Sans Peur", which hangs in their
H.Q. in Stirling Castle as their choice from all their war exploits. This print
shows the last hours of the British in Johore on the evening of Jan 31st 1942.
(On the following dawn, Colonel Stewart and I were the last Britons to leave
Malaya for some years.) The painting by Peter Archer was commissioned by
the Argylls and unveiled by Brigadier Stewart when he was 91 years of age.

Names that appear on the painting:

Lieutenant Colonel Stewart (on the right);

Lieutenant J.O.C. Hayes R.N. (in white in centre);

Captain T.B.G. Slessor (on left).

1960, H.M.S. *Drake*. One man and his dog, Bramble;

1963, accompanying my boss Lord Carrington,
the last First Lord of the Admiralty, on his visit to the Royal Marines H.Q. at
Deal.

H.M.S. *Tiger*. Open to visitors 1965, Hull.

Christopher Tite, the great-great-grandson of Nelson's cabin boy at Trafalgar, was one of H.M.S. *Tiger*'s 1965 visitors at Newcastle-upon-Tyne.

NATO cooperation with our U.S. Navy friends.

NATO exercise in the Arctic with Admiral Sir Charles Madden, twice my Commander-in-Chief.

"It looks to me as though you made the right choice"

My friend and neighbour, the late Eric Linklater, remains the doyen of transfer by jackstay at sea.

Sea Cadets honour me
for a Trafalgar Night
Dinner Speech.

"So d'you think
you *will* join the Navy?";

Routine start for the
Admiral's Inspection;

My two Flag Captains in H.M.S. *Tiger*: Geoffrey Kirkby and 'Harpy' Lloyd.
Their ship was as happy as they look;

H.M.S. *Tiger* leads the Fleet on exercises.

The end of the innings.
Departure as Flag Officer
Scotland and Northern Ireland.

Arabella House, Nigg.

"Where's that?"
"600 miles north of London."

1968: what it takes to run an Admiralty House. My devoted Secretary, Flag Lieutenant and retinue with the family.

June 1987. Her Majesty arrives in Invergordon to a children's welcome.

Chapter 16

Swan-Song of a Notable Old Lady

An hour or so before sailing from Singapore *Repulse* had embarked two war correspondents: O'Dowd Gallagher, a South African working for our *Daily Express*, and Cecil Brown, an American working for C.B.S., both experienced from reporting in every active theatre within recent years. They were rebellious at being assigned "only" to *Repulse*: understandably, because we were incognito by name to the world, whereas *"The Wales"* (as they called her) was headlines and any experience from her decks would be world news, whatever did or didn't happen. As *Prince of Wales* was full they were offered the choice of disembarking from us, but reluctantly agreed to stay, just in case . . . .

Brown subsequently devoted two chapters in his story *Suez To Singapore* to his experiences with us, under the headings "Prelude to Drowning" and "God be with you", the latter being the last words of Bill Tennant to his ship's company. I understand that this book was published in 1942 in America only, because his comments are not always complimentary to the British; yet it is an inherent and ignorant mistake by some of my countrymen to assume that because Americans and ourselves speak a language we can mutually interpret without interpreters–it isn't English!–we therefore share the same views on the world. We don't: and this leads to much disillusionment, which is responsible in turn for many a misunderstanding. *We* grope for an empty railway compartment: Americans seek the one with only one seat remaining.

Brown's job, as a correspondent, was to record; and somehow he managed to preserve his diary despite his adventures during the disaster to follow. We were to share the Flag Deck of *Repulse*–I as Signals Officer and he because that was where he had been told to go–for the latter part of the action. His impressions largely coincide with mine and I am grateful for his timings of attacks which I would not otherwise be able to remember, so quickly did the scene seem to change against traumatic backcloths. His report on this particular drama within his assignment seems to me to be on the whole accurate even if–because of his profession and nationality–over-dramatised. One inaccuracy is his description of myself: "The flag deck Lieutenant is a tough, wiry officer of about twenty five." I must have acted well that day. But I borrow from parts of his narrative because, while I was confined to the 15″ spotting top until we engaged in the final action and I was released for another role, he could be elsewhere in the ship. His job was indeed to record: and this he did in astonishing detail, particularly the timing of attacks, and despite (shall we say) physical discomfiture. You might not expect such a person to get inside the British sailor's phlegm in those circumstances in so short a time: yet he captured an essence.

At 2100 on December 9th our Captain spoke to us over the loudspeakers: he explained that, as we had been spotted before dark by Japanese aircraft, surprise had gone, that the enemy troop convoy would have now dispersed, and that it would be suicide to be found at daylight well within the Gulf of Siam with no air cover. The C-in-C had therefore decided with regret to abandon the operation. "I know that you all share the disappointment... but we are going back to Singapore."

Brown was in the Wardroom. There were groans of disappoint-ment and even bitterness. In the sailors' messes there were tears in their eyes. Over two years in the war at sea, 53,000 miles steaming, and never a chance to fire a shot in anger. A natural reaction. The old *Repulse* cheated once again. Sweep after sweep into the Atlantic for such as *Hipper*: denied the chance to share in revenge for the annihilation of her sister *Hood* by *Bismarck*: day after dreary day at Air Defence Stations in Scapa Flow: convoy after convoy to the Cape and never an enemy in sight: and yet another chance gone to show their mettle against a sudden new enemy. Our Commander Dendy was, according to Brown, at a loss for words, the disappointment on his face speaking for all. Wardrooms react differently from those who carry the ultimate responsibility. Our Captain entirely endorsed his Admiral's decision; nor was it to be long before the guns and action organisation under us wardroom and gunroom officers were to be put to the test against hopeless odds. Is there an ironic yearning in war to become involved in deathdealing activity rather than stand (or float!) idly by? I suspect so.

So the two darkened giants careered south on the moonless night, steering to pass the way we had come, east of the Anamba Islands and back to Singapore some 270 miles away. "Mission completed", as we all had to accept. And so to what was, in retrospect, the beginning of the end, when–however inescapably Phillips had attempted to justify our presence in the area by trying to interrupt the landings at Kota Bahru (how could he have sat in harbour with war suddenly apparent to a complacent population long accustomed to the lassitude engendered by a latitude of 1° north of the equator?)–the lethal mistakes began.

The Chief of Staff, Rear Admiral Palliser, had been left behind in Singapore to advise his Admiral afloat from the shore operations room–the keeping of W/T silence then being an obsessional indoctrination from sea unless breaking it became paramount. Captain Bell had thus become Phillip's chief staff officer on board. This arrangement was to have its weaknesses. (When I subsequently had to have dealings with Palliser, I would not describe him as a jolly man.) Just before midnight on December 9th Palliser sent a signal to his C-in-C to the effect that a landing was taking place at Kuantan half-way up the eastern Malayan coast. That was all. No indication of reliability nor any further amplification. Kuantan was about 120 miles south of our position when that signal was received. If such was true, the Japanese at Kuantan in possession of its airfield and the only road skirting the jungle could have split our land forces in north and south Malaya and been within short-range bombing distance of Singapore itself. Phillips could not disregard such information and to alter course towards Kuantan would add little distance to the passage to Singapore. So at 0052 on December 10th the Force altered course to the south-west to close Kuantan. If in fact landings were taking place there, surprise seemed again to be a factor.

The rest was silence on both sides. Palliser sent no further signal either substantiating or refuting the landing he had reported. Phillips sent no signal to tell Palliser that he would be off Kuantan at daylight or to ask for fighter cover against what he had every reason to expect would be fierce enemy air and surface opposition. Each left it to the other to guess and neither got it right. Number 453 Australian Fighter Squadron was standing by at Sembawang, an hour's flight from Kuantan. They were not called, or not until too late. True, they were antiquated Buffalo fighters against modern Japanese bombers: but piloted by brave men they would doubtless have given a good account of themselves.

So, early on that peerless, cloudless morning of December 10th, Force Z arrived off Kuantan to find–nothing!

I seemed to have been at the top of the foremast surrounded by voice pipes, keyed up, for a long time. It was therefore something of a relief combined with anti-climax when dawn broke upon that picture-postcard scene instead of, as I had imagined possible, observing the effect of the 15″ shells upon the enemy and experiencing the impact of theirs. At 0800 we were off Kuantan: ultramarine sea, a silver beach fringed by dense jungle and a solitary motor-cyclist scooting along the road which divided them: that was all. Our catapulted amphibian Walrus aircraft and a destroyer were sent inshore to investigate. *Express* signalled ALL IS AS QUIET AS A WET SUNDAY AFTERNOON and rejoined. When and how this mistaken intelligence of an enemy landing originated is not known for certain, but it was to prove largely responsible for the ensuing disaster as otherwise, by the time it happened, Force Z would have been beyond the full operational range of Japanese torpedo-bombers from their bases in Indo-China.

Having drawn blank off Kuantan, the natural reaction would seem to have been for Phillips to get to hell out of an area doubtless full of enemy submarines (who in fact had reported us at 0200, steering south-west) and still in range of their aircraft. But no. As *Battleship* quotes me: "So here we were, those two great ships with mighty little surface screen and no air cover, nonchalantly meandering about off that empty coast, executing such ponderous peace-time manoeuvres as 'Turn 135 degrees to starboard in succession'–sitting targets for submarine or air attack for which we were not prepared. Even to the likes of me it seemed extraordinary that we were wandering about the sea so lackadaisically in such circumstances." Moreover, it should be appreciated that Singapore H.Q. did not know where Phillips was. It remains incomprehensible that Palliser did not ask as much–with such R.A.F. help as there was poised to come to our aid–or that by that stage Phillips himself did not break W/T silence. The subsequent acrimony between the two staffs on this point was a classic instance of *"Qui s'excuse, s'accuse"*.

After the non-event of Kuantan we were stood down from Action Stations; yet there seemed to be a sense of foreboding, which was justified when the Japanese reconnaissance plane was spotted high in the sky to the south. Air Defence Stations released me from my role as main Armament Spotting Officer and into my other hats as Signals Officer and Assistant Navigator. The Bridge were fully occupied and needed no sudden addition to add to the activity, so I went down to the W/T office. This was just after 1100, when the first wave of Mitsubishis were spotted approaching from ahead at a height of 10,000 feet. The high-angle guns opened fire. Down in the main wireless office of a ship engaging the enemy the questions, the pithy epithets of my telegraphists, conveyed their disbelief that no enemy report had yet been transmitted by the Flagship. In due course equally incredulous, it was to be *our* Captain who did this–not the Admiral.

Shortly after 1100: "ENEMY AIRCRAFT APPROACHING".

The first wave of high-level bombers flew over *Prince of Wales* and selected *Repulse* as their target, maybe aiming to get the old lady out of the way first before concentrating on her more formidable modern sister. Seven of the pattern missed in fountains of spray and the eighth penetrated through the Marines' mess-deck and into the seventh-aft boiler-room, where it fractured steam-pipes and terribly scalded the stokers; but this hit had not impaired the full speed of the ship from the remaining six boiler-rooms.

The W/T office was in full operational order and so I went up to the other department of my signals domain, the Flag Deck surrounding the forward funnel where the visual signallers were stationed. It was from here that I was aware of our Captain's brilliant handling of an 800-foot battle-cruiser as though she was a destroyer. Waves of torpedo-bombers were launching their attacks at suicidal range and some were being demolished by even our four old single-barrelled anti-aircraft guns and pom-poms. They threw their "fish" into the calm sea and roared away above our susperstructure, machine-gunning as they went so that shipmates fell around me: and still Tennant managed to comb the tracks, those tell-tale bubbles surfacing well behind their lethal origin. It is established that he evaded the first two waves, weaving his great ship at top speed so that the torpedoes—about twelve in all—passed down our side. During the second wave of nine or ten bombers, as during the first, Bill Tennant was saying in the coolest tones, "Port 30. Midships. Starboard 30. Meet her... Steady as you go... Port 30 again... Ease to 15...", zig-zagging to comb those oil-bubbling tracks, as though they were dolphins instead of torpedoes. It was at 1214 that he signalled to Phillips in *Prince of Wales*: "WE HAVE DODGED 19 TORPEDOES THUS FAR THANKS TO PROVIDENCE".

At this moment *Repulse* was still unscathed save for the single bomb hit; but *Prince of Wales* was in trouble and even Providence could not hold his shield above us for much longer. The *"Wales"* had been hit by a torpedo on her port side while steaming at full speed; the force of the explosion had caused eccentricity in her port propeller shafts, which in turn had ruptured the watertight glands throughout her port side and caused severe flooding. Though still steaming she was about two miles from us and down to fifteen knots, so that Tennant was coming to see if he could help. Then a final wave of Japanese torpedo-bombers carried out a classic attack on us. Feinting from the starboard bow until we were committed to the turn, several others appeared to be going to deal another blow to *Prince of Wales*. Three then swung round to attack our port side at short range. We were hit, wounded, but the ship steamed on. That was not quite the end, because our old pom-poms were still embarrassing our attackers into forcing them to drop their torpedoes further away than Japanese bravado teaches: but three more struck home in our port side and the old lady could cope with no more. From being on an upright and defiant even keel at twenty five knots, shaking her umbrella at her attackers, eight minutes later she was gone.

With at least four huge gashes in her port side, including one on the rudder (as a few months before a Swordfish's torpedo had incapacitated *Bismarck*) she listed quickly with her screws still turning and planed beneath the mirror-like sea in a swirl of air-bubbles and escaping oil. Then, like the proud leviathan she was, she lifted her curved, graceful stem to the sky, light grey and terracotta in the sunlight, and hung defiantly for a moment above the surface for the last time before slipping quietly below to become, with *Prince of Wales*, the official war grave she remains to this day, visible in thirty fathoms from the air in certain conditions, with hundreds of her gallant company entombed but undisturbed. Naval divers have since attached a wire to her rudder with a White Ensign flowing out in the current as though still streaming in the winds of the oceans she had weathered since Jutland.

The Captains's calm voice. "All hands on deck. Prepare to abandon ship. God be with you" had been her swan-song.

> "...My movements were then dictated by gravity, like one of those balls on a bagatelle table which bounces off pins–the funnel, red-hot from steaming, then against the port flag-lockers by which time, normally some fifty feet above the waterline, they were almost awash, and so overboard helplessly and down for what seemed a long time. When I bobbed up the great iron structure of the main top, normally some hundred feet above the waterline, skidded just above my head as the ship plunged on and down with the screws still turning."
>
> (*Battleship*, p.241)

Then an oily emptiness as one became aware, among blackened heads and corpses, that one was alive but clogged. Those of us who could swim well set about helping those who could not. Crude oil for boilers is no such fuel for the human lung. There was an inch of the stuff on the calm surface. One did not think of sharks; but in fact they had been deterred by the many torpedo explosions.

It was while in the water that I first had time to look towards *Prince of Wales* She seemed to me to be at a funny angle as though she, too, listed to port. But of course she couldn't be sinking: not one of our proudest battleships? Still, she *did* seem at a curious angle from where I was... hallucination of course... but by the time I next had a moment to look in her direction she wasn't there.

Sub-Lieutenant Geoffrey Brooke, then of the *Prince of Wales*, has recently published *Alarm Starboard*, a chapter of which chronicles graphically his similar experiences of that day. My friend's is the only description I know of the end of *Repulse* as seen from the stalls and I have his permission to quote an extract.

"No doubt the enemy had seen we were crippled and could wait while they concentrated on the indomitable *Repulse*... There can be no more dreadful sight than that of a large vessel, full of one's own kith and kin, being hounded to the bottom. The seemingly inexhaustible supply of aircraft with which this was accomplished indicated to the impotent watchers what could be in store for us too.

"Her tormentors came in individually from all directions... as she squirmed and twisted her way through what we knew was a web of crossing torpedo tracks, guns in crackling defiance. As one plane flew between the two ships, she demolished it and we all cheered as the blazing mass dived into the sea. Another plume of smoke shot up from her port quarter. Her screws and rudder must be damaged by this which one knew was the beginning of the end. Even as the thought registered there were three more hits in quick succession, two on this side of her and one on the other. As the last aircraft pulled away the *Repulse* had a severe list and her speed was right down.

"The sea was calm and grey as was the sky. She was still making headway when her bow began to go under like an enormous submarine and terrible to see. As the waves came aft along her fo'c's'le and then engulfed the great 15-inch turrets she listed further and remained so for a time. Then she rolled right over. She lay on her side for a few seconds, stopped at last. Then her keel came uppermost and she began to sink by the stern. The last thing I saw was the sharp bow pointing skywards, disappearing slowly in a ring of troubled water."

Three destroyers were left floating to confront the catastrophe. *Express* was brilliantly and courageously handled by Lieutenant Commander Cartwright, who actually went alongside the upper side of the sinking flagship, extricated himself astern from her capsizing bilge keel just in time and rescued hundreds to his deck capacity. *Vampire* played her part to the utmost. I was unaware of the name of any saviour I could see who came in my vicinity. Eventually in fact it was *Electra*, who had previously lifted over a thousand from the Dunkirk beaches, and now drifted gently among us. Scrambling nets and wooden ladders were lowered over the side; heaving lines were thrown towards those of us still fit enough to grab them. Oil makes rope slippery.

> "I even had my own moment of humour when *Electra* (and how superb those destroyers were that day) found time to get around to my vicinity where I was trying to help a very large, unconscious Royal Marine, wounded and clogged with oil. Expertly handled, *Electra* glided alongside me and threw me a rope. Wrestling to get it underneath the man's armpits and prematurely anticipating success, I shouted 'Haul away' a little too eagerly only to find that the noose had slid up round his neck. Just in time. There were ribald comments on my performance by friends in the water and already on deck, and then we were both safe."
>
> (*Battleship*, p.263)

Safe but dazed: blackened bedraggled shapes lying on any available bit of deck among outstretched bodies, exhausted figures crouching on depth-charges or any other smooth seat. Was that Bill Tennant? Thank God, yes it was. Was that the Padre, a theologian of repute?... yes... ghosts of old friends and shipmates... scarecrows of men, but alive... why? And why me among them?

Cecil Brown again:

> "There is no bitterness among these men this afternoon about the absence of air protection, just regret that they've lost their ship. One man is wailing that he'd lost the picture of his girl friend, his mother, his dad.
>
> "Another says he's lost his penknife to which a third replies 'Now quit your grousing. Each of us lost the same thing–everything.'
>
> "In the steaming hot wardroom of *Electra* 40 or 50 officers are drinking tea, most naked to the waist. The heat is stifling and as we sit there–I taking notes–the sweat pours out of us as though we were under a shower."

I must admire anybody who can take notes for future reference in such circumstances; yet such tenacity provides the evidence for historians.

A rating from *Electra* sought me out.

"Are you by any chance Lieutenant Hayes?"

"I suppose I still am."

"Will you come to the Sick Bay? There's a boy asking for you."

The Sick Bay was a double bunk compartment at this moment reserved for the most seriously injured who were not already dead. In the gangway outside the curtain I met the camouflaged form of a young doctor of *Repulse*. I have previously described the scene because I was "The Snotties' Nurse" and this incident concerned one of my young charges.

"One of our young doctors was among the survivors, in no great shape himself but tackling his overwhelming task as one would have expected. He sent somebody to seek me out and then told me that he had a little Midshipman in one of the bunks, that he was dying from bullet wounds in the groin, and that although sedated he was in great pain and was asking to see me if I was on board. There was another dying man in the other bunk.

"Among his thirty gunroom colleagues, this Midshipman had hitherto appeared the least developed. Immature for his age and often in trouble–through no intention of his but there are those who cannot avoid it–he had seemed and looked a near child and therefore had needed careful handling. He was insufficiently fledged to have an Action Station of any import and I had therefore allotted him something to do with the secondary armament at which station he had been wounded by a machine-gun bullet.

"Scarcely recognisable myself, I asked to be alone with him and took his hand. He gave me a brave smile which knifed into my heart and conscience for any previous admonishment I had had to bestow. He held on to my hand with a firm little grip as though trying to express the last tangible feeling in the young life he must have known was slipping from him. I have never before or since seen death, or the awareness of death, in that moment of truth so transform youth to man, suddenly adult, brave and silently perceptive of the tragedy in which we were both enmeshed. He died that evening."

(*Battleship*, p.265)

It was early in the Middle Watch of December 11th that *Electra* berthed at the Naval Base in Singapore alongside *Exeter*. The Wardroom took in the motley officer survivors and her mess-deck the ratings. It was the first chance we had really had to find out who was still among us. An old shipmate came up to me and said "You might like this, if I remember," and gave me a pipe of tobacco ready to light. I have it by me now. Such is the friendship of the sea. Bill Tennant was among us. Emotion, as Noël Coward pertinently remarked in one of his plays, is so very untidy. But sometimes you can't help it.

They found us beds in the Fleet Shore Accomodation and for the first time, as I tried to de-oil myself and to plaster the bits which needed covering, I began to realise that the scale of this disaster might become more than a mere incident in naval history. Two o'clock in the morning here: four o'clock in the afternoon in Edinburgh. Normally when ships were sunk, such news was withheld from the world until next-of-kin had been informed and the victims were home on survivors' leave. Rosalind read the placard in Princes Street: *PRINCE OF WALES* AND *REPULSE* SUNK.

It was the first she knew that I was even in the Far East.

THE KUANTAN ENIGMA How did it all happen? This is the enigma–the eventual destruction of the two great ships found wandering off Kuantan on a breathless, sunlit sea by a swarm of Japanese torpedo bombers (very nearly on their last drop of fuel) unopposed except for ship's guns. Is there an answer?

Having reluctantly abandoned hope of disrupting the enemy landings at Kota Bahru during darkness on December 9th, Phillips had turned for home at speed. Shortly after midnight on the 10th he received a signal from Admiral Palliser in Singapore: "Enemy reported landing at Kuantan." That was all.

Kuantan, regarded as a key military position, lies 150 miles south of Kota Bahru, about eight hours steaming from where Force Z was at the time and half way back to the shelter of Singapore and 453 squadron of Buffalo fighters. The Admiral decided to be off that part of the coast by daylight, hoping presumably that his foray might yet prove less unfruitful and thus enable him to justify his Churchillian appointment. He did not tell Palliser of his intentions, who incredibly vouchsafed no positive or negative amplifying information; so the rest was silence. Tragically the fighters were not deployed to Kuantan where they could have been on call by the time the ships arrived to find ...?... nothing but a tug to eastward towing some barges which the two ships were still investigating at slow speed when found and attacked. On finding that the report of any Kuantan landing was in fact false, Phillips could have still got home safely by continuing south at full speed; but the Eastern Fleet was investigating some barges!

And the enigma? How did that spurious report originate?

Even at the time it seemed to us afloat unlikely that the enemy could have staged a second landing as far south as Kuantan in addition to their simultaneous and considerable effort at Kota Bahru without *some* trace being discovered during our run to the north on the previous evening. Only recently have I found a possible answer, conjecture of course, to this puzzle on which I have long pondered: who alerted Palliser to initiate that signal in the first instance?

Quite by chance I have cemented a friendship with someone who joined the Colonial Service as a Customs Cadet in 1934 and was posted to Malaya. He was still there in 1941 in a Pooh-Bah post at Mersing in North-East Johore and *inter alia* answered to naval Intelligence H.Q. My friend met my request to send me his recollections of those days when I must have almost been able to see his base from the Spotting Top of *Repulse* that morning. He writes: "The whole basis of my hypothesis is conjecture but in my view fierce conjecture... I am very happy that you should use it for I feel it should be projected. Only two people can answer why Force Z came in from the Lower China Sea to the coast that morning: God and Admiral Sir Tom Phillips. Neither is available for comment."

My friend became a Japanese linguist, their prisoner when Singapore fell, and further writes:

"Thirty miles upstream on the Endau river was a Japanese owned bauxite mine. The ore was loaded on to barges (possibly including those sighted by Force Z) once every ten days before being transferred to a Japanese freighter. To assist me in my inspection there were patrol boats, some armed and some not, commanded by Reserve officers and equipped for coded communication with the Naval Base on the Johore Strait. Among these were the *Hungjau* under Lieutenant Bill Mellor R.N.Z.V.R. (a great guy) and my own launch the *Pengejar*.

"Then there was the *Klana*. This was a smallish trading vessel owned by a jelutong planter, Windsor, at Kuantan. He had been there since the mid-thirties and traded jelutong up and down the coast which he knew, together with its rivers, like the back of his hand. By early 1939 he had got himself commissioned in the R.N.V.R. when he had mounted a 3 pdr on *Klana's* fore-deck. So his boat became a patrol vessel of which we were very short. He was thus allowed code books.

"I met him often on patrol, a strange fellow: short, fair-haired, pale blue hard eyes, taciturn, almost secretive in a way. He spoke fluent Malay and dominated his Malay crew.

"December 8th 1941. The Japs land at Kota Bahru. I am at Mersing/Endau now openly an Intelligence Officer on staff of 22nd Australian Brigade.

"Morning December 10th. Force Z closes the coast to off-shore Kuantan and to disaster. Where is *Klana*?

"Night of December 11th. I am at Endau wharf. In comes Bill Mellor with his *Hungjau*. We had a drink as the rain teemed and the wind blew.

'Michael,' he said, 'you'll never guess where we're going– . . . Up to Kuantan. I've orders to arrest Windsor.'

'Bloody why . . . ?'

'The bastard's been shooting off his 3 pdr. There is no bloody landing at Kuantan and you know about Force Z. I have to take him back to Naval H.Q. for interrogation.'

"Some time in 1943 Bill Mellor and I fetched up in the same Japanese P.O.W. camp. I asked him what had happened to Windsor.

'He was cleared,' said Bill 'Got away to Colombo, South Africa, I don't know.'

"But by 1946 Windsor was back in Kuantan trading jelutong once more up and down the coast where again I met him on my station. I never asked him about December 10th 1941. Maybe I should have; but sleeping dogs are at times best left to sleep.

You see, Windsor was a naturalised German. His original name I think was Mueller. So what *is* the truth? We shall never know. Your guess is as good as mine."

With this last modest comment *I* cannot agree!

Chapter 17

Adrift, Then Salvation

During the action, to underline the perspective between the way war had to be then conducted compared to the Falklands Islands operations forty one years later, the loss of life from *Repulse* alone (513 out of crew of 1,309) was more than double all British casualties in the South Atlantic from all Services.

On the morning after the sinking, Bill Tennant addressed us survivors of the two ships on the parade ground in farewell, having naturally been ordered home at once to report. He said that he would try to get for us the usual survivors' leave and was cheered to the echo as he left.[1] At that moment the morale of our ship's companies, considering the circumstances, was still surprisingly high; but in view of the mood surrounding us in the Base, stunned and incredulous after only three days of war, there was little optimism among the officers that we *would* be released, if indeed such was practicable for such numbers in any case. Nor did we have to wait long for this to be confirmed: for shortly afterwards we were also addressed by Admiral Sir Geoffrey Layton, whom Phillips had so recently replaced as C-in-C. That speech, still in the ears of those of us who were present, must be among the most disastrous ever uttered by an officer to his men, let alone by an Admiral.

---

[1] He even wrote personally not only to the next-of-kin of the hundreds of casualties but also to the likes of Rosalind, the wives, mothers and guardians of all the survivors: a gesture typical of his compassion. He enhanced his reputation during those grim days which followed, and was never blamed for anything that had happened on December 10th – indeed the reverse. He ended his distinguished career as a full

Admiral and Commander-in-Chief. On retirement he became an equally respected Lord-Lieutenant of his beloved Worcestershire. When he died, twenty two years after his *Repulse*. I happened to be serving as Naval Secretary to the last First Lord of the Admiralty, Lord Carrington, and was privileged, as a new Rear Admiral, to represent Their Lordships for his memorial service in a thronged Worcester Cathedral. Every other attribute of his life was mentioned from the pulpit; but, apart from his rank on the cover of the Order of Service, there was no mention of the fact that he had been a naval officer.

To be fair, Layton was already an embittered man, relieved of his command a few days before by Phillips who of course was substantively his junior. There was clearly no love lost between them. The ex-C-in-C was actually embarked in a liner with his wife and secretary and was due to sail in three hours' time from Keppel Harbour for England when the two ships were sunk. So back to the Naval Base he hurried, re-hoisted his flag over H.M.S. *Sultan* (the base), and signalled Admiralty that he had resumed command. The stranger who appeared on the balcony of the Accommodation Centre to speak to us may therefore be forgiven for being also under duress himself. Forgiven for that, maybe: but not excused for what he said or the way he said it. He told us in a few sentences that we were no longer to be identified as the ship's companies of *Prince of Wales* and *Repulse* but were to become H.M.S. *Sultan IV*, a satellite of the Base, and were to be sent hither and thither in Singapore, throughout the Malay peninsula, "and set-to to help us out of this infernal muddle". With that he disappeared. Morale too disappeared among us all and there were some uncomfortable mutterings among the demoralized men, who were to be scattered they neither knew nor cared.

However successful he may subsequently have been as Military Governor of Ceylon–and I believe he was very successful–I am unrepentant in corroborating what others have already described concerning Layton's performance towards us, foreign as it is to my training that it was wiser for junior officers to keep their opinions of their seniors to themselves. He caused additional unhappiness among so many innocent, loyal shipmates because he allowed his own predicament to outweigh any regard he might have had for theirs. After one incident which followed, involving re-employed survivors manning a small Penang ferry-boat who did not behave, shall we say, "in the highest traditions of the Service", Layton sent a message to Rear Admiral Spooner (Flag Officer Malaya): " . . . I wish to hear no more sentimental rubbish about survivors not being fit for the next job that comes along–they should be only too ready to get their own back."

After the first abortive idea that we should be used to complete the complements of ships of the Dutch Navy in Java, under their Captains and their flag, Layton's staff was then told to fill essential local gaps afloat or ashore and relieve men who had been out East for over two years. True, we had only been out of home waters for two months; but the fact that we had been fighting the war at sea for over two years seemed of no account. A chosen few, such as ratings already selected as officer potential, were sent home–which did not help the morale of the majority who were not.

By V.J. Day three and a half years later, a high percentage of those about whom an Australian Buffalo pilot, who flew over them in the water that day, had written to the C-in-C (" . . . here was something above human nature; I take my hat off to them, for in them I saw the spirit which wins wars . . . ") had not lived to tell their tale.

My own tale began desperately safe and pedestrian as a watchkeeper in the naval ops. room, filing signals, answering telephones and sticking pins into a wall map of the war area–four hours on and eight hours off, within which time another airfield had fallen and our soldiers, outnumbered in the jungle, out-flanked along the few roads within it, had fallen back in the face of those landings which we had failed to interrupt. It was a job which today a Wren plotter rating would probably perform better.

My Captain at *Dryad*, it may be remembered, had been Captain "Jackie" Spooner, who was now Rear Admiral Malaya and who had also been my Captain in *Vindictive* just before the war. He was often in the Ops. Room after Layton eventually did sail for Ceylon with the news that he was "off to collect the Eastern Fleet" and handed over the worsening Malayan scene to Spooner. The three Service Commanders were therefore now Spooner, General Percival, and Air Vice Marshal Pulford, a delightfully web-footed airman with an impossible task. A merchantman bringing fifty crated Hurricanes to our rescue was unloaded scarcely before she had docked, and they were just about airborne by the time she had secured, such was the extended plight of the R.A.F. We were, we knew, simply watching an enemy tide creeping south amid the jungles towards Johore and our island, separated only by the narrow strait and joined by its one causeway. It was just a question of time; but with the arrival of 18 Division of the East Anglian regiments as reinforcements for Percival (deflected from their original destination as build-up for Montgomery's Eighth Army), of course we would eventually fight to the end to defend Singapore as a fortress -wouldn't we?

Then one day towards the end of January 1942–Christmas and New Year had passed unnoticed–my stagnant situation mercifully changed. I was sent for by Jackie Spooner.

"I can now use you better than for sticking in pins. The General has decided to cut his losses on the mainland and the Army will therefore shortly retreat across the Johore causeway into the island. The Japs will of course bomb the causeway. The job of holding the outer and inner bridgeheads in Johore itself has been given to the Australians and the Argyll & Sutherland Highlanders respectively. Colonel Stewart of the Argylls wants a naval liaison officer on his battalion staff. You are to report to him forthwith. Your job will be to collect anything and everything you can lay your hands on which floats–except the White Ensign–in order to get what's left of the Army across the Strait when the moment comes. Off you go and good luck."

My heart lifted for the first time in many weeks.

A bungalow beautifully perched to the east of Johore town and overlooking the causeway had become Colonel Stewart's tactical headquarters. After treading first water and then shifting sands for so long, in first meeting Ian Stewart I regained confidence. Wiry, direct, and imbued still with a controlled energy despite his sapping experiences in jungle warfare during the last few weeks since the Japanese hand landed at Kota Bahru, his frame embodied some coiled, indestructible mechanism which could outlast even the native stamina of his Highland "Jocks"–or what was left of them. The Second Battalion of his Argyll and Sutherland Highlanders, the "Thin Red Line" of Crimean fame, had by then, if they could have known it, carved another chapter for themselves in military history for their performance in the Malayan Campaign of 1941-42.

"How much do you know?"

"Only that the army is to retreat from the peninsula onto the Island, sir, across the causeway in a few days' time; and if the Japs bomb the causeway beforehand your men will need boats of some sort to get across the Strait."

"That's about it. The Japs may not, of course, may want it for themselves: but they may. Now take a look at this,"–going to a wall map where two semi-circles encompassed Johore town to the north. "This operation is called a timed withdrawal. It can be tricky but that needn't bother you. This outer perimeter, the outer bridgehead, will be held by the Australians until the bulk of our troops have passed through it. When they have, the Wallabies will fall back through this inner bridgehead, held by the Argylls. The crunch comes if the Japs are then in contact with my Jocks. As you see, the distance is mighty short north of the causeway; so if they are, it will be a rearguard fight to boats. Is that clear? So do your best to collect anything that floats."

Ever since the foundation in war of Combined Operations under their principal architect Lord Mountbatten, every serviceman has been trained to understand that his own branch is invariably dependent for success on at least one, if not both, of the other two. Joint Service Staff Colleges, Joint Defence Planning organisations in permanent session, in perpetual NATO exercises–these are today part of every officer's natural progress including, for the most fortunate of students of naval Captain's equivalent rank, a year at the Royal College of Defence Studies in Belgrave Square, together with selected civil servants, and military officers from every Commonwealth country and the U.S.A. Apart from teaching the problems, and the differing approaches to them, of fighting at sea, on land, or in the air, people get to know people in the quiet of professional syndicate discussion; make friends, share private social relationships, meet each other's families, and most importantly pull each other's legs; so that when together in the Falklands and up against it, the sea, land and air commanders are probably on Christian-name terms and personally know the Whitehall recipients of their signals.

To take a simple example of such education for a naval officer, which I was quickly to learn one day as Deputy Director of Joint Service Plans: the Captain of a ship, although ultimately responsible for everything within her and anything which happens, right or wrong, good or bad, does not have to worry before sailing on an operation that his engineers have not filled her with the right fuel, that his supply team have not stocked with the right fresh and tinned food, or the gunnery officer with the right ammunition. Having been briefed by your admiral's staff on what may be in store, you are greeted on board by your second-in-command: "Ready for sea, sir." You go up to the bridge and have a quick look at the chart prepared by the navigator: then off you go. "Ring on main engines. Let go for'ard. Hold on to the back spring. Slow astern starboard engine. Stop starboard–" as the bow pays off the jetty. "Let go aft. Half ahead both engines. 100 revolutions. Midships.... steer 275 degrees...." –and you wind your way out of harbour. How different for the Army battalion commander! All those dreaded logistic hieroglyphics about petrol and oil and bullets and rations which he has to think about before he can move his mechanised force and infantry forward, ready to fight. How lucky is the Navy!

Lucky indeed. But not until I found myself among those Argylls during the final stages of the battle for Malaya did I first realise it. When a shell misses you at sea, the fountain splash makes a bang; but when it missed you among the attap huts in the jungle, the bang–for me at least–was much more frightening. My army colleagues didn't seem to worry overmuch. No matter the degree of action stations in a ship, when you *do* get to eat, the butter *has* been in the refrigerator, and there isn't much difference between snacks in the 15″ spotting top or in the Wardroom; but here the margarine was liquid. "Now, sailor, you see how the other half lives"–as we considered a slit trench prudent for the next air attack. I had not met the Highlander before. Subconsciously it may have been why I chose to go and live among his mountains fifteen years later. After similar experiences in slit trenches among the Australians on their outer bridgehead perimeter during bombing raids, I didn't share the same camaraderie; nor the same language when scared.

A motley armada began to assemble, some to the west of the causeway beneath the Sultan's Palace where the embarkation points would be good and the disembarkation hopeless, some to the east underneath our bungalow where the reverse was the case. Sampans, ferries from nearer the open sea, some with engines which did work and others which clearly didn't and would have to be towed somehow, crews who were at first reluctant to be thus commandeered but were persuaded by promise of money (I had no inkling from whence it would come—never mind): they floated, and that was all that mattered right now. Two days before the last troops were to evacuate I could not see how, if the causeway *was* bombed, another catastrophe could be averted. Then suddenly, like a dramatic production at the dress rehearsal, the scene took shape.

There were to be four beach parties on the north shore and four on the south. Boats would be brought round from the naval base a few miles east under cover of darkness and moored on the southern side of the Strait. We reckoned we could lift a thousand men per flight, white crews having replaced native ones, at either side of the causeway. The largest craft were two ex-Yangtsze pleasure-steamers. They were to remain in midstream under way and would be filled early to reduce the final rush. One naval Motor Torpedo Boat was to be held on the west side for the beach parties' final escape. A small but reliable little motor-boat was to be below Colonel Stewart's bungalow for him and the few of us who would be with him at the very end of the operation.

Nature set the scene with her inimitable sense of occasion: brilliantly calm, cloudless days, and at night the moon waxing to full. The cavalcade across the causeway began. Big cars, little cars, black cars, tawny cars all piled high with the pathetic personal trappings of refugees. The stream was interrupted by the demolition squads preparing to blow the causeway after the retreat, if the Japanese had not already done so themselves. Below the waterline the Navy was laying its depth-charges.

The timed withdrawal seemed to be proceeding unmolested, the Japanese not in contact. The Australians abandoned their outer perimeter and fell back through the Argylls and so back into the Island. Colonel Stewart moved into that bungalow with his few tactical staff. From the terrace we could look away to the naval base in the east and Kranji in the west. There was little traffic rumbling across the causeway now—the lull before the storm?

Dusk fell. There was nothing more I could do that I had not tried to do. "Mischief, thou art afoot...." Would the boats creep round to their stations? Would the beach parties get posted? The full moon rose, shyly it seemed. The motor transport began its procession. Lorries, bren-carriers, water-carts, troop-carriers, ambulances, despatch riders—all the paraphernalia of the Army was trundling slowly across. It was a long night. Johore was inexplicably quiet.

Riding pillion, I went round to visit my beach parties. The noise of the motorcycle seemed shattering. None of us could believe that *nothing* was happening. The stillness was eerie. They'd knock hell out of us in the morning, of course; but why not now, in such moonlight?

I returned to the lawn of the bungalow. All tense emotions keyed to action had become suffused by anticlimax and the sheer beauty of the scene: so quiet, so utterly indifferent to what one knew must shortly rage: not quite like the lull before the storm in the Pastoral Symphony but something akin to that: a kind of temporary release between the violence of the immediate past and that of the immediate future which one knew must be inevitable. It doesn't do to think too much ... but confronted with that backdrop ....

Past midnight, the moon made it daylight. The rumbling of the mechanised army subsided and died away. The causeway seemed empty for a little while; and then the infantry began to march across. A slight mist hid their ranks. The tramp of feet on asphalt was the rhythmic sound. It was a tired rhythm.

The dawn of Sunday 1st February ... a sea like glass on the Strait either side of the causeway. To the east our two river steamers were the only movement. The sky was like that of a picture-postcard which is impossibly coloured. The moon was setting among the buttresses of the Sultan's Palace; and then, as the last of the infantry, the remnants of that Argyll battalion, marched out onto the causeway with other Highland "Jocks", a single piper began to play. You could hear every note. It covered the tired beat of feet. Riveted, I watched and listened. I was yet to become mesmerised by the sound of the bagpipe as a conjuror of emotion. One inevitably succumbs to it, Englishman or not. The Highlanders had passed.

Daylight. Still no enemy interference. One by one the machine-gun posts were called in: the last platoon was just coming through. The front line of the British Army in Malaya eventually consisted of two bren-gun posts. I turned to the Colonel.

"May I send our boat away, sir?" The sun was well up by now.

"I think we'll walk after all, sailor. That may be strange for you!"

I signalled to the boat-points: "Finish". Anticlimax. What we had thought would be a challenge had evaporated. As the last of his men filed by, Stewart shook each one by the hand. It isn't like a sailor to have to walk, a fact which amused the demolition squads as the

Colonel and I finally left Johore together to become the last free British on the Malayan mainland for some years. As we passed the lock gates, stuffed with gelignite, at the northern end of the causeway, he said: "That was to have been your air-raid shelter, sailor. Thank you for your help. Glad it wasn't needed."

It was to be forty years before we met again; but after that first partnership he created me an Honorary Argyll & Sutherland Highlander and surely, for an English sailor who was to make his home in the Highlands, there could be no prouder honour?

The timed-withdrawal operation was over, unhindered. As events were to prove, the Japanese had appreciated that the Island would be conquered more easily by keeping the causeway as intact as possible. From its southern end on that Sunday morning we watched. First the northern drawbridge disappeared in a cloud of smoke; then the middle of the causeway disintegrated, spray and falling rock disturbing the peace for a minute or two. Then we all felt rather foolish, "all dressed up and nowhere to go". As at Dunkirk, such as was left of the Army was back in the Island. At least we knew how things stood: nothing left except that Island, said to be impregnable. No longer an Argyll, I was suddenly operationally naked. During those few days I had felt a close affinity with those men, and with Colonel Stewart in particular; maybe because he, like Bill Tennant, had had to watch the decimation of the fighting unit of which he was so proud. When the Japanese landed at Kota Bahru, the Argylls were among the first to confront them. The Second Battalion then held 940 all ranks on its strength. Those killed and wounded during the next few weeks numbered 300. A further near-200 died as prisoners of war, including those *en route* for Japan after the surrender.

Back in Singapore Island the remnants of the Argylls were joined to the remnant of the Royal Marine detachments of *Prince of Wales* and *Repulse* to form General Percival's mobile reserve–probably his best fighting men during those grim final days; they became known as the Plymouth Argylls, after the football team (the ships being West-Country manned); and as such they are remembered to this day.

When in May 1942 I was invited by the B.B.C. to recount my experiences with the Argylls, I concluded with these words: "This has been a narrative of what might have happened. With Dunkirk in

our memory–though what a little thing this was compared to
Dunkirk–we could not imagine that without air superiority an army,
however small after what it had suffered, could retreat unmolested
across the exposed ribbon of road in full moonlight and then in
broad daylight. It was as well for many of us that it did. But
throughout I felt that if there were to be sticky moments, then there
were none with whom I would have more gladly shared them than
with those tough, courageous and business-like officers and men of
the Argyll and Sutherland Highlanders. The country does well to
honour them."

After reaching home by devious ways which I will describe shortly,
I was ordered by Admiralty to report to the Director of Military
Intelligence at the War Office. As one of the few survivors who had
worked closely with the Army during those last confused, often
chaotic days preceding the fall of Singapore, I was told to write what
I had actually seen: no hearsay: no opinion: just a factual account of
what my eyes recorded.

That is now fifty years ago and most official documents have
released their secrecy. In such circumstances even disciplined men
are apt to behave in abnormal ways. Those last days were an
amalgam of acts of supreme individual gallantry and collective
uniformed ill-discipline. I must be careful in what I recount here, for
there were scenes at the end which staggered me, and which
hopefully few are given to see; but those that I do describe are
extracts from a long-hand script by a Lieutenant entitled, "Narrative
of Naval Liaison Officer attached to 3 Corps in Johore and
Singapore–February 1942"–extracts which jog my memory of some
dreadful pictures and are helpful in recapturing their detailed
brush-strokes.

Jobless again on that dawn of February lst and having been in
Johore for the past week, I drove back along the Strait to the naval
base. I had expected to find it at least partly defended, with the
enemy so shortly to be ensconced on the opposite bank. There was
no sign of any such thing. On reaching the base I found it completely
deserted; not a soul about: not even a sentry on the gate. Doors of
dockyard shops were wide open. Office desks had pens and pencils
dropped askew on blotters. The doors of evacuated bungalows
swung in the breeze. It was like any other sleepy Sunday afternoon
in the tropics, with nothing even locked–as if some terrifying film

monster had suddenly said "Go!" and they had, leaving not a ghost of humanity behind. It was an eerie experience...what had happened? This was not the way the Navy usually behaved.

With nowhere obvious to go, I felt rather lonely. I wandered aimlessly about, picturing the activity which had once existed at every turn in what was now like a morgue. Then I was suddenly confronted by a very large and angry Colonel. Venting his spleen on the first naval uniform he could find, he told me in uncensored military language what he thought of the Royal Navy in general, me in particular, admirals, Singapore, the ratting of the Base personnel and the affront to the Army in having to replace them. At least that brought me up to date! Having done so, he clearly felt better. I subsequently was to discover that he was of an East Anglian regiment from one of the brigades of the luckless Eighteenth Division who, *en route* for the Middle East as build-up for what was one day to be Alamein, had been diverted in their troopships to Singapore, unprepared and unacclimatised, precipitated too late into a hopeless military situation and bitter about it. He calmed down on learning that I had only just left the Argylls. I could understand his initial venom but was in no position either to explain or excuse the cause of it.

Looking back on that last nightmare fortnight in Singapore, I roamed in a kind of bemused and (now) khaki-clad role, bereft of any persuasion that my own Service could now have any real contribution to make and desperately sorry for the soldiers who must slog it out and face the music. The least I could do was to continue to try to help them.

I reported back to my Admiral, who told me to switch my naval liaison duties to the General commanding Three Corps, second-in-command to the C-in-C, General Percival; and here again was a man who jerked any temporary bemusement into confidence. General Sir Lewis ("Piggy") Heath, his reputation enhanced by previous exploits in Ethiopia, received me with a twinkling eye, as he put me in the picture–not an encouraging one. His Corps, the backbone of the fighting arm to defend the fortress, consisted of two Divisions with their ancillary arms: the Nine/Eleventh Indian Division and the Eighteenth English Division. The latter, as I have said, were fresh from home but, diverted at sea from their original Middle East destination, were unacclimatised, with no opportunity to train together before action. The Indian Division, or such as was left of it, had fought back throughout the length of Malaya, and their casualties, particularly among the officers, had been heavy. Originally two Divisions, they had now been amalgamated into one. Eighteen Division was fresh, each brigade zestful for what forays across the Strait they could make. The Indians were understandably tired and morale in consequence was low. It was not an easy situation.

My work seemed to alternate between the passive and the active. The first meant trying to pour oil on the bitter attitude of the Army towards the Navy, by cutting the red tape that still tied to the base the abandoned stores and vehicles for which the Army had immediate need. A whole dockyard basin was on fire one night with nobody apparently unduly concerned: such was the inter-Service climate. The rest of my work consisted of arranging raids across the Strait into Johore, now occupied by the Japanese, and co-ordinating these with our ex-*Repulse* Sub-Lieutenant Pool who was a Coastal Forces expert. They were spasmodic and ineffectual, but at least they were offensive. Then on the night of February 9th/10th the Japanese made their successful assault on the Island to the west of the causeway; the gallant intervention of our coastal M.T.B.s could be no more than that of gnats trying to sting a giant, and the Navy's role in Singapore came to an end. Early in the morning of February 11th General Heath advised me that there was no further point in remaining with him nor help that I could lend. Sadly I said farewell to him and to his friendly staff. His patience and consideration towards so junior an officer of another Service, set against the chaotic worries of his impossible responsibilities, are indelible in my memory. It wasn't hard to understand why all under him held him in such affection.

There were no illusions in Three Corps. Many gave me the addresses of their wives and fiancées, should I be able to escape, for they knew that such was unlikely for them. It was the most poignant parting; and as Fate would have it I was in fact to become the only immediate survivor from Eighteen Division and thus an eventual strange messenger to many loved ones at home. The General himself was not to survive the ordeals which he and his men had subsequently to endure. I have never more admired a leader on such short acquaintance.

Chapter 18

Last Hours in Singapore and After

Adrift, with no job and no immediate superior to whom to report–save the Admiral himself, the last person to bother at such a time–it was an inconsequential, helpless feeling: so much to be done and yet how and where? I had been away from the Navy itself for some weeks and had no inkling of any present situation save the despairing mêlée which seemed to envelop the population of Singapore itself, Malays, Chinese, Tamils, terrified thousands as the bombs rained down, beyond either inclination or hope other than accepting the inevitable.

I went to the only place I could think of, the headquarters of General Percival, the C-in-C, at Sime Road. There I found an old friend, Clifford Gill, who had been the Navigating Officer of *Repulse*, now seconded to G.H.Q. Staff. At least we spoke the same language and he took me into a corner of the Operations Room whence I watched for a few minutes a C-in-C whose performance military history has so criticised, even denigrated, and yet for whom as a figure doomed to his destiny I could only feel sympathy. I knew nothing about him, other than that he *was* the C-in-C; but he just didn't look like one to me. There are those whose brilliant staff minds are an essential counterpart to advise, ride on a curb, solve the logistic conundrums for their leaders, yet as unfitted themselves for high command as others who *are* so fitted are disinterested or lazy in staff work. Percival looked to me a sad figure, miscast for reasons well known. His situation was impossible. Maybe such as "Piggy" Heath would have fought a much more traditional rearguard battle before surrendering; but surrender in the end was surely inevitable?

Clifford Gill told me of a last-hope, forlorn scheme to evacuate troops by means of freeing the fleet of Chinese tongkangs (large undecked sampans) moored in the Singapore river. Each could carry a large human cargo provided that each was towed: and by what? On my way to the river I found some sailors, drifting like me and happy enough to find an officer with a suggestion of something they too could do, their morale unimpaired. While trying to free these craft packed tightly together the bombing was heavy and we were watched from the bank by crowds of Commonwealth soldiers who, far from helping, told me they were sick and had lost their units. It was hard to visualise how this scheme could become practical; and an hour before sunset I received instructions from Army Headquarters (presumably through Gill, for surely Percival and his staff had more major problems to consider) to abandon the idea.

I have pondered long as to the wisdom or otherwise of recounting the scenes in the streets of the town I saw during the next twenty-four hours; but on balance I have decided not to be squeamish. It all happened fifty years ago, which releases such events from their pigeon-holed files of secrecy: military history, be it the Charge of the Light Brigade or the fall of Singapore, cannot for ever conceal truth and therefore subsequent judgement by historians upon that truth. This *is* my story which at the time, as I have said, the War Office instructed me (as in fact the sole survivor of Three Corps) to recount. My decision will be criticised, maybe rightly, as making no contribution to Commonwealth relations. I shall not be the first or last to suffer that. If under Her Majesty today the Commonwealth can survive the near-fifty independent approaches towards this planet's problems, loosely knitted and yet part of the same civilised pattern, it must accept individual shortcomings in its past.

When military discipline among uniformed armed troops collapses it is a very ugly sight. The streets were full of debauched, drunken soldiers, deserters from their units, N.C.O.s among them but not officers, breaking their way into any hotel they could find, shouting, "they won't be long now." They stormed H.M.S. *Laburnam*, a local naval reserve H.Q. sloop, only to find that she had no engines. They invaded one of the last liners to leave, *Empire Star*, which was trying to embark women and children evacuees. Morale among Imperial troops can never have been lower. Sometimes they met an ex-planter, a naval volunteer, who would knock them flat on insult or who on another occasion would shoot or be shot. Being unarmed myself, there was little I could do to intervene, and had I tried I would doubtless have been shot too. They were like a crowd of present-day football hooligans, rioting for the sake of it, crazed with ill-discipline and looted alcohol, a shabby advertisement for their nation. Had any of Eighteen Division been present, casualties would have been more numerous and subsequent acrimony even greater.

In mitigation it can be pleaded that these remnants of General Gordon Bennet's Australian force were very young and equally ill-prepared for war, as I had experienced when sharing a slit-trench with them on the outer bridgehead during those final days in Johore. They had been hastily thrown into battle-dress and despatched into a strange, hot hell. There were also acts of gallantry from among them for they are a brave, tough physical people; but discipline, particularly in adversity, is not instilled overnight and when it does crack the splinters are sharply unpleasant.

Statesmen, Generals, Air Marshals, but not Admirals, had meanwhile come and gone with advice as to how to stem the deteriorating position. These had included the great Wavell himself, who had apparently endorsed my admiral's intention to evacuate, if possible, such naval personnel as could continue to fight the war at sea; so that when, as the only sensible act remaining to me, I again reported to my Admiral, he told me to my astonishment that he felt guilty at having held on to me for so long, that there was no further point in my remaining on the Island, and that if I *could* get out I was to do so. He also told me of the best chance of so doing.

In his foreword to the Official History of the Ninety third–those Argylls–Field Marshal Earl Wavell (temporarily their C-in-C of South-West Pacific Command for just a month before Percival's surrender) writes:

"If all units in Malaya had been trained and led with the same foresight and imagination as Colonel Stewart showed in the training of his battalion, the story of the campaign would have been different. It was the realisation of this that led me to order his return to India, after his battalion and brigade had both practically ceased to exist, to impart his knowledge and ideas to units in India preparing for the return match with the Japanese."

Which meant that General Bill Slim, building up his Fourteenth Army in Burma, needed the advice of Ian Stewart so much that the Navy was told to rescue him, if possible, from Singapore before it fell. My Admiral told me to go with him.

A few of us had been told that the cruiser *Durban* and destroyer *Jupiter* were due into Keppel Harbour for a few minutes that night if shelling permitted. For obvious reasons this was cloaked in secrecy. I drove as nice an official car as I could ever hope to own over the edge of the quay (why leave it for the Japanese?) and then sat on an oil-drum, playing dice with the late command naval signals officer, waiting...waiting...with the town aglow with flames behind us, the palls of black smoke from burning oil-tanks obliterating the stars, Japanese shells from the northern outskirts firing over the harbour at the batteries stationed on islands to the south. The few of us maybe felt guilty that we should be so favoured. You just had to still your conscience and tell yourself that *if* you survived it was to continue to fight: and anyhow orders were orders.... The hours drifted on. I clutched my worldly possessions in a blanket, including a bottle originally looted from the evacuated naval base, and gazed at the inky stillness of the harbour. If the ships didn't come....?

Then suddenly two darkened shapes and their dimmed red and green bow lights came out of the blackness to the west. Scarcely a word was heard, just the purring of fans as the engines went astern. Somehow, under Captain Cazalet (later to be in command of *London* in the *Amethyst* Yangtsze adventure and to become Admiral Sir Peter), they had managed to get alongside and now stayed there for the minimum of time. I boarded *Jupiter*. A wonderful feeling once more to feel a deck under my feet and then within a few minutes the throb of the engines as we cast off. I stood on the quarterdeck, letting the night air blow through me, after the suffocating hours of smoke-pall ashore, as the destroyer gathered speed and the fearful sight of the doomed island faded to a distant glow. I stood for a long time, thinking of the Army friends I had left, feeling something of a deserter with their letters in my pocket, and yet persuading myself that I would hopefully continue to be able to fight German or Japanese until their fate was avenged, they and my *Repulse* shipmates who were . . . . ? God and who else knew where.

Jupiter wove her way down through the Banka Strait off the eastern end of Sumatra, running the gauntlet next day of bombs without being hit. She had little navigational room in which to manoeuvre but was brilliantly handled by her Captain "Pug" Thew, and reached Batavia where we passengers were duly deposited. She sailed immediately, after refuelling and was shortly to be sunk in the Battle of the Java Sea, together with that other gallant destroyer *Electra* to whom also I had owed my survival.

Singapore meanwhile had fallen–an event which Churchill called "the worst disaster and largest capitulation in British military history." Some 130,000 British and Commonwealth troops surrendered to a force of under half that number of Japanese after an eight-week campaign which, punctuated by acts of supreme individual heroism, had been an unmitigated débacle. Singapore had fallen, the troops still singing "There'll always be an England" on their way towards those horrendous prison camps; and with the catastrophe came the bitterness which accompanies the end of an era, the demands for inquiries in the House of Commons, for scapegoats, for comparisons between the "spirit of Dunkirk" and other glorious defeats which the British character can delude itself were victories–such judgements on the quick and unexpected end of what had been thought to be an impregnable fortress of the British Empire coming largely from people who had never been there.

Churchill with his supreme oratory and rhetoric had to do his best, but in so doing he may have led those at home to compare a beleaguered Singapore to their own situation at the time of the Battle of Britain. It was not comparable. The stoic character of the Cockney among the fires of London was immeasurably different from that of the panic-stricken natives, by no means all dedicated to British rule, whose fate Percival had to consider. Anthony Kemp in *The Bitter End–The Fall of Singapore* writes:

"The main reason for the surrender was that the water supply for the colony was situated on the mainland in Johore–and that was firmly in the hands of the Japanese. Faced by the problem of a two-million population and with no aircraft to protect them from the almost continuous bombing, Percival had no choice.

The fault lay with previous pre-war governments who failed to face up to the threat of war in the East and the inter-service rivalry that made a farce of sensible defence planning."

To this I add that, despite 15″ guns pointing south to seaward from their impregnable encasements, Stewart was among the few who claimed that any attack would come from the north. But nobody in authority had heeded him.

To end my thoughts about the disaster of Singapore and the many friends, shipmates and army colleagues whom I was never to see again, I marvel at the forgiving, Christian generosity of those I still do know who suffered the bestial and humiliating treatment by their captors in conditions which have since torn at the heart of humanity. We accept today a successful, ruthlessly efficient nation—"Old Friends, New Enemies" as the American historian Professor Marder put it concerning the Japanese and now again "New Friends", so to speak—and why should a younger generation be led to think otherwise? It would be wrong to dissuade them. Western Presidents and Prime Ministers today must pursue their diplomatic relations; but I know of too many whose frames were tortured to find myself able to forgive, while trying in vain to forget.

Adrift again and unwanted. The only Allied military complex here in Java was the Headquarters of General Wavell himself up in the hills preparing, after the fall of Singapore, for the next Japanese assault upon this island and Sumatra. "Distressed British seamen" would scarcely be welcome there. In the town I ran into an old friend, a naval hydrographic surveyor, one of those stocky little men whom no adversity could curb or change, the kind of companion ideal in such circumstances. Bobby Griffiths and I set off to find somewhere to shelter, with no money, no identity save for our squalid attempt at uniform, and no local language. We eventually found something little more than a brothel; but as food was at that point more important to us than its usual fare, and since beggars can't be choosers, we somehow bludgeoned our way, uncouth as we were, into a Dutch business-man's club where one portion of fish would have done for four. One night in our hovel was enough, declining offers, even had we been tempted we had no money to honour, before wandering down to the docks; for there seemed no point in staying here. Somehow we must get to Ceylon.

Alongside the quay we found a small Dutch inter-island passenger coaster called the *Plancius*. She was designed to accommodate 200. On dumping our blanket of belongings on deck we found over 800 refugees already on board: Javanese, white, black, yellow, coffee, women and children with their pathetic trappings packing every inch of deck space and the holds. A full human cargo: but no sign of any crew. Eventually we unearthed the Captain. He was a fine old stolid Dutchman in a state of some confusion. Was he going to sail? No: no convoy. What was the point of staying here, only to fall into Japanese hands? A shrug. Was he ready to sail? Yes, but not enought food for so many. Couldn't we help him to put to sea and help him run his ship? No: he was adamant. So were we, although unarmed. By now a few more naval officers had appeared on the jetty. Between us we persuaded him. We would keep look-out, I would help to navigate, we would run the food rationing: but sail we also would: and finally he yielded. We sailors would sleep on decks under the bridge in return for our help; and so finally we sailed, unescorted and–as luck would have it–through thick fog into the Sunda Strait between Java and Sumatra, where Japanese submarines were known to be lurking. We then steered well south before setting course west for Ceylon.

It was a slow but interesting voyage as part-time navigator, saloon sweeper and cook-of-the-mess in return for two meals a day of soup and Dutch sausage and maybe a potato. But on February 24th we reached Colombo unmolested, parted profusely with our Captain who in turn seemed grateful to us, shouldered our blankets, and began to try to rejoin the Navy. I say "try" because this was by no means straightforward. With the conceit of one who suddenly and for no logical reason imagines that people should be pleased to see him, I went to the only hotel I knew from ten years ago on my way to the China Station as a Midshipman in that P & O–the Galle Face.

A sentry escorted me through the swing doors into the foyer and the comfort and glitter of the world-famous hotel as I remembered it. He deposited me before an immaculate young lady–I can't actually remember if Wren Officers had yet been officially allowed so far afield–at Reception. She was sympathetically kind. — "the mist is dispelled when a woman appears"–but in this case not very much. "I'm sorry, but this is now the Headquarters of Admiral Layton.

Nobody under the rank of Commander is allowed to stay here. I suggest you try the Grand Oriental which is for junior officers." So I went back into the town with my bundle.

Oriental, yes: but Grand, no. At least there was a dormitory floor which was not going to be either bombed or sunk. Reporting to the local Colombo naval authority as an unexpected bonus, I was put into an office to relieve an ailing tea-planter for whom present circumstances were clearly too much, and was told to arrange meal-vouchers for those going on leave to the rest camp at Dyetalawa in the Hills, hardly what Jackie Spooner had meant for me. There then seemed little chance of releasing me for continued service at sea.

Admiral Sir James Somerville, who together with Lord Cunningham was one of the foremost fighting admirals of the war, was coming out to resurrect and command a real Eastern Fleet. His staff preceded him, among them a Commander, an old shipmate from *Danae*, whose eldest child was my godson. Thus I found a camp-bed in his Galle Face room: and through him it was agreed that the likes of me could well do with a week's leave in a tea-planting paradise in the high hills of Ceylon.

At last I had time to tell Rosalind that I was alive and in Ceylon, which seemed unlikely to be invaded by the Japanese even though termed "threatened" by the Press at home.

Back to Colombo and the meal-vouchers until eventually I managed to make such a nuisance of myself that they thankfully got rid of me, under the Dutch flag via the Cape (spoilt again by those kind ladies, who remembered *Repulse* on her way East), and so one lovely May morning to Liverpool. My Far East chapter had ended.

I reported to the Appointments Commander in Admiralty. He seemed more pleased to see me than anybody in Colombo had been. A fit young sea-going officer, unexpectedly on his books, could be useful – as it turned out, as a temporary Staff Officer Operations to a sea-going Admiral.

Rear Admiral Louis Hamilton (known to all as "Turtle" from birth for reasons which he himself could never explain) commanded the First Cruiser Squadron in the Home Fleet based at Scapa – seven 10,000-ton, 8" County Class cruisers including my old friend *Cumberland* of China Fleet days. He had been sent south to plan with the Army an operation, under General Alexander's co-direction, to establish a detachment of the Royal Warwickshire Regiment in a Spitsbergen fiord, in order to secure it as a safe refuelling base for escorts of the convoys to Russia, which were then in their infancy. I looked endlessly at photographs of ice–brash ice, drift ice, pack ice, icebergs–with the Colonel detailed in command who, not surprisingly, seemed luke-warm about his assignment. The supply ship which was to carry the Army's stores, covered by the Navy, was not to be allowed long in the fiord. At my first meeting among the War Office planners I therefore protested that eight tons of stationery seemed excessive. This was cut down to one without demur; in fact the operation never materialised, but I had evidently scored a favourable point with my Admiral, who decided that my temporary appointment as his operations officer should become permanent. I joined him in June 1942 in Scapa where he was flying his flag in *London* (the one modernised cruiser among his other six, which included *Norfolk* and *Suffolk* of *Bismarck*) fame) as an unqualified Lieutenant Staff Officer Operations, a post affec-tionately known as "SOO". Our job was to escort every other Arctic Convoy to Russia, alternating with the Tenth Cruiser Squadron. It was to be for me only six months from the South China Sea to the North Cape of Norway, in the days before regular air travel; and for better or worse, as will be seen, I was to stay with "Turtle" Hamilton for three years. He was an unusual little Admiral, a tiger for action, a destroyer-officer of the old classic breed, a puckish bachelor whose declared intention was to "pop it across the Boche and make Britain safe for fox-hunting." He did both.

Chapter 19

The Destruction of an Arctic Convoy to Russia

Millions of words have been written about the Arctic convoys; by historians with hindsight who were not there and by many British and American seamen who were. I hesitate to add to that library, but as I was present at the only major disaster which attended this seemingly impossible operation of war–I seemed destined to be present at disasters, and from the South China Sea via Singapore to the North Cape of Norway in seven months, with no air travel, was at least an accomplishment–I must include this now historic incident in my personal story. I say "seemingly impossible operation" because if you look at the map and reverse the roles, with the Royal Navy and Royal Air Force occupying the fiords and airfields in the far north of Norway, it would have seemed shameful if any German merchantmen in convoy had reached Murmansk, however heavily escorted. To run the gauntlet between the polar ice to the north, the might of German heavy units with supporting torpedo-bombers to the south and Novaya Zemlya to the east–all of which thus enclosed the Barents Sea into a large Arctic lake–in order to get millions of tons of war equipment to Murmansk, on paper was impracticable, however much Stalin needed Churchill. In fact, only one convoy went seriously awry because the British First Sea Lord, shortly to die of a cerebral haemorrhage, ignored his intelligence advisors and ordered an impractical maritime escapade.

Of those millions of words, should it be feasible for any interested reader to come by them, I know of none more succinct than those from (then) Mr. David Hirst Q.C., Counsel for the Plaintiff in the celebrated libel action of Captain J. E. Broome, D.S.C., R.N., against Cassell & Company Ltd. and Mr. David Irving in the High Court of Justice before (then) Mr. Justice Lawton in early 1970. In his opening address to the jury, Mr. Hirst sketches the background of those Russian convoys, slanted of course towards the context of the action he was defending, in a masterly way. In that legal case I was to find myself as a not unimportant witness for the plaintiff some 28 years after the catastrophe had occurred in the Barents Sea. As it may not be easy for the reader to put his hands on Mr. Hirst's exposition, I quote some of what he said to the jury to set the scene. A house atlas with a map of the Arctic seas is all that is necessary for illustration, as that jury would have found.

In the summer of 1942 the Royal Navy, stretched to its utmost since the outbreak of war, was particularly extended. The Far East, as I have described, took its toll. In the Mediterranean and around the Cape we were trying to hold sea communications firmly enough to support what was to become Alamein. In the Atlantic the U-boat wolf-packs were in full cry, savaging every slow convoy; and on top of all this Churchill had somehow to assuage Stalin's perpetual demands for supplies to be rushed via the Arctic port of Murmansk to the Russo-German front, where so many German divisions were tied down, and thus deflected from their efforts in the West. Hence the Arctic Convoys sailing spasmodically under the code-name PQ from Iceland to the Kola Inlet (Murmansk) and QP to Britain when empty on return.

A glance at the map I suggest will paint the picture for you. At about 8 knots a convoy consisting in this case of 38 merchant ships, British and American, and carrying among them 4,246 vehicles, 594 tanks, 297 crated aircraft and 156,000 tons of general cargo, sailed from Iceland for Russia at the end of June 1942. The route skirted to the eastward of Jan Mayen Island off Greenland some 300 miles inside the Arctic Circle, and then in as wide an arc as possible into the Barents Sea, either to the north or south of the uninhabited Bear Island (latitude 75° N,) south of Spitsbergen, depending on the capricious behaviour of the southern limit of the polar ice; thence west of Novaya Zemlya (Russian territory) and into the Kola Inlet with its port of Murmansk.

The German threat to this provocative and audacious adventure on the part of the Allies was threefold: U-boats swarming in the restricted confines of the Barents Sea; Heinkel and Dornier torpedo-bombers based at airfields (Banak in particular) in the far north of occupied Norway; and—most pertinent to this story—the heavy German fleet units sequestered in the remote fiords of the North Cape, which in this case included *Tirpitz* herself (the most potent battleship in the world), together with *Admiral Scheer* and *Lutzow* (pocket battleships), *Hipper* (heavy cruiser) and a number of their large supporting destroyers. The enforced route of the convoy could never be further north than a few hours steaming from Altenfiord, the advanced base for *Tirpitz* and her colleagues, and so you would think that such as she would revel in the chance of turning her huge armament onto the plodding rectangle of merchantmen. The gamble was: would Hitler allow her to do so? Having lost *Bismarck* in her one brave if abortive foray into the ocean, would he risk his one remaining capital-ship threat? Or would he nurture her as a mother suckles her one remaining issue? Hitler did not understand about sea power any more than Napoleon had done. But *Tirpitz* was there; and while she *was* there it meant that the British Battle Fleet had to cover every Russian convoy from a distance and that every such convoy had to be protected by at least a fast cruiser force, keeping just beyond the convoy's immediate horizon, as well as, of course, by its close escort of anti-submarine ships: destroyers, corvettes, ocean trawlers, anti-aircraft ships, shepherds of their flock amid more hazardous obstacles than in *One Man And His Dog*.

Unlike convoys in other theatres, which sailed of necessity to something of a set pattern, each Russian Convoy was treated as an individual operation depending on, for instance, twenty-four-hour darkness in winter or twenty-four-hour daylight in summer, the disposition of the German heavy units, air and U-boat threat, and the latest ice reconnaissance from the polar region. In the case of PQ17, the close convoy escort was under Commander Broome, independent of the cruiser covering force under Rear Admiral Hamilton (to whom I had now become attached as his very unqualified Staff Officer Operations), who in turn was independent of the Battle Fleet under his C-in-C, Admiral Sir John Tovey. The Admiralty directive to Broome was to get that convoy to Murmansk in the face of U-boats and torpedo-bombers, to make eastwards as quickly as eight knots and ice would permit. The role of Admiral

Hamilton with two British 8″ cruisers and, for the first time, two American 8″ cruisers (*Wichita* and *Tuscaloosa*, whose presence was to have a bearing on the story) and a destroyer screen was to hover within touch but not in sight of the convoy, in order to dart in and deal with any comparable surface force; and lastly the role of the Battle Fleet was to remain to the westward of the cruisers and convoy, near enough to counter *Tirpitz* and other heavy units if the need arose but taking care not to expose such precious ships as *Duke of York* and the American battleships *Alabama* and *South Dakota* to the chance of U-boats torpedoes in the Barents Sea. Such was the scene on the evening of July 4th when things started to happen.

"Knights Move" was the German code-name for the operation to annihilate this convoy, a task which they were virtually to succeed in accomplishing, if in a way they could not have expected. In the event two-thirds of the convoy's ships were sunk. The tales of heroism among the survivors are legion. The catastrophe will for ever remain a source of comment within annals of the Royal Navy.

Admiralty Intelligence rightly showed that the enemy had moved their heavy ships from Trondheim in north Norway up into the fiords in the very north. This was to be expected. As this point Ultra must enter the story. The breaking of German cyphers at Bletchley is now common knowledge, but in those days the names of those allowed to be in receipt of such were available to the Prime Minister. There were four of us in the flagship of that cruiser covering force so inducted: the Admiral of course, his Chief Staff Officer (Captain Servaes, also Captain of *London*), the Squadron Navigating Officer (later to become Admiral Sir John Frewen and a C-in-C) and myself, just a Lieutenant. The Ultra messages had to be unravelled by the Admiral's secretary in person. By this means it meant that I had all the U-boats around the convoy plotted as A, B, X or Y and felt that I knew their commanding officers by their Christian names. I had to be careful to sit on my chart to conceal their positions, just an idle dot of no consequence to whoever came in to see "how we were doing". Thus it was that, when things started to happen the Admiral and his advisors were in confident mood. We had already supported the convoy well east of the conflicting orders from Admiralty. "Don't go beyond 25° East unless the convoy is threatened by the presence of surface forces." "Don't go beyond the B of Barents on the chart." "You are not being urged eastwards against your discretion." (To which our C-in-C added his voice and further counselled his cruiser Admiral as to what extent he should obey Admiralty instructions, depending upon the threat of enemy surface forces. There was no dearth of opinion for Admiral Hamilton.) It was clear from Ultra that the U-boats had dropped astern of the convoy to re-charge their batteries while shadowing and that there was no barrage ahead. One or two merchantmen had been sunk by sporadic attack, as was to be expected, but generally the situation seemed far more healthy than we had any right to suppose. Our tails were up: we thought that we had more than fulfilled our obligation to the convoy in supporting it far further east than originally planned. My Admiral had just decided that we could and should now leave Broome and his escorts to see the convoy through to Murmansk and that the odds on his success were remarkably good. We would stay until the early hours of July 5th.

Then came the bombshells.

From Admiralty to C.S. One (Admiral Hamilton in command of the First Cruiser Squadron). Most Immediate. Cruiser Force withdraw to westward at high speed. Time of origin 9.11 p.m.

This is a very high degree of priority of signal. The time is of little consequence because we were in twenty four hours of daylight.

Twelve minutes later:

From Admiralty to escorts of PQ17 (Commander Broome in *Keppel*). *Immediate*. Owing to threat from surface ships convoy is to disperse and proceed to Russian ports.

Another thirteen minutes later and referring to the above:

Most immediate. Convoy is to scatter.

Had you been in the position of Admiral Hamilton or Commander Broome at that moment, what conclusion would you have drawn on receiving such instructions from the Admiralty? I would venture to think the same as they did: that *Tirpitz*, and who could know what else, was about to appear from Altenfiord over the southern horizon to attack the convoy. That alone would surely account for what seemed to us on the spot—whose achievement so far had been beyond our most optimistic hopes–to be panic in Admiralty; that and the fact that for the first time the cruiser covering force was fifty per cent American, so that politically it would have been an inauspicious start to their co-operation in the Arctic to be cut off and sunk in the east Barents Sea.

When those signals were received on the admiral's bridge in *London* his covering force was well to the north east of the convoy and was in any case about to retire westwards within a few hours to fall back on Admiral Tovey's battle fleet; so now Admiral Hamilton immediately reversed course, collected his four cruisers and accompanying destroyers into a battle formation and careered westwards at thirty knots, into an arctic, icy mist, expecting the superstructure of *Tirpitz* and her force to appear over the southern horizon at any minute. Instead we wove our way among freshets of mini-icebergs and some very surprised U-boats who had been shadowing the convoy and had taken the opportunity to recharge their batteries on the surface. By firing our secondary armament at them they very quickly submerged; while we prepared for *Tirpitz*.

If we are to be sympathetic to the outcome of this story, we must now try to put ourselves in the position of Commander Broome in *Keppel*. He and his convoy had been doing so well. Now he was ordered by Admiralty to do something he well knew was suicidally impossible: to forsake his convoy and let the ships meander their individual ways within that ice-bound lake at the mercy of German U-boats and torpedo aircraft with virtually no White Ensign protection. It was like yielding a personal flock of innocent sheep to the mercy of a pack of hungry and unimpeded wolves. Yet what else could he do? He allocated such protection as he could to the dispersing, or scattering, convoy from his longer-endurance corvettes and "proposed" (this is important) to Admiral Hamilton that his six fast torpedo-armed destroyers should join the cruisers as a torpedo attack force in order to form a more formidable opposition to *Tirpitz* when we sighted her: there would then be more chance to play long-bowls and at least possibly wound her so that our Battle Fleet could have the chance of bringing her to action. (Admiral Fraser's battleship flagship and his destroyers were later to deal similarly with *Scharnhorst* in the same area.)

Admiral Hamilton approved Commander Broome's proposal: and so a force of four 8″ cruisers and now some nine destroyers with their turrets and torpedo tubes at the ready prepared to meet *Tirpitz*. And nothing happened. The rest, as in Hamlet, was silence. No sign of the enemy. No word from Admiralty. No amplifying report. Nothing . . . just the slight lightening of an Arctic "dawn" a few hours later while we were still steering west, all dressed up and nowhere to go. Anticlimax. The cruisers refuelled the destroyers. By now distress signals were pouring in by the minute from the scattered merchantmen being picked off mercilessly by U-boats or enemy torpedo-bombers; and these included the tanker *Alderdale*, the only source of oil from which Broome's destroyers could have re-fuelled to continue their original mission.

A kind of sun was up now on July 5th. What had happened? What had *not* happened? Still no word from Admiralty. It was a very dejected scene compared to just a few hours beforehand. We set course slowly south west. Broome urged returning to protect his decimated convoy; but from where was he to get the oil to do so after what the cruisers had given him became exhausted? Moreover, it was now some eight hours since the moment of scattering, so that such merchantmen as were still afloat, some with a corvette or trawler as their only protection, would have been 100 or more miles apart from each other, and thus beyond all possible hope of being collected together again.

The catastrophe of PQ17 is a classic case in the history of sea power of the threat of a fleet (though in this case really only one ship) "in being" but not used. In fact *Tirpitz*, by being where she was, poised in Altenfiord, had persuaded Admiralty to scatter the convoy. This done, she could leave it to U-boats and aircraft to pick off their prey in twenty-four-hours daylight without risking any damage to Hitler's remaining "Knight Move" unit in relatively confined waters against heavy Allied cruisers and destroyers and eventually, if wounded by them, Tovey's battle fleet. (In fact she only emerged from Altenfiord for a short period on July 5th and then went back again.) And so, of those original 38 heavily-laden merchantmen who originally sailed from Iceland, only 11 eventually reached Russian ports–they and a handful of equally gallant little escorts. By heroism and improvisation, by tucking themselves into the polar ice and camouflaging their own hulls with ice-like colours, by creeping down the coast of Novaya Zemlya, these few, "we happy few" who as of St. Crispin's Day could bare the scars to tell the tale, made Russian ports. In the loss of over two-thirds of the convoy, 3,350 vehicles, 430 tanks, 210 aeroplanes and 100,000 tons of general cargo were sunk.

While this was going on, while every few minutes came the pathetic final death call on the radio from yet another victim on that morning of the 5th, with still no amplifying situation report from Admiralty, bewildered and impotent as we were, Admiral Hamilton instructed me to draft a short Report of Proceedings (i.e. the situation as he saw it at that moment) to send to his C-in-C, who was presumably now within range of our amphibian Walrus aircraft. I scribbled to the best of my ability against the clock in pencil. I took it first to the Captain (also my Chief Staff Officer) who in turn took it to discuss with my Admiral. There was not much time to cavil about the mistakes of grammar, nomenclature or punctuation; for the C-in-C was himself keeping wireless silence and would not have known where his advanced cruiser force was, following the order from Admiralty to withdraw at high speed the previous evening. The waiting Walrus revved up on its catapult. I had to be quick.

'Twenty eight years later, together with a more considered effort written during our dejected return to Iceland, those hastily pencilled words were to be dissected by legal counsel under the microscopes of their profession in The High Court of Justice. At the end of that legal day (or rather years), it was established that, contrary to the allegations of David Irving's 1968 book, *The Destruction of Convoy PQ17*, Broome was not a coward, that he didn't disobey my admiral's orders, and above all that in spite of the disaster none of those emotional traditions of the Navy, jealously guarded over centuries, had been betrayed. At what a price! And all the internal naval post mortems had, of course, now been resurrected.

Great play was to be made during the court case of written messages sent by Walrus aircraft between Admiral Hamilton and Commander Broome concerning the route of the convoy, north or south of Bear Island, the unexpectedly receded iced-limit, the range of torpedo-bombers from Banak in north Norway, and so forth: all red herrings to justify the libellous attack on Broome.

All that had happened was that ice reconnaissance to Hamilton had revealed that the edge was further north than anticipated. This he had told Broome so that he, at his discretion, could route his convoy further north while still making eastwards. Broome's actual navigationl position (understandably in such conditions) was in fact some 30 miles south of where he thought he was: so he didn't alter course as far northwards as Hamilton expected. Typically Mr Irving elicited this as "disobedience" by Broome of the Admiral's orders – that Hamilton was "furious" and so forth. Vicious fabrication. That my Admiral was even cross with Broome is nonsensical.

I had to spend a long time trying to explain to counsel of the Defence that my admiral, who had been dead for some years, was not a "cross" kind of person, that he was doing no more than, with Broome, trying to help the convoy get eastward, such help coming from the fact that the ice was further north than either could have predicted. Mr. Irving in his book had chosen to interpret this as disobedience of orders from his superior by Broome—pure mischief.

Regarding the chain of command, a great deal was to hinge on this in the court case, along the same lines of Broome's supposed "disobeying" of his Admiral's orders.

The question of the Naval Intelligence available to the First Sea Lord also arises. As the aftermath of PQ17 was subsequently to be encrusted as much with law as with the polar ice, it is not inappropriate here to introduce someone who, in the opinion of others (he himself was too modest), was to become a most distinguished Director of Naval Intelligence: the late Vice Admiral Sir Norman Denning, fifth son of that remarkable Whitchurch family which includes his elder brother Tom, until recently an equally distinguished Master of the Rolls.

PQ17 was to involve the Denning family in two ways they could not have expected; first the younger brother's role as Operational Intelligence adviser to the First Sea Lord at the time, Admiral of the Fleet Sir Dudley Pound; and secondly the elder brother's role as Master of the Rolls, Chairman of the Court of Appeal, before whose tribunal naturally came the appeal from Cassell & Co. and Mr. David Irving following the heavy defamatory and exemplary damages (under the Devlin rules) awarded against them in favour of Captain Broome in Mr. Justice Lawton's court of the first instance. To take the subsequent reflections of the younger brother in his own words: "Why was PQ17 such a failure?"

"We knew from information received through Swedish sources that an attack on the convoy by surface forces was planned and that *Tirpitz* would be moved northwards from Trondheim... From the decrypted German signal traffic we knew that *Scheer* and some destroyers had arrived at Altenfiord and that *Tirpitz* had joined them there. Undoubtedly, the intention was to make a sortie to attack the convoy. When the First Sea Lord visited my room no positive intelligence had been received that the squadron had left Altenfiord but the timing was such that if *Tirpitz* had already sailed an attack on the convoy could be expected within a matter of hours. From all my previous experience I was convinced that if *Tirpitz* had sailed we would have had certain indications. Admittedly this was all based on negative intelligence but when the First Sea Lord left my room I was satisfied that he had accepted my explanation of the situation. What made him change his mind if he had so accepted the situation, no one will ever know. Alas!–his decision firstly to disperse, amended a few minutes later to scatter the convoy, was his and his alone....

"Since that time, I have never lost sight of the fact that the lack of my impact upon the First Sea Lord was such that he did not have sufficient confidence in my judgement. This seemed strange to me, as over the months I appeared to have built up the confidence of so many others even including that of the C-in-C Home Fleet."

Strange for Ned Denning, and a tragedy for hundreds of men and thousands of tons of vital material for Russia–because of course the hunch of the First Sea Lord's adviser on Intelligence was right. *Tirpitz* in fact scarcely put her bow out of harbour.

During my interrogation by counsel through the libel action I had frequently been asked how well I knew the admiral for whom I was presuming to act as surrogate. As I had been with him for precisely one month, the truth was hardly at all; and after the three years I was to serve him daily at sea and in Malta I got not much closer. I couldn't even pronounce the names of some of the fox-hunting packs he adored. He was tone-deaf and on occasion had to be nudged to stand up at the first chord of the National Anthem. I can't recall having ever seen him reading a book: we had nothing at all in common: and yet one couldn't help serving him loyally, because he possessed that indefinable charisma called leadership.

Chapter 20

The Devil You Know—1944

Malta. January 1944. The siege was just over, endurance of which was to win the island the George Cross. The people were emerging from their catacombs, tunnels within the sandstone from which all Malta's buildings are built, into the rubble and devastation left by Hitler's Luftwaffe and Mussolini's accomplices. Apart from the crumpled results of bombs, there were the monuments to the efforts of those who had helped the Maltese to survive: the hulk of *Ohio* from perhaps the most celebrated relief convoy, the like of which had been fought through by dint of colossal naval support and bravery: the wreckage of aircraft in memory to *Faith*, *Hope* and *Charity*, the three Gladiator fighters of renown. The siege, the perpetual bombing of Malta, was over. The war was not. Convoys still had to survive submarine attack. The Eighth Army, Tunis and Sicily behind them, were held towards their advance up the Italian mainland, where the Headquarters of Allied Command had moved. The Mediterranean theatre may have become less dramatic but nevertheless was still on the world's stage.

Fort Lascaris, an ancient stronghold of the Knights of Malta, damaged but not destroyed by bombing and commanding a superb view overlooking the Grand Harbour and Calcara, Vittoriosa (or what remained of them) beyond, became the Headquarters of the Vice Admiral commanding the waters of the Central Mediterranean. For the next year my being, my whole life was to be contained within a sandstone cell with two casement windows overlooking Grand

Harbour. A ping-pong table as the operations plot with portable telephone wires dangling beneath it, a chart or two pinned to the walls, a camp-bed, a table for signals and another for occasional food was my world; for where else and for what else was there to escape? This in itself was comfort. There is indeed comfort, I found, within a world encompassed by prison-like conditions. Worries become so utterly confined to the moment. The world shrinks and thereby poses few demands beyond the moment–provided you don't think too much.

Before dawn on any day: still dark; wearing a kimono to protect me from the sand flies, I would stand at the casement overlooking the harbour. From far below would come the metallic cries of the young boy goatherds, goading their emaciated flocks up the strada steps to sell what they could from their udders to hovels along their route. Then surreptitiously the beginning of the day would creep up as the bells across the harbour began to chime, calling Catholics to awake: the sandstone barraca cliffs began to shed their black battlements to reveal at first a dim russet, which then turned into an ever-brightening ochre and yellow. With the light extinguishing the glow of churches, the bells quietened, the goatherd stopped his exhortations, the sun gathered heat. Another day had begun. Lovers of *Tosca* will need no prompting as to where I was in my reveries: on the battlements of Castel Sant' Angelo not all that much further north in Rome: and as the bells silenced I too used to choose that uninterrupted moment to write to my loved one only to be roused, not by a gaoler with "*L'ora*", but by a Wren Plotting Officer with, "Excuse me, sir: Convoy M.R.S.16 is threatened by submarines south of Sardinia and what are you going to do about it?"

So I passed 1944, unhappily frustrated at being thus confined ashore while my friends and contemporaries were fighting at sea. Their brief appearances and assurances that somebody had to do what I was doing kept me going: but it could have been done, and probably better, by somebody unfit for sea. I felt a fraud as somebody who had survived *Repulse* and Singapore, surely for a more active contribution than this? It seemed a heavy price to pay for being the devil you know in the eyes of my Admiral. Then, as invariably happens when least expected, frustration evaporated.

When the Fifteenth Cruiser Squadron under Admiral "Jack" Mansfield in *Orion* was ordered to support the liberation of Greece (and so ensure the best chance to return democracy, as opposed to Communist, government there), I was lent to him as a replacement for his sick Staff Officer Operations. I never welcomed fortune more. My temporary appointment as the devil my Admiral did *not* know was to be among my most happily constructive during the war – and for once not in defeat.

Between my return to Malta in early 1945 and V.E. Day a few months later the maritime war in the Mediterranean was little more than dealing with spasmodic, desultory attacks by exhausted U-boats upon convoys still passing through on their way to the British effort in the Pacific War, still far from over. V.E. day in Malta was tame compared to London's, but at the end of my war service the thrill of my first sight of my homeland coast was as keen as ever. Now, together with millions of others like me, I could begin really to know the girl I had married and meet our first-born (in my case, now two years old) virtually for the first time.

Sometimes my generation may be forgiven for wondering: as we watch the struggle domestically between Left and Right, about the character of our own national self-denigration. What exactly *did* we fight to preserve? But it only needs one second of common sense to recapture confidence in ourselves; for one knows – for all the increase in crime, for all the understandable reactions of an over-populated island whose natural resources can no longer sustain its work-force, and whose outlets into the business of the world are now so contracted – that the youngsters so frequently in trouble through boredom today would not fail their country in adversity (of which the Falklands incident is an example) any more than their fathers and grandfathers did. Small wonder that foreigners find it hard to gauge the British: for we find it hard enough to gauge ourselves. Therein lies the mystery of our national Enigma Variations, albeit in a different sense from what Elgar was trying to say.[1]

---

[1]Those sentiments were expressed a decade ago. The performance of our Boys and Girls in the Gulf War would seem to justify them.

FACE THE MUSIC

A SAILOR'S STORY

Part 3

1946-1968

...and Peace, a Miscellany

War ends in peace, and morning light
  Mounts upon midnight's wing....

Michael Wigglesworth, 1669

Thank God for peace! Thank God for peace!
  When the great grey ships come in....

Guy Carryl, 1873-1904

PART III

.... and Peace, a Miscellany

Introduction

If these recollections of a naval life should only reach as far as war and, as a regular officer trained for such beforehand, include such training as prologue and stop, then at the age of thirty two I should. But to fight a war, although of course it must constitute the kernel of a service life if and when it happens, was no more my purpose in entering the Navy than it was to the millions of reservists who had not but likewise found themselves having to do so. The only difference, as I have previously hinted, is that my life did not have to turn a professional somersault whereas theirs did. In presuming to try to write my story, of which war was an inescapable ingredient, inconspicuously performed as a junior officer, my reason was to try to re-live the colours and the shades of a fortunate life more concerned with the environmental changes within a great Service over some forty years rather than to describe battles in which I seemed invariably to be on the losing side! Colossal geniuses like Mozart or Schubert terminated their lives at comparable age; and who can guess what either would have achieved had they lived as long as Liszt, Wagner or Brahms? Would Nelson have faded under political controversy had he not died at the crescendo of his destiny? But most ordinary mortals have their testing times somewhere in the middle of an ordinary life and then, still on their professional shelves in so-called retirement, or an advanced Age of Man, experience anti-climax which is nonetheless still part of their *raison-d'être*.

Although even war can stage its occasional lighter moments to punctuate its tragedies, somehow it did not seem becoming to include them overmuch in chronicling the several catastrophes with which fate decided I should be confronted during those six years. They were sombre times during which hopefully I grew up. I watched the heroism and stamina of others overcome what I have repeatedly asked myself if I could have thus surmounted had Providence been less kind to me. I cried much inwardly and laughed little outwardly. So when release from strain finally encompassed me, I found myself before the spiritual mirror a very different person: still dressed in dark blue as a serving Lieutenant Commander, and so to the Navy just a slightly less junior officer; I could continue to be of use. Yet to myself I was flotsam with no longer the specialised Alma Mater of my original Navigation Branch to nurture me: no particular expertise to direct me up any particular channel: I thought about quitting together with the countless others in the Reserves going back to their original professions. But as I *had* no other profession this did not seem practicable.

So I stayed—in fact for another twenty three years after the War. It was an entirely orthodox ascent of a ladder of the kind any normal man or woman should accomplish if he or she is lucky enough to remain in one profession for any length of time. There were few fireworks, endless fascinating personal relationships, a great deal of luck and sustained happiness which together eventually took me into the higher branches of a tree I felt I had no modern technological qualifications with which to climb.

That being the case, I felt I could not, having had the conceit to embark upon this facing of personal music, end on the tragic movement of war. As symphonic custom often dictates, I am ending with some kind of rondo: and so this last movement scampers in time over more than half of my years in navy blue while dwelling in fact only shortly on the lighter escapades. Every now and then there was the bar of the high jump which you might or might not be able to surmount, even for the third time of asking or more: promotion; but generally life became a flight of hurdles which we may all jump, given a rhythmic stride: and if you knock one down it only temporarily checks, as distinct from elimination from the race.

I dwell therefore in this last Act, as it were, mostly on the lighter side: the sailor who is inimitable and the environment of the ships which make him so.

I do not use chapters, because life wasn't like that any more – just the scenes which linger from some of the differing and successive appointments I was fortunate enough to hold between 1946 and 1968 when I left the active list.

1946

Bringing home the boys – *and* girls

The end of the War found tens of thousands of Service men and women overseas, waiting to be demobilised and returned home to their previous way of life, professions and families. The owners of liners, requisitioned as troopships during the conflict, were clamouring for their return to be refurbished into their original role. The Navy therefore removed the aircraft from every carrier it could spare from such operational commitments as remained and used their vast accommodation potential to bring home its own. Between V.E. and V.J. days, our largest Fleet Carriers had at first been grudgingly accepted by the Americans in the Pacific to help their Fleets under their great Admiral Nimitz in the final Allied confrontation with the Japanese. Our contribution under Admiral Sir Bruce Fraser was regarded in more complimentary vein when the Japanese Kamikaze pilots penetrated the unarmoured decks of the American carriers and bounced off the armoured decks of ours. Such were *Indomitable, Indefatigable, Illustrious, Victorious, Formidable* – now stripped of all air-arm potential. I was appointed First Lieutenant of *Indomitable* in early 1946. It sounded something of an also-ran appointment. It turned out to be as fascinating an exercise in tactful personnel administration as one could wish for.

My job was the internal running of this vast, converted carrier for people of both sexes instead of aeroplanes: their accommodation, their well-being, their entertainment to keep them out of mischief with nothing to do but relax throughout a ten-thousand-mile voyage in a warship in sunshine and with no responsibilities other than to behave themselves, the tensions of war behind them, their families and a return to peace-time conditions ahead.

The way these temporary troopships each approached their artificial task depended of course upon the Captain's outlook on the problem. By the time we reached home from the Far East we were carrying 3,000 passengers, who included some very attractive young ladies—Wrens and V.A.D.s—well out-numbered by unmarried sailors who had enjoyed no social contact with their like for many past moons. It was therefore a nice administrative balance to decree the places and times, often under moonlight on a calm sea, when the two sexes could, as it were, overlap. In *Indom* under my enlightened Captain William Andrewes (later Admiral Sir William) we decided that, within reason, the less repressive the rules the more likely they were to be observed—with severe consequences to either of the sexes who kicked over the traces.

People were very happy and co-operative. They were going home from war stations and therefore, with reason, stood little upon seniority in accepting my accommodation on offer—with one exception throughout our three ventures to Australia, Colombo and Hong Kong. On the latter voyage our passengers included two Captains of precisely equal seniority, a Paymaster and an Engineer. I had two single cabins to allot them, one with a scuttle and no running water and the other vice versa. The Paymaster was charming, the Engineer recalcitrant. He belly-ached from the start. It was the only occasion on which I had to tell my Captain, on my evening visit to him in his sea-cabin, that I was in trouble.

My Captain suggested to the Engineer Captain that he should go ashore in Aden and wait for the Woolworth Carrier coming along a week behind us. He took the point, and harmonious relations were restored.

Home for Christmas to end *Indom*'s temporary trooping duties. I couldn't see what channel within the Navy I could next pursue which led to any particular harbour. Fun as all this had been, it led nowhere. Since I was unqualified for command of a destroyer or any specialised role, the future looked bleak; so when next day my Captain informed me that I was to become the First Lieutenant and Cadet Training Officer of *Frobisher*, the cruiser converted for this purpose and successor to my beloved *Vindictive* of pre-war days, the sun came out. I did know a bit about how to navigate this challenging channel; and it was generally accepted that officers appointed to train ex-Dartmouth fledglings, at sea for the first time, had hitherto to have conducted themselves, if only to their own satisfaction, also to that of Their Lordships.

On docking alongside at Portsmouth after one of these Far East excursions my first job was with the Customs Officers; and it *was* a job. Three thousand passengers with every kind of luxury to declare (or not), over past years unobtainable in rationed Britain. By hanging the sword of Damocles over would-be prevaricators, on the whole the sailors behaved well, and Customs were more than fair. With the ship "cleared", families were allowed on board. I had just greeted mine in my cabin, popular for what I had brought home, when the officer I was to succeed in *Frobisher* appeared. Well known as a bachelor and a training fanatic, he began to tell me even then what would be expected of me after my fortnight's leave.

At that time there was curious creed that those best qualified to train the young should have neither wife, nor therefore (presumably) any young of their own–such philosophy supposedly stemming from the idea that in non-working hours they would not therefore be distracted from their attentions towards their charges, day or night. There were those of us who felt that a family man was perhaps more experienced in the problems confronting the young; but be that as it may, my predecessor was rabidly of the old school. Casting a perfunctory glance at Rosalind and our three-year-old arranging the tins of ham and fruit in patterns on the deck, he weighed right in.

"You won't be able to do this job married, you know."

"What do you mean, Walter?"

"Well you just won't have the time."

"But aren't we at sea most of the year?"

"Yes, but it's twenty four hours a day, seven days a week."

"I see. What am I to do? Divorce Rosalind?"

Silence. Then I ventured: "You know, Walter, if it wasn't for the ladies, you wouldn't have any little cadets to train."

"See you in a fortnight," he said. And went.

1947

Ten years on in shaping embryos

January. The windswept quarterdeck of *Frobisher*, moored astern of my late *Indom*. Walter was pacing rapidly up and down while I tried to keep up. Around us ran, or lurked in feigned cleaning operations, scores of Naval Cadets dressed in motley uniforms, half officer and half sailor. This was what was called a turn-over between him and me.

"Look at that," he shouted. "That's what you're up against. Come here, You"—as a very small figure shuffled before him. "Look at those boots! One laced horizontal and the other criss-cross. Go and shift at once."

"Dreadful," I said, concealing my own shoelaces which had a knot in them. "We must put that right . . ."

As soon as were plunging into a westerly gale heading for my birthplace, "putting it right" merely meant removing the fear of punishment from the youngsters under training, so that they could begin to regard themselves as human beings of some potential instead of butts of censure for trivial if traditionally nautical indiscretions. *"Plus est en vous"*—as years later I found the motto of Kurt Hahn's Gordonstoun to be and which I believed even then. Remove fear from the average young and they will generally blossom. Some of my charges, the sword of Damocles removed, did so promptly.

I suppose it isn't surprising that, even at that age, those who were likely to reach the highest rungs of the ladder displayed some distinctive characteristics. War of course had taken its toll of many whom I had first known in *Vindictive* as Cadets in 1938; but for example, I see among my notes of that time that I had written against a certain Cadet Lewin of the Foretop Division: "promising." As he is now an Admiral of the Fleet in the House of Lords, ex-Chief of Defence Staff during the Falklands Task Force conflict, perhaps I wasn't far wrong; and there are many who, in the course of their ascent to distinguished Flag Rank or the Victoria Cross, I may be forgiven for watching over the years with some interest. Perhaps the Navy, despite its reputation for philistinism, some critics might even say sadism, did conjure the best out of its young by a process of survival of the fittest; and whatever it did so conjure acquitted itself not too badly when confronted by the test of war.

Yet if our methods were thought to be tough, a visit by *Frobisher* up the Chesapeake for a week of exchange methods with the American Naval Academy at Annapolis adjusted the perspective. Each day a hundred of ours changed places with a hundred of theirs who were several years older. Interesting. By indoctrinating our British youth to the rigours of discipline so comparatively young, we could take it gently. By waiting until nineteen, not only well past puberty but often already engaged to be married, the Americans had to use shock tactics during that first year when their raw naval recruits were known as "Plebes", in order to drive out any pretensions of individualism as a start to their four years' training. Plebes, to my way of thinking, were dressed like convicts in white dungarees. They were not allowed to converse except among themselves. At table they were not allowed to start eating before their seniors, yet had to finish first. They couldn't just walk down a corridor without what was called "squaring the corners". Dartmouth, let alone *Frobisher*, seemed a feather-bed by comparison. The visit thus served its purpose in persuading our youngsters that they were not so harshly treated.

But by now *Frobisher* had become an octogenarian and thus transferred her maternal role to *Devonshire*, a 10,000-ton County Class cruiser with superb class-room and mess-deck accommodation, three funnels and still a single 8-inch turret for'ard (which didn't have to work). At least we thought she looked superb; she looked the part which prompted a documentary film crew to ask if they could spend a week with us to demonstrate how this naval crèche conducted itself at sea. We spread and furled that quarterdeck awning until our hands were raw. Guards and bands, bugles and pipes blew endlessly as we approached anchorage in Loch Broom at Ullapool in Wester Ross. My wife had come to meet me and was sitting on the point, watching, when she heard a tourist "wifey" comment, "Maybe she's a kind of a carrrgo boat . . . ?"

Cargo boat or not, we were then sent to represent Britain for the ninetieth birthday celebrations of King Gustav V of Sweden in

Stockholm. Of all the inland voyages in the world, that from the Almagrundet light vessel in the Baltic, through the miles of a narrow tortuous channel in the archipelago which eventually debouches into the great amphitheatre of Stockholm harbour, is of the most dramatic. There is no question of navigating apart from radar and the leading lines or beacons which point the way as precisely as when driving a car between the white lines. From the thirty foot freeboard deck of a 10,000 ton cruiser you look down on the roofs of the chalets, each on its own little holiday island of wealthy and scantily clad waving Swedes who, shall we say, whetted the sailors' appetite for the girls they were to meet; then suddenly you are underneath the waterfront of the capital, royal palaces, spectacular and beautiful of their kind and today bathed in June sunshine.

We moored in a privileged position because, for all their national military inferiority complex, in this century bred of neutrality, they seemed to hold a certain respect for our Navy; maybe because their own had also suffered their disasters. (Most notable was in the case of *Vasa*, The King's Ship, which must have made the shortest voyage in history by any man-of-war.) Came the day when in brilliant sunshine on his ninetieth birthday the old King drove among his people in an open carriage, his great-grandson aged two—now the present King—on his mother's knee beside him. They are an undemonstrative race. There was mild clapping from those lining the route. Imagine the euphoria in London for our Sovereign in similar circumstances. In command of the British contingent of cadets and sailors I was at attention, minding my own business with sword at the carry, when up drove a plumed Duke of Plaza-Toro who leaped from his carriage and suddenly pinned a medal on my breast: then on to our Lieutenant carrying the Colour. To "Hearts of Oak" behind our Royal Marine Bank we marched through the streets in step to wild applause. Next day a headline in the press was BRITISH SHOW THE WORLD HOW TO MARCH. Whenever admonished the Cadets were to throw this back in my face for months to come. It transpired that we were the only two British citizens to receive this personal medal from the King and I did not see it again worn for thirty years when, standing with my bow and arrows on the staircase of Holyrood Palace as a member of the Queen's Bodyguard for Scotland, I witnessed again that little child, now the King of Sweden, on a state visit to Her Majesty in Edinburgh.

We sailed next day. At that time, when you left Sweden direct for Norway, you had to be circumspect not to advertise the fact to either nation: particularly so in our case as when offered asylum by the Swedes when Germany invaded his country, King Haakon had given a one word answer and with his government had come to Britain in this very ship *Devonshire*. We were therefore accorded a tremendous welcome in Oslo harbour into which I was thrown at midnight daylight on 30th June 1948. In those days a signal from Admiralty twice a year announced promotions to Captain and Commander at the drop of a hat. You pretended not to worry unduly, but of course you did. The brass hat was the first real hurdle in a naval career when within the zone of eligibility.

1949

French Leave

My appointment as the Naval member on the Junior Directing Staff of that élite military establishment in Belgrave Square, the Imperial Defence College (now the Royal College of Defence Studies), had meant that after ten years of marriage Rosalind and I could see the seasons round together for the first time and even plan a holiday together with certainty. Paris in the Spring for a fortnight on a permitted £25 each ...*les marronières* in blossom ... the *haute couture* ladies with little dogs on leads lifting their little legs on every tree in the Champs Elysées... the contrast of the berets and little cheroots hanging over the Left Bank ... the sheer delight of what you could see for nothing of some of the masterpieces of the world in such differing settings ... to bask in this climate for a few days, all thoughts of Navy dispelled with no likelihood of any recall telegram, is why this little interlude became a punctuation mark in our life together.

From the trivia of the personal to the serious; the creation of the I.D.C. was a brainchild of Winston Churchill between the two Wars, when Imperial Defence was a less illusory concept than it is today. Winston established the I.D.C. for senior military officers of high potential in order to give them a chance to become whole people in their respected exalted spheres, with time and opportunity to think as opposed always to be having to be doing. And so it has turned out that—with the conspicuous exception of Montgomery, who may not at the time have held with such interruptions to physical preparation for war—there are few if any other officers to have held high command in any of the three Services who have not benefited from their sabbatical year; bereft of responsibility, subjected to lecturers of the highest expertise in their respective careers—ambassadors, economists, Cabinet Ministers, Prime Ministers themselves, leaders of Commonwealth and foreign countries—students are asked to listen, think, produce their syndicated judgement on the world's problems, visit many parts of the world as onlookers and individually try to equip themselves beyond the calling of their respective individual careers. As a junior Staff Officer whose job was to help arrange their curriculum and various demands on journeys overseas, I was entranced by the happy irresponsibility of the established leader when divorced from such leadership. The most distinguished, who were to become even more distinguished, revelled in their temporary abandonment of pressures in the most hilarious, if sometimes, embarrassing ways There were few who did not mislay their passports.

Winston's vision has been justified. The original small number of senior British military officers as students has now grown to include not only Civil Servants of every Ministry in London but also representatives of any Commonwealth country, black or white, of any Service, and with a sprinkling of officers from NATO countries to inject the leavening.

I ought of course mostly to remember this exalted aspect of my two years in such august company, but I did admit that this part of my story would be a soufflé. Came our last day on that Paris holiday with mighty little left of the allowed £50 between us. A lovely Sunday...could we go to Longchamps and not bet?...of course...the last race...let's just risk a *few* remaining francs and hell to lunch from Le Gard du Nord next day. We chose a name and I went to the *guichet*...it wasn't running, so I slid one down to Cosmo de Medici. We found him cropping the grass, the most moth-eaten animal you could imagine mounted by an even more decrepit jockey. So that was that?

The race ended not even in a photo finish but a *"photo generale"* among the ten runners, from which mêlée emerged . . . Cosmo de Medici at 100 to 1. Rosalind wore the lovely lace blouse from the Rue Saint Honoré for many years and we lunched well towards Calais. So—maybe for less laudable reasons than higher military education, I have affectionate memories of Imperial Defence.

1950

Operational Aircraft Carrier

My two years of sophisticated respite in Belgrave Square were brought to an abrupt end and jerked me down, if not exactly to earth, then onto the flight deck of a light Fleet Carrier, H.M.S. *Ocean*, on Christmas Eve. Ten years ago to the day I had asked if Boxing Day would do to join *Repulse*; it didn't then, and nor apparently would it do now. I released a disinterested predecessor in Plymouth, who clearly had had little stomach for the trooping role, ex-Reserve Fleet, of this "flat-top", and spent Christmas Eve wandering around a dead ship; and when one of H.M. Ships is dead it is very dead, horribly quiet, eerie, as if pleading like a deserted dog: "Why don't you want me any more?"

But they did want her. I had been given six months to transform her into the operational flagship of the Admiral (Air) of the Mediterranean Fleet after a refit at Rosyth. As I wandered around the rusting, dirty hangars and gangways and empty messes, the trappings of what had once been alive, somewhere on some lone loudspeaker the voice of that single King's College chorister fluting "Once in Royal David's City . . ." stimulated me to think that the impossible must be possible—somehow. It was a hollow Christmas Day, at best survived, and with hardly a soul on board. A sympathetic Captain might have tried to ease my strangeness as a new second-in-command—but not this one. I had served under him twenty years before, during my destroyer training on the China Station, and so knew his idiosyncracies, which now included getting out of this crate as quickly as possible. Somehow we got to Rosyth, where he left me and the ship at a buoy in the Firth of Forth in a Force 8 gale and went to bed with a cold. He then thankfully disappeared; and I began. But *where* to begin...? The little dockyard would of course take care of operational transformation, and did; but there are furbelows which are not in such remit. For a start, the Wardroom would consist of over a 100 officers of diverse professional expertise, from flying aeroplanes rather fast to making their aerodrome move along at more than thirty knots, all equally important and who would expect their Mess to be suitably equipped as their home at sea. There were no funds for this project.

Came the day when *Ocean* was beginning to look respectable and when, having been hitherto responsible only for her face-lift, I welcomed my new Captain (the late Admiral Sir Charles) Evans, whom his beautiful and deliciously unorthodox and controversial wife invariably and affectionately referred to as "the red fellow" on account of his arresting beard. Charles Evans, a naval fighter pilot and a hero of the Taranto raid, was equally unorthodox and therefore refreshing; he was in fact the first fighter pilot to command a carrier. His lack of experience in the running of any ship, let alone one of this size, was equalled by mine in aviation. Such maybe are the best partnerships. Under him, in spite of, or maybe because of, his whimsical yet efficiently successful approach to the command of that polyglot community, the aircraft carrier, I count my experience in *Ocean* as one summit of all my happiness in the Navy, and for a variety of reasons.

Even by naval standards the running of an operational aircraft carrier—the most precious of our ships, as recently proved yet again in their role as Flagship of the 1982 South Atlantic Task Force—presents an enthralling challenge. Their main armament is of course the Air Group they carry, a comparatively small number of highly skilled and trained intrepid young men, whose role is to fly sophisticated machines rapidly about the sky in defence of the Fleet by engaging the enemy in combat or attacking their ships or territory, before returning to base—which to them looks like a tiny ribbon of undulating airstrip on the high seas. This achievement requires a certain kind of approach to life, and in the case of those who fly fastest demands a panache, a compelling sense of the dramatic coupled with the finest judgement concerning the limits to which they can drive themselves consistent with the rules they must obey. They are stimulating people who can outwardly cast care aside and yet inwardly are hightly responsible to their ship and to each other.

So that they can achieve that role, their aerodrome has to steam for days on end, often at high speed, in all weathers. Beneath their life on and off the flight deck, in the air briefing rooms within the "island" superstructure, there exists another world. Hundreds of engineers in the engine and boiler rooms: hundreds in the hangars and aircraft workshops maintaining those machines: hundreds cooking and arranging the food from victualling stores so that all shall be fed well and on time: hundreds of electricians supplying enough power for a small town, of those who must arm the complexity of weapons, of those who tend the sick and injured. The enormous population of the wardroom, from its President and Commander to Midshipmen under training, Padres, doctors, plain sailors like myself–all these constitute a fascinating cross-section of special people, all dressed alike in dark blue maybe but very different in their respective contributions to the common task of making their carrier work efficiently.

The challenge for him whose job it is to blend this community on behalf of his Captain (who at sea can never leave the Bridge) is just that: a challenge. You must make the airmen realise what they owe to those below decks whom they may see infrequently–for once in harbour they disembark to a shore Air Station–just as you must make the stokers realise to what purpose they are sweating out their guts in the tropics. There are ways and means. Accommodation was spartan in dormitories of twelve for junior officers. By making air crew share fifty-fifty with ship's officers, each had to learn the problems of others. By making air-arm ratings live in close contact with the sailors who had to clean, work anchors, ropes and wires, man communications in W/T offices–so did each come to respect the others' contribution towards a common end. This may sound ridiculously easy to arrange: but it was not always so. As we arrived in the Mediterranean to embark the Air Group and begin our work-up, I knew that carriers tended to be either very happy ships or rather unhappy ones.

On their television screens during the Falklands operations, the viewing public watched the Harrier jump-jets rise vertically from the flight decks of *Hermes* and *Invincible*, swoop over San Carlos Bay at near sonic speed and then gently alight at the end of their mission like hawks alighting on their nests; but it was not always so. Before the days of the jump-jet and the angled flight deck–so simple an idea that like so many revolutionary inventions it remains a wonder why nobody thought of it sooner (before a naval aviator did)–arrangements for landing-on were less sophisticated. Across the after end of *Ocean*'s flight deck were stretched six or seven wires which, hydraulically controlled, acted like pieces of elastic. Stern down and with a hook lowered, the aircraft, still flying fast, had to catch one of these arresters to jerk itself to a standstill. If it did, well and good; if it didn't, it crashed into a wire barrier half way along the flight deck to prevent it running into those already landed and in the deck park for'ard. This was known as "barrier prang", which could have minor effects or, equally, result in the engine catching fire. It was matter of honour that pilots avoided such ignominy: but it happened.

Not being an aviator myself I never ceased to admire the skill of those boys as, at one-minute intervals, they brought in their machines onto a heaving flight deck, ninety nine times out of a hundred successfully; and because I was thus unskilled myself, they knew I was in no position to censure them for aviation malpractice if and when they did prang. Thus a kind of amateur bond grew between me and my junior wardroom with no disloyalty to our Captain, who was likely–and rightly so–to be less sympathetic in his judgement, being so distinguished an aviator himself. This all added to the psychology of running a carrier, for there were those who were accident-prone and those who were not. When a pilot realised that he had enjoyed hundreds of accident-free deck landings, even the best would become apprehensive that on the law of averages his turn must soon come; and when it did, please God and the Captain, it would not be fatal.

It was one horrid twilight off Malta as the last of the Air Group in his Sea Fury was due to land-on. The deck was heaving, wet, and visibility was rapidly dwindling. Tony was the best pilot of the lot and I knew he was twitched. He bounced between wires, hit the first barrier with his lowered undercarriage, somersaulted while his engine cavorted forward in flames... Silence while we held our breath. He lowered himself out of the cockpit upside down and unhurt. I sent two scribbled notes via my Midshipman; one to Tony telling him where the whisky was in my cabin before he reported to the Captain; the other tactfully to the Captain himself, just asking him to dwell a pause before professional admonishment. I presume to recount this incident because I believe that the sheer charisma of the Fleet Air Arm at its best is unquestionable and because my many friends within it taught me so much then of what was to stand me in inestimable stead later on.

President Truman having had the courage to mobilise NATO in defence of South Korea, a British light Fleet Carrier was then part of our contribution. *Ocean* would presumably therefore take her turn after service in the Mediterranean? I was promised by the Admiralty that this would not happen, as we were to become the Flagship of that fleet and that therefore our families could safely come out to Malta. They did, including my own; hundreds of them; so that when of course *Ocean* was ordered to Korea, at least I could confront my sailors and say that I had been ill-advised in all honesty, witness the presence of my own wife and child. They sucked their teeth and just accepted my explanation. A sailor's wife alone in Malta with her husband off Korea tends to watch the horizon for his return like Madam Butterfly; and like Pinkerton he won't appear, if ever, for a long time: but that's naval life, if less traumatic than in Puccini's opera, for which I am ever grateful that he did not make the tenor a British naval officer!

Worse was to come: within a week of the ship sailing for the Far East I was suddenly ordered home to an Admiralty desk. This I could not expect my beloved ship's company to stomach, although it was as unpredictably true as it was embarrassing. It was the most difficult admission of circumstances I have had to confront. Clearly they thought I had betrayed them. Miserable, I was succeeded within days and left the ship to acquit herself brilliantly in her NATO operational role. Before I left it was decided to give a small "intimate" dance in the hangar by way of a swan-song for our families. A carrier can do anything: waterfalls and ducks on ponds (temporarily " borrowed" by the Midshipman from the Palace in Valetta, for which I had to answer); bowers of shrubs and plants; every kind of coloured electronic device blinking, every diversion to which expertise of aircraft technicians can be harnessed–and the next Sunday was my last on board.

1952

Appointing my contemporaries

"And in my court I sit all day,
Giving agreeable 'jobs' away.
With one for him—and one for he—
And one for you—and one for ye—
And one for thou—and one for thee—
But never, oh! never a one for me!"

—which possibly apt if prostituted quotation seemed to describe my tether to a desk overlooking St. James's Park tube station for the next two years.

My unexpected recall from *Ocean* to a London office had been because the Commander responsible for arranging the appointments of some 500 of our own rank and over 1,000 Lieutenant Commanders had himself been promoted, and needed an immediate successor. As I arrived he handed me a closely typed file. "Get this out of your system," he said, "and then we'll start the turn-over." "This" was a catalogue of confidential reports—and in the Navy they really *are* confidential (unlike in the Army), unseen by the victims—on my performance under umpteen commanding officers since I first went to sea. It was an embarrassing document to read, with every fault and indiscretion laid bare among the odd virtue. Little had they concealed: devastatingly perceptive were comments on what one had naively hoped had gone unnoticed by others. I was left to ponder them until I could stand no more, and put this dreadful testament back among those of my colleagues, never wishing to see it again.

During my time at the I.D.C. I had been questioned by many highly placed Civil Servants on the Navy's system of what every one knows of as the S206. It is worth a moment of print as the envy of many. Every time an officer leaves an appointment, one such report has to be written by his C.O.; and every time that C.O. leaves his command, sometimes embracing hundreds in his wardroom, he must write on each of his officers, detailing their qualities for higher rank or otherwise. The recipient does not see this unless–and this is the kernel–it enumerates faults he can rectify. "This officer has an unfortunate approach to his men. Efficient enough himself, he lacks the light or understanding touch to encourage those with less. The result is that he spoils himself in the eyes of those he should be leading with a brash confidence in his undisputed professionalism. Unless he can temper this he will not succeed in higher rank." Such is underlined in red ink, which means that the C.O. has sent for the officer, read the remarks aloud to him and discussed them with him. The future is then up to him.

Conversely there are drawbacks which an officer cannot help. "His crowning ambition is to become a naval attaché. He could probably accomplish this himself as a linguist, well read, professionally adequate and socially acceptable. Unfortunately his wife shares none of these attributes and would, in my opinion, immediately get under the skin of his Ambassador's wife to the detriment of whatever contribution that officer might subscribe. Not thus recommended but he'll be all right in a more mundane environment." This is not underlined in red because, short of ridding himself of his wife, there's nothing much the husband can do about it! Fair . . . ? At any rate these were the criteria on which I now had to work in interviewing officers for their next job every half hour.

It was daunting work because one held in one's palm–subject to (generally) perfunctory corroboration from my Captain, who had a thousand other things to consider–the fair chance of promotion for the majority of one's clients in the running. They all came eager in anticipation. Some you could satisfy: many you would have to disappoint, because it was already clear on past performance that no springboard was now going to lift them over that first five-bar gate to the coveted brass hat: and so they went sadly away and made me sad in their going.

1954

Command at The Cape

You virtually *had* to be promoted from that particular chair. Having had to read every detail about your contemporaries, it would be expecting too much to send you straight out into the civilian world, no longer bound by naval loyalty under a bowler hat; and so I was on my way as a newly promoted Captain to combine the post of Chief Staff Officer to the C-in-C South Atlantic with command of his frigates and, subsequently, tactical command during exercises of ships of the South African Navy. Rosalind and our youngest had been due to sail with me by Union Castle Line, about the last of the wives allowed to accompany sea-going husbands; but our daughter elected to give this world three extra weeks before arriving in it, and so I sailed south alone in May, out of season in a near empty *Winchester Castle*, where I hid myself in the corner of the smoking lounge to sketch the outline of this story. This mitigated the presence of the duty-free bar and eased my conscience in that, whether a word should ever see the light of day or not, at least I had tried to do *something* . . .

On arrival at Simonstown, still then the British naval base at the Cape, I called on my new C-in-C who already knew me. I was to take over command of a *Black Swan* type frigate next day.

"Nice to see you, Joc," he said. "Have a drink. You may need it." I raised my eyebrows. "I don't want to be unfair to your predecessor. He's had a difficult time beginning with South Korea straight from U.K. where the ship did well enough. Then she came here to the Cape where brandy is cheaper than beer and she's been in commission for nearly two years. The contrast has, I'm afraid, been too marked for her ship's company–an armchair job after limited war–and it's gone to their heads. I sense serious ill-discipline, which I hope you will forestall from becoming the ultimate. All I can say is that whatever you decide to do, I will support you. Good luck."

Soldana Bay is a natural inlet well north of Simonstown, the Scapa Flow of the Cape as a harbour and nothing else. There I took over my command on a Sunday evening and within the hour my predecessor had gratefully departed.

There are three moods within a warship. If your sailors are going cheerfully about their work, or if they are by habit declining a four-letter word more or less as a punctuation mark in harmless complaint about everything in general and about gunnery exercises in particular, then there is no cause for worry; but should they be quiet, there is. They were sizing me up, naturally, and the best place for them to do this was at sea. I didn't like what I saw or heard. The ship was filthy, and so it became clear in what areas in the first instance I would need the support of my C-in-C. I landed my Second-in-Command and the senior Lower Deck rating unceremoniously: appointed their immediate subordinates in their place: and cleared Lower Deck, which means addressing your whole ship's company except those on essential watch.

They shuffled aft, rebellious. I told them that there was now a line drawn beneath everything before my arrival, including a punishment return larger than in my aircraft carrier. I described my approach to leave-breaking: they could try it on if they chose and find out if I was bluffing. They and our ship were not to my liking. To be brought up to R.N. standards within a week ... " ... And as for your language, I am used to sailors' expletives since running a picket boat over twenty years ago as a Midshipman; but yours is nauseating. My cabin is above your mess-deck for'ard. My scuttles look out onto your fo'c's'le. You have to pass the little weather decks on either side of me to reach it. I will shut all my scuttles except those on the starboard side, for we are in hot weather. I like ladies and they may be in my cabin from time to time; so in order to remind you that you are passing my quarters on the starboard side, where my scuttles will be open, I will have a red line painted on the deck. Between those lines you will mind your tongues—or else . . . . "

They sucked their teeth again and shuffled for'ard.

Next morning a seaman was painting the boundary outside my cabin as instructed. He well knew I was within. A stoker who had evidently been on watch when I had addressed the ship's company stumbled over the paint pot, and the ensuing conversation went as follows:

"What are you f.....g doing?"

"Paintin' a f.....g line."

"What f.....g for?"

"Cos the f.....g skipper says we ain't to use such f.....g language."

So I poked my head out of my scuttle and said: "Fifteen-all"

Thus we started to get to know each other and didn't look back. We began in the best possible way with the annual anti-submarine exercises off Durban under my new C-in-C in his flagship, a distinguished, taciturn Scot. Admiralty sent out a conventional British submarine as target, and on this occasion she was joined by an uninvited guest, a Soviet submarine whose presence was subsequently corroborated by Naval Intelligence and which spent some time beneath me. The South African Navy were under my tactical command, their ships still commanded by ex-R.N. officers. All began well. I was the senior officer on the anti-submarine screen of the main body, but early on I managed to get this into a chaotic tangle. The exchange of naval signals are noted for their laconic brevity.

From the C-in-C: "What exactly do you think you're doing?"

From me: "Regrettably misinterpreting your intentions, sir."

From the C-in-C: "I am disappointed."

—which for me was to become a classic admonition in later life. As I was also, when ashore, Chief Staff Officer to Admiral Sir Ian Campbell who was frequently away visiting his huge parish, it was as well that he should have become quickly aware of my limitations. I did not know the Scots then, but through him I began to learn of their economy with words—at least at sea.

My successor in that London appointments chair eventually sent me out another Second-in-Command, an unusual extrovert whom I had known as a very junior R.N.V.R. and who is now a retired Admiral. He quickly transformed the ship for me. Rosalind meanwhile had been allowed to come and join me in Bosky Dell, an enchanting little original Boer house with a pillared step overlooking a Simonstown cove.

Having recuperated from weeks in dock, during which time the frigate had been torn apart and re-assembled, we had to sail for home. It was sad to have to say good-bye to Bosky Dell, its stoep and the happiness it had seemed to give to many of my company; but at least I got the impression that my C-in-C was no longer "disappointed" as, with Paying-Off Pendant flying, a foot for every day of the two-and-a-half-year commission, we left Simonstown one January morning for Plymouth via the Cape Verde Islands and Gibraltar. Only the albatross, the dolphin, Mother Carey's chickens and other stray birds (who somehow sense that the sailor loves them and thus perch on the upper yard-arm) accompanied us at our twelve knots.

Gibraltar was full of the combined Home and Mediterranean Fleets gathered for their annual manoeuvres. Our strange little uninvited addition with its white hull and single dark grey funnel crept apologetically between the moles and was told to berth alongside the flagship of the Admiral commanding flotillas. No sooner had I achieved this than I was sent for by the C-in-C, an awesome little man of naval renown, Admiral Sir Michael Denny, recently Controller of the Navy. What had I done to deserve this summons? He received me personally on his quarterdeck and congratulated me on the appearance of my little ship—*such* a little ship among the throng under his command.

Apparently there was stringent criticism in Admiralty about refits in other than H.M. Dockyards. Ships had been rejoining the Fleet improperly rejuvenated. He would therefore send his technical staff next day to comb the outcome of my Simonstown experiences. He gave me more than one drink and was kindness itself. Then I lunched with the Admiral whose flagship was accommodating me, an old friend. By this time I was a little heady and had to shift berth into the "Pens" where all small ships berth in Gib—one parking space left in a car-park otherwise full. I do not recommend driving a ship in confined waters unless sober, but on this occasion it was a case of "I drive better when I've had one or two". No engine order less than full ahead or full astern. No wheel order other than hard a'starboard or port. We shot round dredgers' wires, cruisers at anchor, carriers alongside, and safely into our allotted car-park without cracking an egg. "Ring off main engines"—to the relief of my shaken and perspiring navigating officer.

When we reached Plymouth to pay off, my Ship's Company gave me an inscribed, framed parchment describing what we had done together, containing every one of their names, some of them the most lovable "skates" I have known and who to this day sometimes write and tell me what they are doing. In the four corners are painted the flags of the International Code: "God Be With You."

I need hardly add that there had been times when I had been glad He had been.

1955

H.M.S. *St. Vincent*–a Naval Kindergarten

The row of symmetrically stark yet warm red-brick blocks, which once housed prisoners of the Napoleonic wars, overlooked the huge asphalt parade ground and the blue-domed belfry above the archway, which was the entrance to one of the two naval crèches for boys of sixteen who had chosen, or been persuaded, to join the Navy from Secondary Modern School. *St. Vincent* in Gosport held a mere 800; our larger sister, H.M.S. *Ganges* near Ipswich, held 2,000, and in those days (for alas neither of them live today) they together prepared the future Able Seamen, Chief Petty Officers and Warrant Officers for the Fleet. The teenagers in their first bell-bottoms were not the cleverest from grammar schools who would become Electrical or Engineer or Air Artificers and receive more advanced schooling: they were just enthusiastic, honest, generally lovable and at other times intractable, humorous, run-of-the-mill sons from every kind of decent working man's home in Britain, who were entrusted to our initial training methods for eighteen months before joining any kind of White Ensign ship in every corner of the world. I have since regarded command of them as among my more cherished experiences, for they were indeed honest and without guile; their devastating directness of reaction without emotion was often flattering and made one realise that if you are consistent and fair, while playing to the rules, such young charges will respond with respect. They asked so little and gave so much, invariably encouraged by proud parents who had that photo of the smiling face beneath the first cap-ribbon on the mantelpiece. I think it was the vexed subject of corporal punishment which first alerted me to the importance such sensible parents attach to the discipline of their young.

Punishment No.20 under the Naval Discipline Act of Parliament applied only to these two Boys' Establishments and consisted of not more than twelve and not less than six cuts of the cane for serious offences—"serious" in that context being, for instance, stealing half-a-crown from your neighbour in *Drake* dormitory. It could be awarded only by the Captain after hearing both evidence and defence (or otherwise) from the boy's Divisional Officer and, if so awarded, was executed only by the Master-At-Arms within half an hour, in the presence only of that officer, and after a medical check: I never awarded more than the minimum for a first offence and during my two years in command never had cause to repeat it to any boy. I had no more than two complaints from parents who accused me of being a sadistic bastard to be reported to their M.P. and the popular press. I had boys before me with tears in their eyes, begging me to award them the cane instead of stopping that precious one afternoon's leave a week. Precious indeed . . .

The daily parade on weekdays was taken by me. On Sundays a visiting admiral from the Portsmouth Command or from sea added lustre to the ceremonial inspection in the Boy's best uniform prior to the march-past led by the bugle band playing "Marching through Georgia". This was followed by church in the gymnasium, in those days compulsory.

In vain did I often suggest to my distinguished guest, who may not always have been familiar with the repartee of the young sailor, that the smaller the frame the brighter he was likely to be. There is a temptation always to single out the smallest in the middle of the front rank for such questioning and which invariably received the riposte it deserved.

On this occasion the impressive tall, rather pompous admiral in full sword and medals regalia, stopped before five-foot-nothing, rigidly at attention.

"And what, my lad, did you have for breakfast this morning?"

"Bacon and eggs, sir."

"And how often does your mother give you that at home?"

"Never, sir."

"Well, that's one good reason for joining the Navy, isn't it?"

"I *hate* bacon and eggs, sir."

"Smart boy that," said the admiral as I led him to the saluting dais for the march-past.

The boys shared the yearly wardroom dinner to celebrate Admiral Jarvis's 1797 defeat of the Spanish Fleet off Cape St. Vincent with the customary ju-ju—dressing up as seamen of the time to receive the guest of honour, parading the platters with the chefs—doubtless wondering what it was all about. Many Admirals don't look the part; but if ever one did it was my C-in-C, the late Admiral of the Fleet Sir George Creasy, who with his white hair, warm smile, throaty voice, arresting stature, and G.C.B. ribbon across his Mess Dress, could not have been anybody but what he was. His knowledge of naval history was enthralling, his affection for St. Vincent unstinted; his love of G-and-S dated from his first historic appearance at school as Pitti-Sing. Never did I serve a more lovable man from my first days under his command when I was told he wished to see me at once. I went in trepidation.

"Ah yes, Hayes, now what was it I wanted to see you about? Yes—I was going to the Trafalgar Day dinner last night in my car in full uniform and we stopped at a traffic light. Three *St. Vincent* boys were leaning on the pavement balustrade and looked at me, chewing, with no other form of salute. I expect they'd only been in the Navy a few days but would you explain to your lads what a uniformed Admiral of the Fleet looks like?"

At the end of my reign after two years as their "boss", the boys harnessed the field-gun's drag-ropes to our car and pulled us away beneath the archway gate for the last time, through the avenue of smiling faces. I knew then, as I still know, that I could never have had a more rewarding appointment. It *was* that uninhibited honesty, along with their enthusiasms, their camouflaged pride in their first bell-bottoms, their certain humour, their loyalty, which I had come to realise was the essential ingredient of the sailor in the making and why to this day, when so frequently asked, "Do you miss the Navy?" my reply is invariably "Not wind Force 9 at sea; but for ever Jolly Jack."

1957

Incarceration in the M.O.D.

Meanwhile Their Lordships had suddenly announced a decision which had sent cataclysmic shock waves throughout the ranks of all Captains and Commanders, particularly those of the seaman branch, and caused to at least half of the latter deep distress. In a nutshell it meant that they were divided into two categories, those who were still considered eligible to serve in the Fleet at sea, and those who now knew they would never do so again: sailors who would no longer sail. They, together with the non-seaman branches, were amalgamated into a General List; those more fortunate few were named the Post List after the traditional term for a seagoing command, a Post Captain. The ripples of outraged disappointment and disillusion mounted into no mere storm in a teacup but dominated the outlook of those so affected throughout the Service. The underlying reasons for such drastic measures may have been sound enough; but the brash and insensitive way in which they were introduced was out of character with what is frequently called "the highest traditions of the Service."

What had prompted this step was the inescapable fact that –because of the shrinking size of the "Fleet in which we serve"–if "buggin's turn" continued for every Captain and Commander in command at sea, the allotted time for each would be so short as not only to react on their ship's companies but also insufficiently to equip them with experience for sea command in higher rank. As the number of ships could not be increased those eligible to command them must be reduced: as simple as that: but nobody was warned or asked, for instance, whether personal circumstances such as a sick wife or disabled children would in fact remove the barrier of separation which would have led some, albeit reluctantly, to opt for shore appointments. The Executive, or Seaman, Branch were clearly the sufferers although, and perfectly fairly, those on the dry list would be given such coveted jobs as a naval attaché in one of our Embassies instead of the unpopular staff imprisonments in Plans or Operations. Moreover, Engineers or Supply Officers became eligible for shore commands previously regarded as sacrosanct to seamen: so that I was succeeded at *St. Vincent* by a friend and ex-shipmate Engineer, one of the first such plums so to be awarded. My C-in-C was dubious, as the kindergarten was for young seamen and not engineers, and sought my opinion. "Sir," I said, "Raymond is an old friend, a first-class individual, and happens to have played rugger for the Navy. That is what will matter to his boys." And so it did. But for me it was now a choice of the Pentagon or Deputy Director of Joint Plans in the Ministry of Defence. Although I believe that no British officer who will perhaps receive a NATO appointment before long is fully equipped without serving in America, such were our domestic circumstances at the time, very small children included, that I opted for the latter.

The J.P.S. was an organisation, as usual originated by Churchill, whereby the three Services were made to realise that no one of them could generally operate without the other two. Today such creed is accepted by us all and applies in general to the vast majority of service activities: the Falklands Task Force is a recent and classic example, when all the senior officers were probably on Christian-name terms, thanks to their enforced time together in such institutions as the Royal College of Defence Studies or the Defence Staff in the M.O.D. Sandy and Jeremy, you name them, would have been old friends, together with their wives on social occasions, and this is now what makes the military world go round; but it was not always so, and will probably never pertain to in-fighting when it comes to rivalry for slices of the Defence Budget cake. That can tarnish the closest friendships.

So my lot for the next two and a half years was to be incarcerated in a small room looking across Whitehall and shared by a Colonel and Group Captain, each of us with his own telephone and each answering to different bosses leading eventually to the Chiefs of Staff themselves. My good friend the Colonel did not need a telephone to make himself heard to the Army Council on the other side of the Cenotaph.

The set-up was simple enough. A joint Service plan was initiated and processed for every likelihood of operations world-wide as envisaged by the Joint Intelligence Staff. (Doubtless this included– well after my day–an Argentinian invasion of the Falklands.) A skeleton outline of what was required by the planners was then first given to the appropriate joint teams at Commander's level responsible for that part of the world. Their draft was then discussed with us, their Deputy Directors. Ourselves agreed, it went to the Directors at Brigadier level to be chewed over again, the relevant Foreign Office and Commonwealth Office experts having by now been involved. The Directors then submitted the plan to the Chiefs of Staff themselves. After final to-ing and fro-ing it became a Chief of Staff paper, pigeon-holed as "C.O.S.(53) 333: Invasion of Bongo-Bongoland" and forgotten. Then, when Bongo-Bongoland *was* invaded, which invariably seemed to happen late at night by G.M.T. the Joint Planners were summoned to look at the plan again until dawn, to see if what had been originally agreed was still operative.

It was after one such all-night sitting and gin time next lunch-time that, as I have already hinted, it became clear to me how easy it is to take a ship to sea or a squadron of fighters into the air compared with advancing a battalion a few miles. The plan in question had no naval content, and by the time we came to drafting Appendix One my thirst and appetite were clamouring for attention. Glancing down the columns of hieroglyphic gobbledegook of army abbreviations about PoL and Ammo I ventured: "This doesn't concern me, Jacko; what'll you drink in due course?"

"You sit here, sailor, and if you don't understand you can at least try to learn"–which I did, and was subsequently the wiser for it.

At the end of two and a half years, and because I was on that Wet List, I received news to cement the ambition of any naval officer (in particular a non-aviator) to command a large aircraft carrier. Here was the consummation of years of endeavour embracing hopefully my love for the sea and, thanks to *Ocean*, the Fleet Air Arm. Could I meld the two into what was any such Captain's ambition, an efficient and happy carrier? I felt contentedly humble and thought it wise, having been reading into the small hours for years, to strengthen those spectacles which had first been necessitated off Flamborough Head twenty years ago. Aircraft carriers don't have open bridges. You sit in a high chair behind windscreen wipers. You are physically impervious to the elements while looking at charts: but ceaseless C.O.S. papers had become an eye strain and I had stupidly sought to equip myself.

"You are well below standard for command at sea," said the naval ophthalmologist. I appealed to civilian consultants and lost. So I crept away: although Wet, condemned to be Dry. That, I presumed, was that, as far as any continuation of a naval career was concerned.

1960

Drake as opposed to Nelson

Not surprisingly, that piratical buccaneering Devonian of the first Elizabethan era (whose exploits today would have occupied a deal of time before the Admiralty, Probate and Divorce Judges, the Court of Appeal, the Law Lords) in addition to playing bowls on the Hoe has bequeathed his name to many a gathering of trainees but most permanently to the naval shore complex in Plymouth. There, as the next best thing to a capital ship command, Their Lordships now sent me as a Commodore. In the Navy, unlike the Army, this is an honorary rank to mark certain appointments; it is not substantive promotion.

If H.M.S. *Drake* had heard of the Battle of Trafalgar it did not then admit it. The defeat of the Armada first established the Royal Navy in the ascendant some forty years after its foundation by Henry VII, and that exploit is what is annually celebrated. The Wardroom's heirlooms contain the coconut presented to Elizabeth I as palliative to one of Drake's more illicit escapades. Alas, admirals of today are not encouraged to present such loot to her twentieth-century successor! But Armada Night in the Wardroom is the big occasion.

It was my first appearance among some 200 of my officers, as a guest because I was not of their Mess. To cater for such shades of religious belief as the sailors might occasionally require we had three padres: Church of England of course, Roman Catholic, and that miscellaneous pack known as the Free Church. Tonight it was Father

Steven O'Connor's turn to pronounce Grace. This is usually short, in English, and to the point: "For what we are about to receive, thank God," to which most of us inwardly add "hopefully the chefs too"; but Steve now rose opposite the President–a robust Commander but, like us all, no classicist–and said it in Latin. As we sat down the President boomed:

"I didn't understand a word of that."

"Nor" said Steve with a benign smile "was it directed to you."

The command of a large depot accommodating a shifting population of thousands of men, changing every day as they arrived or left to commission their ships from dockyard hands, was a run-of-the-mill job, utterly different from commanding a ship. Apart from my few permanent Wardroom Officers and key ratings they were all temporary strangers; and although life seemed to be non-stop, at the end of the day one often wondered what exactly it had all been about. No crises; no moment when your ship narrowly escapes collision: nothing to excite: and yet it had to be done–President of Boards of Enquiry and Courts Martial, endless Commissioning Ceremonies, and of course thousands passing through one's official residence. Never dull.

A naval Court Martial, unless involving the Official Secrets Act, is a public Court of Law, a fact not always appreciated. The ceremonial is akin to that surrounding the arrival of the Judge in the circuit days of Assize: but instead of Bishops and High Sheriffs there is a one-gun salute at 0800 on the day, the breaking of the Union Flag, a Guard for the President in sword and medals, the entry of the whole Court of five, and the full panoply of Naval Law. There have been notable Courts Martial in history. The luckless Admiral Byng after his defeat off Minorca in 1744 was found guilty of such and shot on his own quarterdeck. *Royal Oak*, shortly before I joined her in 1930, had staged an abusive exchange between her Commander and Bandmaster on another quarterdeck, an incident which had hit the headlines. But such titillating situations for public curiosity are rare; generally Courts must by mandate probe into the running-aground of H.M. Ships, which are after all the property of the taxpayer and whose misadventures are therefore open to public scrutiny if desired.

I hated the Presidency of such a Court, especially after the judgement on a friend in command who may have just "taken the ground" in an awkward situation and in foul weather. Rarely, I suspect, does a Judge on the Bench think "there but for the grace of God...", whereas that is frequently the thinking of the President of a Naval Court. You do not *have* to sum up as a civilian Judge has to, but I found it fairer to do so and to underline that fairness towards the accused: he was after all being tried by his own, who frequently may have been no less *guilty* but at the time were just more fortunate.

Another novel experience was having to take Wren defaulters for the first time: there were several hundred Wrens within the Plymouth command. Every naval officer and rating respects, often loves and sometimes marries our female Service counterparts: they hold an earned respect among us: but they are not always angels. When they broke their leave, generally for obvious reasons, they duly appeared at my defaulters' table. I have a soft heart, as the Chief Wren Officer well knew. "This little monkey will use every trick," she cautioned. "She's well known on the Hoe. Don't weaken. You can see from her record that this is not a first offence." A pretty little girl was stood before me. Tears welled in her eyes. The lashes fluttered and the lower lip trembled. The Chief Wren gave me a kick under the table. Here was no Cordelia or Miranda .... "Leave stopped for a week." "Quite right," said the Chief Wren afterwards.

Run-of-the-mill or not, my indelible memory of *Drake* is my daily association with the Devonport Field Gun Crew when they were training for the Royal Tournament. It is a recognised hazard that it is near enough impossible to portray what the Navy actually does at sea to justify the thousands of millions of pounds spent on it by the taxpayer*: and yet every year they come in their thousands to Earls Court to see that patriotically moving example of Service drill and stamina, bringing their children who in some cases are sufficiently impressed to join. The Field Gun Competition dates from the relief of Ladysmith in the Boer War, and the public still won't let it go. Suffice it to say that those Field Gun crews are for their year the stars of the Navy: once a Field Gunner, always remembered and respected.

*Since writing the above there *has* been a BBC TV documentary programme, called *Submarine*, which in my opinion convincingly portrays what one very important branch of the R.N. does as sea.

There were no professional actors, just the officers and their men of a conventional, a hunter-killer (or Fleet) submarine and finally an insight into what life is like during the eight-week submerged patrol of the Polaris boat—in fact the successor to my old *Repulse*. The series was widely acclaimed and I think rightly because those taking part didn't try to act: they were just themselves in the daily round, the common task, behaving before the cameras as they do every day on the job. It also touched on the reactions of their families without emotion or sentiment—just what they have to endure through periods of long separation.

1962

Naval Secretary to the First Lord of the Admiralty

Having defaulted, for medical reasons, on the one chance to command a capital ship, I had no right to expect other than that that was the end of the naval road for me. The post of "Wet List" Commodore who had driven nothing bigger than a frigate must have seemed to many a poor passport to flag rank. Yet Their Lordships after much internal debate (as I was to discover) not only generously forgave me but sent me to the most fascinating appointment that a brand new Rear Admiral could receive.

The Military Secretaries of the three Services share the same intrinsic role, that of appointing or submitting for appointment to their respective Board or Councils the senior officers of their respective coloured uniforms; and in this age of joint cooperation they must be friends so as to balance the personal merits of those appointed to tri-Service responsibilities and to those appointments which each take in turn. The Treasury assesses allowed complements in terms of one-third of an Admiral, General or Air Marshal.

To the amusement of the other two, and by no means exceptionally, the Navy plays the tune in a different and minor key. Whereas the Army and R.A.F. have two very senior three-star officers on the same level as their Councils, the Navy has always held to a newly promoted two-star Admiral, the servant equally of the

First Sea Lord, his uniformed master, and of whoever was in those days politically responsible to the Cabinet solely for naval affairs as the "Head" of the Navy: the First Lord of the Admiralty, a post once held by Churchill. As the Naval Secretary's responsibilities to both included the appointment of Captains, among whose ranks were friends he had only just left, and the jigsaw of planning the Flag List years ahead principally for the First Sea Lord to consider, there was method in the system. On a summer's day I arrived in my new office overlooking Horse Guard's Parade and adjoining that of the First Lord. Scanning with awe the portraits of my predecessors over the years, who included the great Beatty himself when looking after Winston, I felt a pygmy. As had once happened before, my friend whom I was relieving pulled cardboard sheets out of a file. "Get this out of your system and you'll see why you're here." That drawer of files held the personal histories of every Admiral and Captain still serving. I felt even smaller, a sense augmented by the fact that the Naval Secretary is also the go-between to the Board for every retired Admiral, octogenarian or older or younger, who was delightfully to write his opinion of what was wrong today; and forceful opinions they were too.

On reflection thirty years later, I hope that the shade of the one master and the vibrant and very much alive personality of the other will forgive modest comment from someone who had to serve both equally without fear or favour: two very distinguished men: the late Admiral of the Fleet Sir Caspar John and Lord Carrington. The latter's wit is no less rapier-sharp and pungent than was the former's, a factor which tautened the tightrope I had to walk between them. "His foe was folly and his weapon wit," is true of them both while neither, in any characteristic whatsoever, resemble the cynical, irascible mountebank Gilbert whose epitaph is thus inscribed on his statue. Throughout the Navy's long history I doubt if there can have been two more contrasting characters who had to work together day by day, or who more sincerely shared its well-being throughout an anxious chapter in that history, when the future of the aircraft carrier was in jeopardy—and no early advocate of that ship had done more than Caspar to preach its potency as well as that of the airborne torpedo-bombers, which Phillips in 1941 would have done well to heed. Poles apart in background, the ability of each was mirrored in their respect for the other. My role was to "look on both indifferently".

Caspar John, the son of Augustus, had rebelled at the early age of 12 against Bohemian domestic unorthodoxy and joined the Navy. This was one day to lead the "gentle rebel" under the influence of his hero, the renowned Jackie Fisher, through naval avaition and the Board of Admiraly, to become a most revered and unusual First Sea Lord. It took little time to realise that you had to stand up to him or he would bend you.

One such example of our relationship will suffice. In 1963 the Prime Minister had agreed with President Kennedy that Britain's independent deterrent within NATO would be transferred from Vulcan bombers to Polaris submarines in five years time. I received a message at noon that by 1430 the First Sea Lord would like the names of those admirals from whom he could select the Chief Polaris Executive for the whole of that time and, moreover, endure working closely with that American nuclear legend, Rickover. I duly presented my proposals.

"Is that the best you can do?"

"In the time, sir, I don't think I've done too badly."

"Ah well: it's always nice to meet an officer who *thinks* he has done well. Which of these would you suggest and why?"

Likewise, when suddenly I would receive a message via his secretary that if I had nothing better to do would I lunch with Caspar at his Club, not surprisingly I never had.

My official appointment was as personal servant to the Head of the Navy which was itself, strictly speaking, a political post. For eighteen months I had the good fortune to answer a Victorian clapper bell at his calling, to accompany him wherever he visited his Navy in any part of the kingdom or the world, to experience for the first time some of what goes on in the higher echelons of our country's government–though never of course did he involve me politically more than "the Prime Minister would like to know..." or "We seem to have a little problem with the Secretary of State for Air" (not unusual!). Above all, it was an experience to work closely with a man whose charm and humour camouflaged a puckish demolition of waffle, had an eye which unerringly distinguished what matters from what doesn't, and a fierce loyalty for whatever happens to be in his charge at the time. For this particular moment it was to run the Navy with Caspar.

I count it as a luxury that I was able to serve two such men simultaneously, not only for the increased knowledge which came from the experience, but also as a yardstick within myself. When the future was to present me with awkward decisions I could wonder: "Now what would *they* have advised?"

So Sir Caspar was promoted to the pinnacle of naval rank; and Peter Carrington, already in the foothills of power, began his ascent of higher peaks. (He has recently climbed, as Secretary General of NATO, a very high peak indeed: and there may be those who would agree with me that there could have been no greater service to Britain, internationally regarded as he is, which he could have performed). The old order traumatically changed when the three separate Service Ministries left their historic portals and in 1964 merged together amid the soulless modern corridors and umpteen floors of the new Ministry of Defence. It had to be. With the Chief of Defence Staff, Lord Mountbatten as architect, the three coloured uniforms became a tricolour in every top organisational cell, the C.D.S. properly wielding supreme military authority. Reorganisation doubtless produced colossal financial savings and cemented the cooperation between khaki and the two blues; but no longer did one feel the ghosts of those who had gone before you questioning: "Who are you?". Atmosphere vanished. My two new bosses were, shall we say, different. I daily groped in the dark as to what the one had confided in the other, if anything. My relief was profound when I was appointed as one of the only two Admirals who then lived afloat.

1964

Flying a Flag at sea

In one respect only can an unremarkable Admiral lay claim to have followed in the footsteps of that remarkable predecessor by fifty years, the great Lord Beatty himself, in that he too had been Naval Secretary to a certain First Lord called Winston Churchill at the outbreak of the First World War, and had then hoisted his flag in his renowned *Lion*; from her bridge he exerted that flair in command of the battle cruisers of the Grand Fleet which culminated in the Battle of Jutland, and his subsequent succession of Jellicoe as Commander-in-Chief. There the footsteps stop! Yet I too hoisted my flag in the modern successor to his *Lion*, a 6″ cruiser, in Malta's Grand Harbour in October 1964. I was conscious of the dashing shades which must have smiled wryly down upon the new Flag Officer Second-in-Command of Britain's Western Fleet. "Western Fleet" meant every White Ensign afloat of any kind west of the Suez Canal. The only other Admiral living afloat was he who commanded in the Far East, so to be thus appointed was for me a genuine surprise. Such a progression was customary enough, all things being equal; but my own steps had stumbled, and my experiences with the successors to Peter Carrington and Caspar John had been far from happy, and so things were far from "equal". Nevertheless, here I was, apprehensive but helped by those who knew my failings of old, reading the Lesson for Quarterdeck Church on my first day: the story from the Acts of the Apostles when Paul was shipwrecked at Melita Bay just up the way from our berth, as if to remind me that nothing which happens at sea is new....

My first exercise–and life with NATO is inclined to be one long exercise with few bright lights–was to have been west of Gibraltar, embracing the Spanish Navy under my tactical command. Spain was then thinking of joining NATO, a prospect which had taken months of painstaking diplomacy to arrange; but at the last minute some new Gibraltarian controversy had arisen, the exercise was cancelled, and *Lion* was sent to kick her heels at Marseilles, to the delight of the sailors. From there I contacted my Spanish admiral at home on the telephone.

"I am sorry," he said, "but what you can expect? I am now shooting partridges instead."

Here, it could be said, is where we came in: for in my opening chapters I switched from the alpha of my childhood in Bermuda to this omega, my last daily acquaintance with the sea. I dwelt then on sentimental reflections; the interim has been an ordinary story of peace and war leading to the fulfilment of most naval officers: flying one's flag at sea. I touch now therefore on the operational demands as opposed to the emotional ones. In doing so I invoke the title of my book; for to command a large NATO fleet at sea, embracing many nations, is akin to what I imagine must be the challenge confronting the conductor of an international orchestra. You will be an expert instrumentalist in one section and possibly semi-expert in others; above all you must by experience be able to read the score or know every line by heart. The latter is more common in a classical symphony than in the unexpected at sea!

In my personal case I knew how to perform in navigation and its minor keys, but the remainder—gunnery, torpedo and anti-submarine warfare, electronics, communications—were a closed book professionally, and all clamoured for attention under my baton, understandably disregarding the general orchestral effect. So one brought in the strings, silenced the brass, muted the woodwinds and allowed the percussion their moment according to the situation. The Leader was of course the Captain of the Flagship, also Chief Staff Officer. I think I would relate the percussion to the Staff Officer Operations, who would nudge if not actually hit me when I created discord by misreading the score. The pizzicato movement could contain humour, the allegro was deadly serious; and nobody clapped at the final chord.

The spectrum of such a life contained many colours, mostly NATO assignments ending either in the Arctic mists of Norway or the sunshine of Portugal—a routine conclusion which in every case provided a halycon escape for Admirals, while the said orchestra had to dissect its conductor's contribution in what is known as a "wash-up" of an exercise, preparation for which prohibited my presence. Instead of rehearsing the next concert one either went ski-ing in Norway or sun-bathing in Portugal, awaiting a politely explained analysis of one's mistakes. There were two unusual departures: the first resulted from somebody's enlightened idea that for once the Navy should try to demonstrate what it does at sea—"show the flag"—to the citizens of our own Island for a change instead of abroad. The outcome was Operation "Jack Tar", with my flag moved to "Tiger", sister to *Lion*. The two ships were a contrast: the former was not particularly immaculate but was happy and efficient, whereas the latter was so spotless that you could have eaten a meal off any of her decks. The squadron of cruisers, a carrier, frigates, submarines and minesweepers went from port to port around our coasts, taking those in local government to sea by the hundred and opening daily to thousands of the general public. Public relations blossomed, as when, in Newcastle, I entertained the great-great-grandson of Nelson's cabin boy at Trafalgar; we still correspond. The hiccups were occasioned by the media; for around our coasts past history has conferred upon local Mayors and Provosts such honorary titles as, in this case, Admiral of the Humber. The Lady Mayor had been assured that she would fly her flag in *Tiger* when I took her to sea. Our relationship had to cool when I assured her that there was only *one* lady who flew her flag in any of her Ships!

The other departure from routine remains in my memory as being among the most evocative and emotive experiences. In 1965 I was sent in *Tiger* to represent the Admiralty at Narvik for the twenty fifth Anniversary of the first battle in those huge Arctic inlets, when Churchill left it to the discretion of Captain Warburton-Lee in H.M.S. *Hardy*, with his handful of H-Class destroyers, whether or not to attack a superior German force already ensconced up the fiord as part of Hitler's occupation of Norway. The gallantry of that action resulted, posthumously, in the first V.C. of the War. A second Battle of Narvik ensued, conducted conclusively by Admiral Sir William Whitworth in the battleship *Warspite*. I was privileged to take him in *Tiger*, together with General Sir Hugh Stockwell and Rear Admiral Micklethwaite; the latter, then in command of H.M.S. *Eskimo*, had chased the remaining German destroyers up Rombak's Fiord, had his bow blown off, came back stern first and won his umpteenth D.S.O.

The mountains of the fiord in April were starkly iced in the sunlight. The local civic reception was moving, yet was eclipsed by what was to follow. Norwegian naval M.T.B.s took us down the fiord to the war cemetery, past the wreck of *Hardy* to whom they piped the "Still" as a war grave. Normally at this time of year under ten feet of snow, the graves had been dug out so that their ranks of dressed granite rose from a flat white carpet encompassed by parapets of snow in brilliant sunshine, with Norwegian and British flags held by schoolchildren as a surround. There was Warburton-Lee, V.C., next to his cook in *Hardy*. There were personal friends I had known who had been instrumental in chasing those Germans up the fiord in a blinding snowstorm. Their little ships, sunk or disabled against hopeless odds, had yet given Britain a boost to morale badly needed at such a time; it had been the first true successor to the Battle of the River Plate. There are times when emotion is not out of place. I was relieved that for some unexplained reason I was ordered to sail home immediately, for small-talk even among the most faithful of allies would have been trite after such an occasion.

And the lessons learned after such experiences, as my coveted turn as a NATO Sea Commander drew to its end? Presumably I had by then learned a bit about my own Service, but rather less about other nations' approaches to our mutual problems. I already had a cursory understanding of how the U.S. Navy conducted its affairs, thanks to having worked with them on those Russian Convoys, but only as a junior officer; so perhaps above all else I did come to appreciate with sympathy how and why it is that we sometimes misunderstand each other. Because we do not need interpreters to communicate in our common lingo, we are prone to thinking that we are the same kind of animal. In terms of culture our histories differ so markedly compared with, say, our relations with the French, with whom even perfidious Albion shares a far deeper affinity: yet as a military man, of course, one's experience is the opposite. Whereas in 1916 it could be said that Britain held in its Navy the most powerful weapon that the world had known since Napoleon's armies, and yet failed at Jutland to manifest that power in an action whose controversies no historian will ever resolve, America's Navy was then still learning. Now the roles of sea power have been more than reversed–Britain is No.3–and it is thus sometimes hard to stomach brash criticism of the R.N. by those cousins who could not, perhaps, be expected to be sensitive. Yet we should always be conscious that despite their overwhelming superiority in weapons, tonnage, manpower and every

other statistic, America nevertheless has a deep affection for the
Royal Navy and what it was once able to achieve when no other
could. Whereas militarily (and possibly politically too) France will
probably never feel able to forgive the nation who twice rescued her
this century, she *has* somehow managed at least to condone–in a
modern *entente cordiale*–the nation who has twice conquered her.

In 1917, in the aftermath of Jutland and concerning America's
entry into the War, the Editor of the *New York Tribune* wrote to the
late Arthur Pollen, our most distinguished naval correspondent of
the time and the harshest critic of the lack of offensive spirit
displayed by the Jellicoe school and their disciples:

> "Like minded as we are, your people and mine, there are yet
> many points at which we seem to miss sympathetic comprehen-
> sion of each other's moods. We look askew at each other for
> the most ludicrous reasons. Wherein we are alike, it is
> fundamental; and wherein we are not alike it is superficial.
> More is the pity."

Whether it is the different way we approach battles at sea or the
razzmatazz of a Presidential Election compared to a British General
Election, I fancy those words hold good in the education of both our
younger generations towards each other, now as then; for in the end
the future freedom of their lives does depend on such philosophy,
like it or not.

It is well over twenty years since I hauled down my flag in *Tiger*, as
previously flippantly described; so as an appendix to this paragraph
in my life I include some armchair reflections of an older man.

Had the predecessors of General Galtieri decided then to invade
the Malvinas, there was no other Admiral at sea in a position to take
command of a Falklands Task Force at the drop of a hat, and so
presumably it would have fallen to me. I may therefore be forgiven
for fireside dreaming on how I would have been placed compared to
my successor by many innings, Sir "Sandy" Woodward, *vis-à-vis* the
Argentine forces of the time. Some up-to-date opinion agrees that I
would, on balance, have been better off.

On the credit side I would have had larger carriers, a commando
carrier, several unsophisticated guided missile destroyers (of

Devonshire class), plenty of frigates, perhaps a couple of nuclear attack submarines, and above all that old veteran sea-bird of an aircraft, the Gannet, which could have flapped around the ocean with its heavy radar set in its belly to give me a wide picture of the theatre of operations before alighting on the deck of my carrier and (literally) folding its wings. I would of course also have had superbly trained Royal Marine Commandos, paratroops and landing craft crews.

On the debit side, I would not have had the Harrier jump-jet, so that the protection of my flight decks would have been even more crucial. I would not have had the same sophisticated overall Fleet Support R.F.A. ships to give me everything from oil to ammunition and food. I suspect that the Commando training, now regularly undertaken in the Arctic and elsewhere, would then have stretched that "yomping" from San Carlos Water even more than General Jeremy Moore's brave men were stretched; and no R.A.F. aircraft such as the Hercules would have been able to contend with the 8,000 miles from Britain to the Falklands via Ascension Island.

But what would the "enemy" have had? Experienced readers interested in such hypothetical conjecture may like, with me, to ponder.

So that revel ended. I must have been almost the last cuckoo to usurp two such welcoming nests in *Tiger* and *Lion*, of such different character but always among friends. I had to curb my innate laughter in the one and appear to be more seriously minded in the other; all in all, I believe the light touch at the right moment to be an essential ingredient of high command. He is a dull dog indeed who cannot smile with the sailor; yet you have to be yourself to win his respect: he sees through you like a piece of cellophane in your every mood.

1966-1968

Naval Finale

All the world's a stage, naturally. We have our exits and our entrances, for naval officers generally every two years, and one man in his time plays many parts. My last before bowing before the final curtain was as Flag Officer Scotland and Northern Ireland, Their Lordships having been kind to me to the end; for by now our home had been in the Highlands for ten years and I had been lucky enough to come to know something of that great little mountainous area as well as any Englishman is like to be vouchsafed.

FOSNI (as the Navy calls him) is virtually a Commander-in-Chief though he cannot thus be called. It would be tactless to do so because, politically, of Ulster and more importantly because the Governor of Edinburgh Castle is the G.O.C.-in-C in Scotland; but with a parish stretching from the Humber to the North Pole the naval area is a rather larger command geographically than others whose admirals carry the title.

With this had to be blended those who go down to the sea in ships ... the fishery protection squadron often off Greenland's ice, the perpetual coming and going of operational visits, a dockyard refitting scores of every shape and size (traditional if not strictly economic), Polaris submarines from their base at Gairloch, in whose inauguration I was one of three architects—by and large one felt it to be a consummation of all that one had been taught or experienced, to be allowed to do one's best far enough from London to avoid Admiralty interference in an appointment I knew was the end of the road, albeit at an age when a little wisdom was perhaps beginning to permeate.

That is adequate description of the operational aspect of that life which in fact was the easiest part of it; for the stage upon which one must strut, an Admiralty House, isn't yours and it isn't you. You must act out a part in a huge, beautiful mansion overlooking the Forth, while literally thousands flit through it during your reign—naval officers, of course, galore: Cabinet Ministers wondering whether they should obey the three-line whip or get paired that night and changing their minds every few minutes: Edinburgh dignitaries (the bridge having now joined the capital to its Navy): an endless succession of visitors, some welcome and others less so, to be welcomed as though the hearth was really your own. It was an act but a very rewarding one.

He is a vain man who imagines that he can achieve success in such a role without the help of a devoted consort. It is she who has to carry so much of the burden of the day—and night! Party after party in which, of course, one has the help of a devoted retinue of naval stewards and cooks. They were all friends, some having served with us before. "Chef," Rosalind would say "I just can't bear the thought of to-night." "Never mind, madam: two o'clock in the morning is bound to come," and which surprisingly it did, inevitably successfully.

Looking back, it was an extraordinary household. You can't run it like a ship because its a house, while yet embracing naval discipline and attention to detail. The retinue are officially there to serve the Navy, in which your wife is not. Loyalty to the net result is therefore paramount to her as much as to her spouse. There are codes of behaviour which you trespass at your peril; never penetrate that green baize door to their quarters and the kitchen: never fish around to see what's there as one would in one's own house: Rosalind's morning meetings with the Chief Steward and Chef were just as important as mine with the Air Marshal in M.H.Q.: often more so.

The household was enhanced by the outstanding character within our family over the last fifteen years—Nanny Bain. Nan was ample, pink, grey-haired, round, Protestant and Scot, in her seventies. Every officer and sailor we had introduced to her, anxious parents in Malta or South Africa, wild bachelor fighter pilots, those separated from their families who wanted to talk about them, all had confided in her about their love life or their children's skin ailments. Our guests called into her nursery before our sitting room. Her near-extinct breed has been painted by Nancy Mitford in *The Blessing*. She could by her soothing experience anaesthetise the squawking, mewling, unappeased infant as a conductor will silence the tuning-up of his orchestra by the lifting of his baton. In short, she was a lady for all seasons.

Her last contribution to the Navy concerned Ben. Ben was that rare relic by 1968, the three badge Able Seaman, a "stripey". He had somehow managed to linger in FOSNI's Barges crew (FOSNI has had no Barge since the bridge was built) for years, until suddenly unearthed by the naval drafting world and appointed to a large aircraft carrier. There of course he would die and as the day drew closer Ben got drunker. Yet that day inevitably had to come; for I naturally resisted all the protestations to spare him the sea job he had evaded for so long.

His final call in uniform was on Nan where he was found with his head in her lap singing gently to her after a sojourn in the North Queensferry Arms.

"Dear Ben," said Nan, "he's unusual, y'know", a classic understatement.

Having aged gracefully in her original Highland environment, she died as she had lived, beloved by all who owed her so much. She had brought up forty two children, starting in the British Consulate in Peking, our younger two being her last. She had lost her Gordon Highlander fiancé on Armistice Day 1918. She never complained. "Maybe I was meant to bring up more than I could have had myself." She was among the greatest ladies we have known.

So to the last of my dramatis personae to wag his way under the proscenium of this stage, the last of our dynasty of springer spaniels, a breed as contemptuous of authority as Launce's good dog Crab. He had come to us as a puppy five years ago in *Drake*, advertised as "strong and bold", already fighting the grip of two vast Army Provost sergeants who had brought him from khaki to dark blue. "'Ere's your dog, sir. Likes ice cream. We call him Butch." We called him Bramble.

As life for us without four-footed friends is not life, despite the contrasting pomp of an Admiralty House compared to his normal habitat, Bramble had to be accepted by the staff. He and the Chief Steward, who secretly respected him, fought a running battle. Bramble's methods were subtle. The Gents at the end of the passage was full of family clutter from golf clubs to dog-feeding paraphernalia, too much to clear away for *every* lunch or dinner party when Bramble would retrieve the odd boot to bring in among the aperitifs: but today was Royalty. The Chief Steward meant business and cleared the lot except for the one essential face towel.

Before the social ice was broken Bramble arrived with it, circled the company, sat on the Royal foot, offered it and smiled at the Chief Steward.

Although in his prime, eleven o'clock was, he considered, bedtime for a springer. He would then stretch from the hearth and rub around the assembled company of both sexes, in and out of skirts or trousers so as to make everybody thoroughly uncomfortable. If this failed to flush them, he went out into the hall to find the invariable pyramid of naval caps. Carrying the top one by the peak he would then perambulate, sniffing, until he found the lap of the owner into which he dropped it.

"Thanks for the hint, old boy. Of course you're right. Time we went."

The point had been made. During the pleasanteries of what a lovely evening it had been ("Two o'clock in the morning is bound to come, madam") Bramble took his place in the hall alongside the duty steward, saw each guest into their car and when the last had gone gave an approving bark before going up to his basket.

Small wonder that our greatest authors have focussed their skills upon such company. *Indian Summer of a Forsyte*: old Jolyon's peaceful end: "At his feet lay a woolly brown and white dog trying to be a Pomeranian–the dog Balthasar, between whom and old Jolyon primal aversion had turned into attachment with the years."

The same may be said of our Chief Steward and Bramble.

As if with an innate sense of affectionate timing, at the same time as I was leaving the Navy my beloved mother left this world. The restless spirit of my father had been freed to flit who knows where a few years earlier. Having demanded her every hour for years past, as is the way of such strong yet mercurial husbands, the vacuum of his passing left her bereft of purpose. She fell, didn't die but mentally joined the fairies. In her lucid moments her humour remained unquenched, but in her fairyland it was the Nuns who came to my rescue and cherished her to an octogenarian end. She was far from being a Catholic (I can't remember having seen her enter even a Unitarian church except for a wedding) but this made no difference to the Mother Superior. They nursed her as if she was of their own and loved her for her gentle Christianity and her sense of the ridiculous. One Ash Wednesday, Sister Philomena was standing at the end of her bed.

"What shall we give up for Lent, Mrs. Hayes?"

My mother, for whom Lent had never exactly featured, said: "Food."

"You don't eat very much you know. Couldn't you think of something more practical?"

My mother smiled sweetly. "I know," she said, "I'll give up religion"–and quietly departed. The Nuns attended her cremation. I could never adopt Catholicism: one change of creed is enough: but as old Nan would say, "They're guid people", and they were the only people who could and would have so laid my mother to her final haven.

"Last things... last things... how they hurt." More so if it really *is* the last time. The Guard, the Band, swords and medals outside my Maritime Headquarters: perfunctory farewells and handing over the reins to an old friend, Ian McGeoch. (He and I, when Commanders of ships anchored off Kyrenia in North Cyprus, had together in my cabin heard of the death of King George VI. You remember such moments.) Then away to the traditional departure in my Barge manned by my senior officers. Across the Forth for the last time and into our own car without the Royal Marine driver but with our inimitable Bramble, who had defied the Chief Steward throughout his reign with mutual respect, Bramble proudly upright in the front seat, as much as to say, "Enough of all that."

It had been a wonderful innings. I couldn't claim to have carried my bat: but, as a Vice Admiral, shall we say eighth wicket down? I had been nearly run-out twice because of eyesight; but my friend at the other crease always seemed to see me through. When you are seven you don't wonder what is going to happen to you as a retired man in your middle fifties, having to carve out a new life just when you are beginning to gain some experience. But that's the way of the naval world. Middle fifties are quite old enough to presume to serve at sea in this NATO age.

1968-1988

"Retirement" in The Highlands

In about 1770, Hugh Rose, fifth son of the little town of Tain's manse, set out to find his fortune. He went from this little town on the southern shore of the Dornoch Firth, in the County of Ross & Cromarty (which, dating its Charter from King Malcolm Canmore in 1066, claims to be the oldest Royal Burgh in Scotland), to become a Naval Victualling Officer in the West Indies. There, in fairy tale fashion, he did find that fortune by successfully feeding the fleets of

Admirals Rodney, Hood and, as he was then known, Jarvis. The latter was Hugh Rose's main saviour. His fortune made, Hugh returned to his native Easter Ross while Jarvis was to become Lord St. Vincent after defeating the Spanish off that Cape in 1797, brilliantly assisted by a certain young Captain Horatio Nelson. In due course St. Vincent became Godfather to Hughs' first daughter.

Hugh purchased superb agricultural land, planted avenues the remnants of which still just stand, and in 1798 built on to a seventeenth-century croft a beautiful house which he named "Arabella", after the lovely Arabella Phipps whom he married. But Arabella's happiness was not to last. Legend has it she was murdered by a vengeful mistress of Hugh's Caribbean days: according to Arabella's carved marble tomb in Tain's beautiful twelfth-century Chapel of St. Duthus, she "while administering physic to the poor suddenly expired". Her tragic ghost is said to flit within the local mansion.

Some 150 years later, as I have recounted, I was ending my command of H.M.S. *St. Vincent* in Gosport. Our little Wiltshire home had become too small to hold our increased family. Knowing that I was about to become entombed in the M.O.D. in a job frequently to involve the small hours, we had thought it prudent, as Scots would say, to move temporarily nearer Whitehall. Trustees baulked all our efforts. We became impatient.

One morning as I was about to take the morning parade ground salute from the *St. Vincent* boys, Rosalind asked, "How would you like to live in Easter Ross?"

"Where's that?" I said in a hurry.

"600 miles north of London".

"About the right distance from the M.O.D. but scarcely practical," and gave it not another thought.

A week later she suddenly asked again, "How would you like to live in Arabella House, Nigg?"

"It's rather a nice address. Where's that?"

"Easter Ross." The rest can be guessed. The previous owner queried my sanity to a former shipmate. "Why?" "Because he wants to buy Arabella and he hasn't seen it."

He wasn't the only local so to wonder but Rosalind had

done her homework. Among other extraordinary coincidences subsequently to be discovered was that I should have been commanding the Navy's memorial to the great man, H.M.S. *St. Vincent,* when we bought Arabella. There followed over thirty supremely happy Arabella years. We did not disclose that her grandfather had been M.P. for Nairn & Inverness Burghs at the turn of the century, with his home along the road in Nairn in whose Council Chamber his portrait now hangs as Lloyd George's Lord Chancellor: or that her mother and father got engaged on its golf course. I did not confess to falling in love with Scotland during that first Christmas of the War protecting the mined *Nelson* in Loch Ewe; nor, other than to myself, my innate love for the Highlander dating from my association with the Argyll & Sutherland Battalion in Johore.

So much for naval past: what of the future? unqualified in aught else: long before Easter Ross with its historical agricultural quality became such a pioneer in the colossal construction of rigs on the advent of North Sea Oil: and yet still aged only 55 but thus maybe also beginning to acquire a modicum of wisdom from life experience. What now? You don't think about such when you decide to join the Navy at the age of seven! Yet I need not have worried.

Scarcely had my last day on full pay passed than a local sadness occurred in the death of a distinguished farmer and Councillor. Would I replace him unopposed? What could I say? Hardly that I was too busy! In vain did I protest my utter ignorance. "You'll learn," they said. "We'd like a fresh face." The humourless County Clerk of years standing was not so sure.

"Ah, good morning, Admiral. So you have been asked to succeed Mr. Ross. How sad. I don't suppose you know much about what it entails."

"You're right there."

"Well, you'll sit on all the committees of your late lamented predecessor. Planning: Property & Works: Highways: Diseases of Animals. All right?"

"Please, with so many farmers on the Council, couldn't I possibly be less useless on whatever committee considers, say, the Cromarty Firth?"

"No. Rules are rules." So that was that and came the next full Council meeting with me the only newcomer. The Convener, a Free Church Minister of local notoriety, having expressed the sympathy of all in the death of Mr Ross, welcomed his successor.

"I understand, Admiral, you have agreed to serve on all his committees?"

"Not quite, Convener. Could I possibly be spared the Diseases of Animals?" whereupon the youngest member jumped to his feet with, "We can't have a brand-new member arguing the toss as to what committee he does or does not sit on. If he doesn't know anything about animal diseases, he can learn."

The Convener twinkled at me. "What do you feel?"

"Just that I will make myself the best informed Admiral in the Fleet on artificial insemination." The light touch relaxed the atmosphere and needless to say I was soon allowed to contribute instead some nautical expertise.

How easy and cheap to mock: for there was to follow for me five years of the happiest enlightenment in various spheres. Firstly, of course, I came to learn about what hitherto I had never considered–how one's own surroundings were governed and financed. Secondly, because subsequently as Chairman of the Highways I had to learn about roads instead of sea: and what roads! Up the precipitous narrow hairpins to the summit of Applecross Forest, 2,500 ft in two and half miles, there to find a way by radio beacon so that marooned snow-blower crews could at least tell their families below they were stuck in the corrugated iron shelter for the night. And then there was the Hebridean relationship....

Just to make things easy, Lewis was part of Ross-shire in Local Government whereas Harris, Uist, Barra, the Inner Hebrides and Skye were part of Inverness-shire. So, when seizing on any excuse to visit Lewis, this introduced me to the unique moors, bogs, swamps, bothies, indifference to time or date, native individualism, religions, hospitality, generosity and friendliness extended to all who can appreciate the Hebrides from the Butt of Lewis Lighthouse in the north to Berneray Island in the south, beacons I had often been comforted to find from seawards. I loved it all; and when council matters became tense it was invariably the Lewis members who charmingly debunked–generally after lunch!–with the necessary humour. Now they rule themselves in Local Government and Ross-shire is the poorer for their absence.

"All the world's a stage... And one man in his time plays many parts", as pertinently observed by the melancholy Jacques 300 years ago, and as I have already quoted accurately relates to a Service life in particular. Short of reaching such pinnacles as First Sea Lord or his fellow Chiefs of Staff, whose reigns will be remembered for one reason or another, our appointments of about two years are ships that pass in the night. You hope you have done your best while, as it were, on the bridge, but have few illusions that there will be an aftermath. Ironical therefore that possibly the only exception for me should have been when I was least expecting it. I happened to be the right man in the right place at the right time to lead the Council in the creation of the Cromarty Firth Port Authority at Invergordon. It took three years.

The Firth's most remembered role in naval history is as the safe haven from which Lord Beatty launched his famous battle-cruisers into North Sea actions against the German High Seas Fleet which culminated in Jutland itself. The lethal magazine explosion which destroyed the large cruiser *Natal* during a children's party on Boxing Day 1916 remains for ever a mystery. Her wreck became a war grave until the recent attention of naval divers. In 1931 occurred the mutiny, hatched in the canteen because of the unheralded cut in the sailors' already mercilessly small pay packet by an incompetent Board of Admiralty; but apart from being a convenient exercise base, the Firth became less and less of an absolute naval necessity and even in the Second World War it was geographically on the wrong side of Scotland, with the entrance too deep to protect against the modern submarine.

All of this was naturally clear to me during my final appointment as Flag Officer Scotland; and then came the exciting impact of North Sea Oil. This was what triggered my determination at least to persuade the Navy to share the potentials of the Firth with a separate Port Authority; and such determination was strengthened one day when I was enjoying with my spaniels our favourite walk together among the Nigg sand-dunes belonging to our near neighbour, close friend and distinguished author, the late Eric Linklater. A little party had erected a sheer-legs and were drilling, obviously to determine the depth of the water table beneath though naturally they wouldn't admit that to a stranger.

I went out and stood on the spit jutting out into the Firth entrance, watching the oyster catchers wheel their circuits and the countless waders busily darting at the water's edge; and I wondered.... When I asked Eric what was going on he said pontifically, "They tell me they want to dig a big hole", "in the shape of a vast dry dock" which was some under-statement in that he had no option but to sell his fine house and land, which included those dunes, to the Anglo American Company Highland Fabricators. They have since constructed the huge complex under the North Sutor where some of the first 30,000 ton jackets for the first Rigs were built. Within it seemed so short a span in time, the little green lane from Arabella to Nigg had become an arterial road where now, at the change of shift, over 400 cars thunder along.

And so industry came to what had only been agriculture.

So on 1st January 1974 I found myself as Chairman of a small Board under an Act of Parliament and nothing else: no roof, no capital, no income and no staff. A condemned Nissen Hut and a ping-pong table for a chart were our first acquisition. Among my first visitors was an infuriated manager of the local whisky distillery whose harbour dues, last assessed in 1936, I had apparently increased by 1,200 per cent; but the need had been met and life began to prosper through portakabins to the impressive building of today with its twenty-four-hour operational control under expert staff and a commanding presence overlooking its historic harbour, in which as many as thirteen non-operational oil rigs once replaced the very occasional White Ensign.

Then once again and just when, after three anxious years, I dared to think my dreams were beginning to come true–and which indeed they since have–my life was suddenly changed. My friend and previous colleague Captain Alick Matheson of

Brahan, a universally respected Highlander throughout the County where his family was long established, had been a natural choice for its Lord-Lieutenant for the previous six years when, after a normal morning on his beautiful estate, he suddenly and tragically died. That was five months before, to my astonishment, I received a letter from the Prime Minister (now Lord Callaghan) asking me if he might submit my name to The Queen to succeed Alick.

It will surely be understood that such a thought could not have crossed my mind–that I, an Englishman from Birmingham, unkilted without a dram of Scottish blood in my veins, a comparative newcomer of a mere twenty years in the Highlands when not at sea, should presume to become Her Majesty's representative for Ross & Cromarty, Skye and Lochalsh, 3,000 square miles of the most dramatic High Hills in the world. Yet how could such an honour be refused?

So, in January 1977 I bequeathed the Port Authority and found myself at the outset of The Queens' Jubilee Year responsible for arranging all events throughout my vast "parish". I shall never forget the wonderful and enthusiastic support I received throughout it; and there began eleven years in work I could not have dreamed about. "Emotion is so very untidy" runs a typical Noël Coward line; yet I might be forgiven for yielding to such when (say) investing the British Empire Medal on behalf of Her Majesty to a grandfather in the presence of his five married children and fifteen grandchildren in the vicinity of Loch Ewe, where that young Navigator had had his first view of Scotland on that first Christmas Day in the War.

"What exactly does a Lord-Lieutenant *do*?" is a very usual and perfectly understandable question to which there is no answer apart from what is generally known: arranging every detail of a Royal visit, such as when my cup was filled just before the end of my allotted "reign" by The Queen's visit to Invergordon to open the new Wet Dock for accommodation of Rigs by the Port Authority; but otherwise it is a different and personal ball-game for every one of the hundred of us, depending upon your particular environment and what priorities you choose among endless possibilities in order to be worthy.

Personally, I set my cap at trying to gain reward for the unsung heroes and heroines within remote corners of my huge area who had devoted his or her life to helping others, and who would selflessly never have thought of recognition; and when pinning that pink medal on the left breast, my invariable inclusion amid congratulations to the married was to stress that it is a vain man or woman who supposes that they achieved such on their own and without support from a devoted consort; and in such I was expressing my own experience.

Prior to leaving the Navy my knowledge of the magical Isle of Skye was little more than that a bonny boat had once sped thither over the waters of the Minches, long ago immortalised by one Flora Macdonald's initiative in contriving the escape of that ever-romanticised Prince in the Heather. My only visit had been in that Cadet Training Cruiser *Devonshire* thirty years ago to Portree shortly after the war, when a few officers decided it would do Cadets no harm to accomplish the Cuillins walk from Sligachan to Loch Scavaig whence the ship sailed to receive a wearied hundred of us or so: but proud to have accomplished it.

Now, and since the re-organisation into two-tier Local Government in 1974, Skye had become part of Ross-shire's Lieutenancy; and perhaps of all my memories within my "reign" the happiest was the Investiture of the late Mrs Catherine MacPhie–Katie to all. She was seventy eight, had first joined the Post Office in her native Dunvegan sixty years before as an assistant and had not left the counter since. Moreover she insisted that she had no thought of retiring as postmistress "so long as my health keeps up".

Katie was beloved by all and so we were generously lent the Great Hall of the historic Dunvegan Castle by the successors to the late Dame Flora MacLeod, herself partly responsible for her friend achieving so richly deserved an honour. There was not a spare square foot to be squeezed tighter and most of the rest of Dunvegan waited outside to acclaim their hitherto unsung heroine.

Katie was dressed in pink from the hat above her whitened curls to her toes. Her cheeks were the pink of roses: and the medal was pink. I joined her admirers and we visited her thereafter whenever in that corner of Skye.

On such memories one can for ever sentimentally dwell.

It is made perfectly clear in Her Majesty's original appointment that it must stop on your seventy-fifth birthday: and high time too! We have our "exits and our entrances". And so, from that first childhood day in irrevocable naval uniform to my last at Investitures, sixty one years of unbroken Crown Service in one role or another gently closed in the major key, which is not to say that hopefully there won't still be plenty of useful occupation in the minor. To that same Providence to whom I unashamedly prayed when in command of something small in severe ocean gales, presumably I owe with profound gratitude the colourful innings vouchsafed me. With Prospero I must now really concede that my revels are ended; but as to leaving "not a rack behind", only a posthumous jury can consider their verdict on that. Hopefully, it may be slightly more flattering than the uninhibited, warm-hearted comment of an ex-*St. Vincent* boy, years afterwards and by now a chief Petty Officer, who peered into my car as I waited on Invergordon Pier during some local naval visit:

"'Scuse me, sir, weren't you at *St. Vincent?*" I, immensely touched: "Yes indeed; how clever of you." "Thought so, sir. Reckernised the dog."

Perhaps my final Advocate could advance before my Judge a more lasting memorial concerning the historic water, over whose length from the Hill of Nigg (that compelling little word which first attracted us to Ross-shire) I now gaze from our present lawn, in the ever-changing Highland lights of sunshine and storm, away to the western Farrar Hills from whose ridge Sgurr Vuillin asserts its authority in diurnal varieties, sometimes glittering in snow-clad predominance, sometimes the last silhouette against a crimson sunset; and in so doing I feel fulfilled.

The Closing Chord

Such as it may be, my story is told. Presumptuous to try...? most likely; but I felt that if one was lucky enough to decide what one wanted to do in life at the age of seven, do it, survive a war, savour the colour of the world and live among inimitable characters then, while memory can still hold the door ajar, one should not slam it shut.

There is hope for me before memory quite fades. In the village where our granddaughter lives there also resides the inevitable embarrassment to every charitable amateur concert, that earnest and well-meaning lady who plays the piano execrably and is hurt if not invited to do so. "Mummy," asked Philippa after one such catastrophe, "how old is Miss—*really*?"

"I don't *really* know but I should think not far short of eighty."

"Eighty! But that's even older than Grandpa and *still* in good condition!"

I think it was Nancy Astor who, towards the end of her life, was being interviewed on television and asked whether she believed in the after-life. "Well," she replied, "as nobody has ever come back, have they, I don't really know."

I have a simple-minded approach to this spiritual conundrum which my religion affirms in its creed, a kind of fairytale belief that there is some guiding purpose, some almighty conductor who decreed the music each of us individually had to face, the pace at which we played it, and did not mean it to end in a final earthly chord. I wonder how certain characters of contrasting genius will be getting on? What kind of repartee might occur between (say) Beethoven and Nelson? These two I am sure would mutually approve of the Eroica Symphony and Trafalgar. How would Robbie Burns and Shakespeare reconcile their differing national approaches to dramatic poetry and song? It is an absorbing and quite irrelevant mental charade, inexhaustible in its possibilities.

Yet within it I share the curiosity of the restless questing soul of Gerontius. I too shrink from the devils, hope for the angels and imagine my faltering footsteps towards the Presence. What will He look like? As the Book of Revelation describes and as Blake painted? Will He be so awesome? I'm sure He's got a sense of humour; He must have to ordain the ironies of this planet; and as Elgar's music ascends the lower slopes of harmony towards that shattering chord, I wonder if I will have the courage to stand firm, having faced my earthly score, or will I too shout:

"Take me away, and in the lowest deep
There let me be . . . . "?

If that must be, then I ask no more than that Kathleen Ferrier, who I am sure is divinely cherished, will lead me gently by the hand to the soaring chorus of "Praise to the Holiest . . . " and in that mellifluous richness of tone soothe me with:

"Softly and gently . . .
In my most loving arms I now enfold thee . . .
Farewell, but not for ever! . . . .
Swiftly shall pass thy night of trial here,
And I will come and wake thee on the morrow.
Farewell! Farewell!"